INVESTING
FOR
SAFETY'S
SAKE

INVESTING

FOR

SAFETY'S SAKE

MICHAEL D. JOEHNK

Harper & Row, Publishers, New York
Cambridge, Philadelphia, San Francisco
London, Mexico City, São Paulo, Singapore, Sydney

FIRST EDITION

Designed by Karen Savary

Library of Congress Cataloging-in-Publication Data

Joehnk, Michael D.
  Investing for safety's sake.

  Includes index.
  1. Investments.   I. Title.
HG4521.J63   1988   332.6'78   88-45035
ISBN 0-06-055129-1   88 89 90 91 92 CC/FG 10 9 8 7 6 5 4 3 2 1
ISBN 0-06-096293-3 (pbk.)   88 89 90 91 92 CC/FG 10 9 8 7 6 5 4 3 2 1

This book is dedicated, with love, to my wife,
Charlene.

Thanks!

M.

Contents

Preface

When it comes to investing, caution does have its rewards. And that, in a nutshell, is the message of this book—that there's absolutely nothing wrong with being a safe, conservative investor. For some reason, a lot of people look down their noses at safety-conscious investors. They somehow have the idea that unless you're investing in the latest financial products and aggressively trading in and out of securities, you're just not investing. Well, that's hogwash. The fact is, whether you're investing for retirement purposes, for the down payment on a new home, or for any other reason, following a safe, cautious approach to investing makes a lot of sense—for the simple reason that you *can* make some pretty serious money over the long haul by following such an investment philosophy. Let the gunslingers play in the street all they want; let them dabble in options, futures, and margin trading. You don't need to. Not if your investment objective is to earn a nice, comfortable return on your money. Now understand, by nice, comfortable return we're *not* talking bargain basement rates.

By now you're probably thinking there has to be a gimmick here, so what is it? Quite candidly, there is none. We have nothing to sell, nothing to push, no gimmick to promote. This isn't going to be another one of those books giving you a blow-by-blow description of how you can make a million bucks in your sleep by investing in condemned buildings or Third World bank notes. Nor are we going to insult your intelligence by telling you that the best way to make money is to buy low and sell high. Instead, this is a book about making money slowly but surely, by making *safe investments.* What do we mean by safe investments? Securities like federally insured CDs, Series EE savings bonds, U.S. Treasury notes, prime-grade corporate bonds, blue chip income stocks, and certain types of mutual funds. When it comes to investment vehicles, these are about as basic as they get. And no, we don't advocate some complicated trading strategy to enhance your returns. Quite the contrary. We advise you to follow a simple buy-and-hold approach to investing.

The keys to success are knowing what kinds of securities to select and how to use them. Unfortunately, not all securities are alike; as a result, to get the most from your investment dollars, you have to know what kinds of features to look for. It's *not* terribly difficult—it's just a matter of becoming an informed investor and then putting that knowledge to work for you. That's where this book comes in. For it shows that if you know what you're doing, even ordinary rates of return can lead to rather substantial sums of money. You can have *both* safety and return. Indeed, there's no reason to settle for anything less.

Following a safe and sound investment philosophy that's based on simplicity and fundamentals can lead to long-term results that may not be spectacular but are certainly respectable. Consider, for example, a 9% return. That's certainly respectable. Do you know that at 9%, your money will double every 8 years? Translated into dollars, that means that $50,000 will grow to some $400,000 in 25 years. That's substantial! And that's what *Investing for Safety's Sake* is all about.

I would like to thank several people for their help and support in the production of this book:

Tammy Johns, for putting up with all those changes in the manuscript.

Terrence Joehnk, for lending his artistic talents to the graphic presentations.

Dave McLaughlin of Chase Investment Counsel, for his many helpful suggestions throughout the development of this book.

Roger Oldenkamp, for his help in carrying out some of the research.

Helen Moore, my editor at Harper & Row, who deserves a special token of appreciation for all her help in marshaling this book through from proposal to finished product.

PART ONE

BUILDING
THE
FOUNDATION

This book offers only general investment observations based on the author's experience and makes no specific recommendations.

It is intended and written to provide the author's opinions in regard to the subject matter covered. The author and the publisher are not engaged in rendering legal, accounting, or other professional advice, and the reader should seek the services of a qualified professional for such advice.

The author and the publisher cannot be held responsible for any loss incurred as a result of the application of any of the information in this publication.

Every attempt has been made to assure the accuracy of the statistics that appear throughout *Investing for Safety's Sake*. In some cases, data may vary from your reports because of interpretations or accounting changes made after the original publication. Please remember that *Investing for Safety's Sake* is a *guide*, not a definitive source of financial information. When you have a question, check with your broker or investment advisor.

1

Safe Investments Don't Have to Mean Dull Returns

Do a little daydreaming for a moment and try to picture yourself in the following situation: You've just been notified by a very official-looking letter that you're the lucky recipient of a $50,000 windfall. For a variety of reasons, you decide to invest the whole amount. Now, assuming that the markets are all performing well, which of the following investments would you be most comfortable with: a 3-year U.S. Treasury note or an aggressive, high-flying, growth-oriented mutual fund? Your choice says a lot about how you feel about risk. And your choice of this book says you want to make investments that are safe.

Granted, there's more to making an investment decision than what we've included in our daydream above, but it's very likely that if you chose the Treasury security, you tend to be fairly conservative in your approach to investing. There is, of course, absolutely nothing wrong with that: being cautious doesn't mean you have to be condemned to some kind of investment purgatory where respectable rates of return simply don't exist. The fact is that over the long haul, most investors would be pleasantly surprised at just how much can be earned by putting their money into good, sound, safe investments. The trick is to know what you're doing—to know where to look for investments that will give you a bit more yield, to know when a shorter maturity is

3

better than a longer one, and to know how to build a well-balanced portfolio that will give you an attractive rate of return from a tolerable amount of risk.

Don't misunderstand: there's no easy road to fat profits, nor is it all a sure thing. But if you know what you're doing, if you're a well-informed investor, then even ordinary rates of return can lead to substantial sums of money! And it can be done without following some absurd, off-the-wall investment strategy. The whole philosophy of *Investing for Safety's Sake* is to keep it simple, stick to the basics, be consistent, and above all, get into the market for the long haul. Don't try to time the market, and unless you really know what you're doing, don't get fancy—because more often than not, fancy techniques in the hands of a novice can lead to devastating results.

Not All Investments Are Alike

For investors, 1987 will go down as one of the wildest years ever. First, stocks literally skyrocketed in price, shooting through one record level after another, only to take the biggest single-day plunge in history on October 19th, which has since become known as Black Monday. Now while all this was happening in the stock market, bond prices were behaving quite differently: they started nose-diving in the spring of the year and then staged a powerful rally in October and November. We could go on, but the point is that even during this tumultuous period of time, we saw once again that not all investments behave alike—for the simple reason that not all investments are alike.

Better to Be Safe Than Sorry

While American investors today can choose from a full menu of investment vehicles, our concern here is with safe investments—those low-risk security or savings vehicles that offer a solid, steady return to investors over the long run. Safety of principal is, of course, the single most important feature of these investments. There should be no question about whether dividend, interest, and/or principal payments can be met in a prompt, timely, and effortless fashion. Does that mean such securities will never go down in price? Unfortunately, no. Short-term price fluctuations may (in fact, probably will) exist with some of these securities. Indeed, total protection from price volatility is hard to avoid in all but the shortest securities (like bank CDs and money funds). Carefully selected safe investments should offer some price protection, however, as they should be less price volatile than their more risky counterparts. They may not be price leaders when the market is rising, but they don't tend to fall as much or as fast in down markets either.

In addition, safe investments will generally derive a greater portion of their total return from current income, in the form of annual dividend and interest payments. Capital gains don't even exist with some of these investments and, with many others, are little more than a pleasant byproduct that occasionally accompanies the principal source of return. The level of current income from a safe investment is usually fairly substantial and acts to shore up total returns when markets are soft. There's a final element you should look for when putting your money into safe investments: when you're buying securities that are traded in the market, try to confine your investing to securities that offer plenty of liquidity. A liquid investment is one that can easily be bought or sold at, or close to, prevailing market prices. Liquidity is important because it provides you with a safety valve in case you ever have to bail out in a hurry.

Some Safe Investment Outlets

We can identify four general categories of safe investments:

1. Savings and Short-Term Investment Vehicles (like CDs, money funds, Treasury bills, and savings bonds)
2. U.S. Government Notes and Bonds, and high-grade Corporate and Municipal Bonds

3. Blue Chip and Quality Income Stocks
4. High-Quality Mutual Funds

All these securities are easy to buy and sell, and market information on them is readily available and widely disseminated. And, they don't require any specialized skill or know-how—they are about as basic as you can get. Furthermore, they cover the full range of maturities, from short-term to long-term to no maturity at all, as in the case of common stocks. Each of these four types of securities will be explored in detail in chapters 4 through 7, where we'll look not only at important issue characteristics, but also at how these securities can be used in a safety-oriented investment program.

There are some investments that are conspicuous by their absence from our list; for example, annuities and other life insurance products, which are touted chiefly for their tax shelter features. No matter how they are packaged, these are still primarily insurance products—that also happen to have features of an investment vehicle. There's no question that some annuities (particularly fixed annuities) are, indeed, low in risk. But there's a *serious* lack of information about the quality and long-term performance of these investments, so it's hard to know what you're really getting into—and to make matters even worse, they're far more complex than most securities since they combine an insurance policy with an investment vehicle. What's more, they're generally considered to be highly illiquid, because you're expected to tie up your money for extended periods of time (many annuities have substantial withdrawal charges if you take your money out early), and there may be severe tax penalties if you take your money out ahead of schedule. Limited partnerships also lack liquidity (they're *very difficult* to sell), and they can involve some pretty hefty commissions; these things, too, are fairly complex, and they're equally tough to evaluate.

For some reason, gold seems to hold a special appeal to many investors, especially the doomsday market-newsletter writers. It's left off our list of safe investments because it's strictly a capital gains-oriented investment (unless you buy gold stocks or mutual funds, there are no dividends or interest payments with gold). What's more, it's a fairly speculative investment vehicle, subject to wide swings in market prices. True, gold can at times act as a nice hedge against inflation, but there are other investments that can do that, too. Other types of investments (like options, commodities, and financial futures) were left off the list quite simply because they're just too speculative and require considerable investor sophistication.

So Why Take a Lot of Risks?

Contrary to what some people may believe, you don't have to be a rich speculator to make money in the market! There's nothing that says you need a lot of money to play the game, nor is there some unwritten rule that you have to take on a lot of risks in order to earn an attractive rate of return. Indeed, if you just put the principle of compound interest to work, you'll discover you don't need astronomical rates of return to produce big dollar profits.

Letting Compound Interest Work for You

They call it the eighth wonder of the world. And all those things they say about compound interest are true. For example, it's true that if you had put *1 cent* in the bank a couple thousand years ago, and just let it grow at some reasonable compound rate of return, today you would be worth megamillions. There are, of course, two obvious flaws with this anecdote: the first is that it's very likely the bank would have failed long ago, and the second is that even if the bank had survived, it's very unlikely that you would have. Even so, the moral of the story still holds—that compound interest is a powerful ally to have on your side.

In very simple terms, compound interest is nothing more than a process of growth. For instance, when you put money into an investment, you earn a profit on your capital; but when you

start earning money on your profit, that's when you start compounding your return. Compound interest, therefore, refers to a
process of generating earnings from the original invested capital,
as well as prior-period profits. With compounding, your capital
base gets larger and larger over time as you continue to plow back
earnings. As a result, even though the percentage rate of return
on your capital doesn't change, the dollar amount of profits will
increase.

The net effect of compounding is that *even ordinary rates of
return can lead, over time, to fairly substantial sums of money!*
Consider, for example, an investment that offers a 6% compound
rate of return—let's face it, finding a 6% investment today is not
all that difficult to do. Put $10,000 into this investment and in
10 years, you'll have almost $18,000. Not a bad return on your
money. But look what happens if you leave your money in for 25
years, rather than 10: without putting up another dime in fresh
new capital, your investment will grow to nearly $43,000. That's
a $43,000 payoff from an original investment of just $10,000—
and it's all been achieved from a very modest 6% rate of return.

Now let's see what happens when we increase the rate of
return. Since we don't want to be greedy, let's increase the return
on investment by just 2 percentage points—from 6% to 8%. Big
deal, you say. What impact is a couple of percentage points going
to have on our return? Well, look at the accompanying graph and
decide for yourself. The graph contrasts the rewards from two
investments: one yielding 6% and another earning 8%. Notice
that at the end of 25 years, the extra 2 percentage points translate
into another $25,000 in profits—that's a 60% increase in profits.
Clearly, when it comes to compound return, a couple of percentage points can lead to big differences in the dollar amount earned.

Two facts are worth repeating here with regard to compound
interest: First, even modest rates of return can lead to big profits.
And second, it pays to try and pick up a percentage point or two,
since even small differences in return can lead to big differences
in profits. These facts are key elements in safe investing, because
they mean you don't need to take a lot of risks to make a lot of

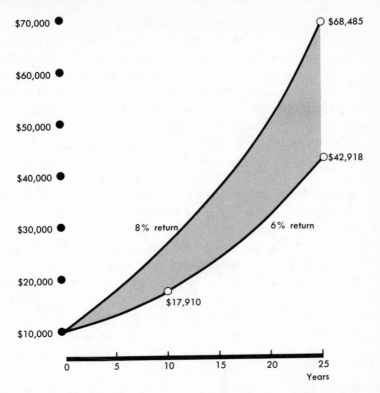

money. Stick with sound, secure investments and then just use some safe, commonsense ways of adding a point or two to your return. As shown in the graph, you may be pleasantly surprised at the results.

Sophisticated investors learned long ago to incorporate the concept of compound interest into their investment programs. Yet as powerful as compound interest is, it is still ignored by a large segment of the investing public. This is unfortunate, since achieving a fully compounded rate of return is a fairly easy thing to do. All it really takes is discipline—the discipline to systematically plow your earnings back into your investments, to *reinvest* any and all investment income (be it from interest, dividends, or capital gains). In that way, your capital base will grow over time and you'll be able to reap the full benefits of compounding.

You can reinvest your investment earnings in one of two ways. First, you can confine your purchases to investments that will automatically reinvest your earnings—CDs, for example, as well as some types of bonds; also, mutual funds and common stocks that offer automatic reinvestment programs (all of which will be examined in later chapters). Alternatively, you can do your own reinvesting: when you get that dividend check or realize a profit on the sale of a mutual fund, just resist the temptation to spend the money. Instead, put it back into your savings/investment program. Buy some stock with it, or another mutual fund; if nothing else, put the money temporarily into a short-term CD or money fund. There are a lot of things you can do with the money, but the most important thing to remember is to keep it fully invested. Putting compound interest to work for you is a giant step on the path of setting up an investment program that is not only safe, but lucrative as well.

2

The First Step in Making Money Is Not to Lose It

To a lot of people, the notion of a safe investment means nothing less than a fully insured savings account or bank CD. But to others, it conjures up a totally different image. Consider, for example, the front page story in the December 2, 1987, issue of *The Wall Street Journal*. Seems that some investors were lulled into believing that selling put options was a low-risk, sure-fire way to make money in the market. Now most individual investors—and many of the brokers who were selling these things—don't even know what put options are, let alone how they behave.

Very briefly, put options give their holders the right to sell a certain number of stocks (or some other financial asset) at a specified price for a specified period of time. Who has to stand behind these options and provide the buy side to this transaction? Why the person who sold the option, of course. And that, unfortunately, is the catch. For the holders of the puts are betting that the market will fall—that's the way they make their money; but that's the last thing the sellers want, since they'll lose money if the price falls. Now, according to *The Wall Street Journal*, many brokers were selling their customers on the idea that selling put options was as close to a riskless sure thing as you could get. After all, they reasoned, how could you lose from betting that one of the strongest bull markets on record would all of a sudden come to a screeching halt? You guessed it: enter October 19th, 1987, Black Monday! In a matter of just a few hours, many of the people who thought they had a sure thing had to face up to the reality that they were literally wiped out. One investor reportedly lost his entire nest egg of around $100,000 *and* ended up another $70,000 in debt. These weren't paper losses, either. They were the real thing.

This, of course, never should have happened, and certainly not to safety-conscious investors. For one of the key ingredients of a safe investment is preservation of capital. Obviously, when you make an investment, at the very minimum you want to be able to get your money back! You certainly don't expect to lose it because the company or institution that issued the security goes out of business, or because the market value drops so much you're forced to sell out at a big loss. Preservation of capital is concerned with avoiding these kinds of dollar losses, and with minimizing temporary paper losses. After all, what good does it do to worry about the kind of return you'll earn *on* your capital when you don't even know if you're going to get a return *of* your capital?

Getting to Know Risk

"There ain't no free lunch." This colorful phrase is used in the field of investments to describe one of the key facts of life about the market; namely, that higher returns and higher risk usually go hand in hand. Put in another perspective, it also means that you, as an investor, shouldn't accept higher risk without getting more return. The principle at work here is that, for the market to operate efficiently, the negative factor—increasing risk—must be offset by a positive factor—increasing return. Such a trade-off is necessary to get investors to take on more risks. And even though it's not always so obvious, this same relationship applies just as much to short-term savings vehicles as it does to other sorts of investments. For example, why do you think some savings and loans offer such high rates on their CDs? It's certainly not because they're in a generous mood. Rather, it's often the only way that the generally weaker institutions can attract needed deposits.

Given its importance in the marketplace, just what is risk? In very simple terms, it's the chance that something will go wrong; that the actual return from an investment will turn out to be less than what you thought it would be. Risk pertains not only to the preservation of your capital, but also to the return on your capital. In this sense, it's important to keep in mind that you can have a secure investment and still be exposed to risk as far as return on your capital is concerned. *The trick in safe investing is to stick to the sound, secure investment vehicles, and then get the maximum return you can from the level of risk (albeit small) that you choose to assume.*

The Different Kinds of Risk

Risk exists with investments because, as far as return is concerned, the only thing that matters is how a security performs in the future. So what if Southern California Edison paid $2.33 in dividends in 1987. If you didn't own the stock, it didn't do you any good. Now, because the future is subject to uncertainty, you have risk—and as we'll see, this applies to even the safest of investments, like Treasury securities. The total risk of a security results from a combination of several different sources. For savers and investors, there are four major sources of risk:

- Business and Financial Risk
- Market Risk
- Purchasing Power Risk
- Liquidity Risk

Let's look now at each of these and see how they can affect your return.

BUSINESS AND FINANCIAL RISK When you invest in a company, you may have to face up to the possibility that the issuing firm will fail. That's exactly what happened to investors who bought Braniff, A. H. Robins, L.T.V., Gulf States Utilities, and U.P.I., to name just a few. Corporate failure may be due to economic or industry factors or, as is more often the case, to poor decisions on the part of management. Companies that are subject to high degrees of business risk generally experience wide fluctuations in sales, have widely erratic earnings, and can, in fact, end the year with substantial operating losses. In a general sense, *business risk* may be thought of as the degree of uncertainty surrounding the firm's earnings and subsequent ability to meet principal, interest, and dividend payments in a prompt and timely fashion. For safety-conscious investors, business risk is something to avoid, or minimize, as much as possible: to do so, stick to financially sound companies that have solid sales and earnings records.

The same holds true for *financial risk*, which relates to the amount of debt used to finance the firm. Look to the company's balance sheet to get a handle on a firm's financial risk. As a rule, companies that have little or no long-term debt are generally viewed as being fairly low in financial risk. This is particularly so if a company has a healthy earnings picture as well. The problem with debt financing is that it creates principal and interest obligations that have to be met regardless of how much profit the company is generating. As with business risk, financial risk can lead to failure (as in the case of bankruptcy), or a rate of return that is sharply below your expectations. Again, such risks can be avoided or greatly reduced by sticking with high-quality, highly rated investments. (*Note:* Although our discussion here has been couched in terms of business firms, it should be understood that these risks can also affect other types of issuers—such as various types of financial institutions, or state and local governments.)

MARKET RISK Sometimes the prices of stocks and bonds will change even though business and financial risks, and other intrinsic factors, stay exactly the same. Such changes have nothing to do with the securities themselves, but instead are due to so-called exogenous forces—such as political, economic, and social conditions and/or investor tastes and preferences. These are the market forces that combine to make up what is known as market risk.

Virtually all types of marketable securities (from stocks, corporate bonds, U.S. Treasury securities, and municipal bonds, to different types of mutual funds) are subject to market risk. Short of keeping your money in some kind of short-term savings vehicle, there's just no way to avoid it. Fortunately, the impact of these market factors on security returns is not uniform. Thus, it is possible, through careful security selection, to at least minimize the impact of market risk.

With common stocks, it's estimated that about 35% to 50% of a stock's price volatility is due to the impact of market risk. Obviously, a force that powerful is something to be reckoned with! Luckily, it's fairly easy to get an idea of how much market risk there is in an individual common stock, since over the past 15 or 20 years, the investment community has developed a very effective (and reasonably accurate) measure of market risk, known as beta. Actually, beta is derived from a fairly sophisticated statistical procedure that relates the historical price behavior of a stock to the historical returns for the market. Most large brokerage houses, as well as many of the major investment advisory services (such as Value Line), publish betas for a broad range of securities, so you don't have to trudge through any of the laborious calculations yourself.

Using beta to assess the market risk of a stock is fairly easy. All you have to remember is that the beta for the market is equal to 1.0, and all other betas are viewed relative to this value: a beta of less than 1.0 means the stock is less risky than the market, while a beta of more than 1.0 means the stock is riskier than average. *In general, the higher the absolute value of beta, the riskier the investment.* While the measure certainly isn't perfect, it does a reasonably good job of indicating the type of responsiveness you can expect from a stock. For example, if the market is expected to go up (or down) by 10% over the next year or so, then a stock with a beta of, say, 0.8 should undergo a change of around 8% (10% × 0.8 = 8%). Now you can see why stocks with low betas (less than 1.0) are considered to be less risky: their prices are less volatile. And less price volatility means, of course, less exposure to loss. That's why, if you're a safety-conscious investor, you should stick to high-quality, low-beta stocks.

Market risk takes a slightly different form for fixed income securities, such as investment-grade bonds. For these securities, the most important market force is interest rates. So long as it's an investment-grade security (such as a U.S. government bond, or an investment-grade municipal or corporate bond), it will respond more to market interest rates than anything else. In a nutshell, *market interest rates are what cause bond prices to move up or down.*

In essence, as interest rates move in one direction, the prices of fixed income securities will move in the opposite direction. Thus, if interest rates go up, it's virtually guaranteed that the prices of long-term bonds will go down—it's just a question of how big the fall will be. (As we'll see in chapter 5, that depends on several key factors.) Just as beta affects the price volatility of common stocks, interest rates affect the price volatility of fixed income securities, and as such, they should be closely monitored by safety-conscious investors. In addition, whenever you use fixed income securities in a safety-oriented investment program, there are steps you can take (covered in chapter 5) to minimize your exposure to interest rate risk. These steps can do wonders not only in preserving your capital, but in enhancing your rate of return.

PURCHASING POWER RISK They say that nobody really gains from inflation, and that's certainly true when it comes to saving and investing. Purchasing power risk pertains to inflation—the tendency for the general level of prices to go up over time. Purchasing power risk, in one way or another, affects all types of investment and savings vehicles, and becomes a real problem when inflation starts heating up, as it did in the mid-1970s through 1981. Look what happened to stocks and bonds during most of this era: long-term bonds did terribly and, more often than not, stock returns fell far short of the rate of inflation. Then, as inflation was brought under control in 1982 through early 1987, stocks and bonds both took off in record-breaking fashion.

Now, don't fool yourself into believing that savings accounts and other short-term vehicles get off scot-free during times of high inflation. They don't. For while it's true that they don't experience the kinds of capital losses that stocks and bonds do, you can hardly say you're preserving your capital when the rate of return you're earning on your money is less (and in some cases, substantially less) than the rate of inflation. You may have more money, but it's worth less and as such, won't buy as much as it used to. There's little doubt that over the past 10 to 15 years, inflation has had a very real and substantial impact on price volatility and security returns. Whether dealing in short-term savings or long-term investments, purchasing power risk can have a dramatic effect on both the return of and the return on your capital.

LIQUIDITY RISK Some securities are easier to buy and sell than others. Ideally, you should be able to buy or sell a security anytime you want, with little or no delay or inconvenience, and with little or no variation in the prevailing market price. The less likely you are to be able to do this, the more liquidity risk you have to bear. For *liquidity risk*, basically, is the risk of not being able to liquidate an investment conveniently and at a reasonable price. Simply being able to sell a security quickly, in and of itself, is not a measure of liquidity, since you can sell just about anything quickly if you cut the price enough. Instead, you also have to be able to sell it at or near the security's current market price. Don't underestimate it! Liquidity risk can have a direct and at times significant impact on your return—as, for example, when you have to take a loss simply because you can't get out of an investment in a timely fashion.

Having to take a loss because of an illiquid investment is particularly unfortunate since liquidity is one risk that you, as an investor, have a lot of control over—you can easily avoid it. Simply confine your investing to those securities and savings vehicles that give you the kind of liquidity you're looking for. As a rule, *avoid:* (1) small companies, (2) small issues (few securities outstanding), and (3) thin markets (little supply and demand for the securities). Although safe investing generally takes a long-term perspective, liquidity is still important as it provides you with a safety valve just in case you ever have to get out, for one reason or another. Real estate, limited partnerships, and collectibles are three investments notorious for their lack of liquidity; in sharp contrast, widely traded common stocks and mutual funds, Treasury bills, and Treasury bonds are just a few examples of highly liquid investment vehicles.

Treat Risk Both as an Adversary and as an Ally

Some people just can't take any risk; they don't like it and they want nothing to do with it. To them, getting a good night's sleep is far more important than having a comfortable bed to sleep in! And there's nothing wrong with that. For it's better to recognize such an intolerance for risk and devise an investment program accordingly. But unless you're one of those who can't tolerate any risk, don't let risk be the sole factor in your investment decision. As we said earlier in this chapter, there are two important elements to consider in an investment: risk *and* return. Risk is undesirable; indeed, you realize just how unpleasant risk can be when it actually materializes—when you watch the market price of your investment tumble to new lows, or when you actually lose money on an investment. These are situations that nobody likes, and explain why risk should be considered in every investment decision. In this sense, treat risk as an adversary—something to be avoided, or at least minimized.

Trying to avoid or minimize risk, however, is not the same thing as trying to *eliminate* it. For most investors, that's an important distinction. They recognize that in the world of investing, it's hard to totally eliminate risk. And that's precisely where return comes into the picture. As an investor, you have to determine your own tolerance for risk. But it's probably safe to say that, as a safety-conscious investor, it's on the low side. You don't want to take on a lot of risk and you don't have to. Just remember to get compensated for any risk you do incur, no matter how small it may be. The more risks you take, the greater your returns should be. *There's only one kind of intolerable risk, and that's where risk is incurred without regard to return.*

This applies just as much to safe, conservative investors as it does to speculators. A bit more risk should lead to a bit more return. As we saw in chapter 1, when you've got compound interest working for you, even small differences in return can lead, over the long haul, to big differences in the amount of dollar profits made. In this light, it's easy to see how risk (so long as it's kept to a safe, tolerable level) can also become an ally. For if properly employed, it can become the vehicle through which you can earn a greater level of return—not a lot, perhaps, but enough to make a real difference over the long haul. Understand, we're *not* advocating that you sacrifice safety for return; not in the least. Rather, just make sure that any risks you incur are offset with added returns.

Strike a Balance between Preserving Your Capital and Increasing Your Capital

What would you think of an investment that offered nothing more than the chance to get your money back? Specifically: would you put $25,000 into an investment if all it promised to do was pay you exactly $25,000 in 10 years? Almost certainly the answer would be a resounding, "No way!" Yet this is exactly what you will get if all you are going after is *preservation of capital.* Certainly this is better than losing money, but that's not what saving and investing are all about. You put money into an investment in the hope that it will generate a rate of return greater than zero; in other words, that you'll be able to earn a return *on* your capital.

Consider once again the hypothetical $25,000 investment mentioned above. You'd surely find this to be a far more attractive investment if it promised to pay you, say, an 8% return on your money. In 10 years, such an investment would grow to nearly

$54,000 and provide you not only with a return of your capital ($25,000), but also a return on your capital, in the amount of $29,000. Thus, just as minimizing risk is important in preserving your capital, generating an acceptable rate of return is important in increasing your capital.

Key Components of Return

If we were to put the notion of return into the form of an equation, it would look something like this:

$$\text{Return} = \text{Principal} + \text{Profits} - \text{Taxes}$$

The first element of return is recovery of principal. That's what return of capital, or preservation of capital, is all about. Don't underestimate the importance of this element of return, for as the title to this chapter suggests, the first step in making money is not to lose it. But clearly, if it all stops there, you have done nothing more than break even. In order to end up with a positive return on your money, you have to move to the next component of return, and generate a profit. Profits are the vehicle through which you can earn a return *on* your capital. Without profits, you're back to a break-even situation, or worse.

Finally, taxes are important in our return equation since they determine how much of the profit you get to keep! Of course, because they're a drag on our return, you'd like to be able to minimize your exposure to taxes as much as possible—legally, of course. Except for some of the more obvious ways in which taxes affect investment return, we don't go into detail on taxes in this book—there are plenty of books devoted to the subject of taxes. Suffice it to say that taxes are something you shouldn't overlook. That brings us back to the first two elements of the return equation; we've looked at principal (preservation of capital), let's now look at profits.

Any investment vehicle—be it a bank CD, a bond, or a share of stock—has just two ways of turning a profit:

- Current Income
- Capital Gains

Some investments offer just one of these sources, though most offer both. There's more to it than that, however, for to get the most from your investment program, you need a third element:

■ Interest-on-Interest

Whereas current income and capital gains make up the profits from an investment, interest-on-interest is a measure of what you do with those profits.

CURRENT INCOME The income that you receive periodically—whether it's monthly, quarterly, or over some other time period—represents the current income from an investment. As a rule, it's money you receive, or expect to receive, every year, on a fairly regular basis. For most securities, current income takes the form of either interest or dividends. The interest that you earn on your passbook savings account or bank CD, the dividends that you receive from your stocks, and the interest that you earn on your long-term government bonds are all examples of current income. Such income can be substantial and have a dramatic impact on the amount of return you generate.

CAPITAL GAINS You have capital gains when you're able to sell a security for more than you paid for it, or when one of your security holdings goes up in value. So long as you continue to hold the security, any capital gains that have occurred are strictly *paper profits.* That's an important distinction since, except for certain types of bonds, you don't owe any taxes on paper profits—so far, Congress and the IRS haven't been able to come up with a way to tax paper profits, though they're probably working on it! Thus, you could own a stock for 15 years and it could appreciate five-fold in value; until you actually sell that security, you don't have a *realized* capital gain, and therefore you don't owe one dime in taxes. Growth-oriented common stock and mutual funds are often acquired for their capital gains potential. Generally speaking, capital gains may give you more bang for your investment dollar, but they're also a far more uncertain (and therefore more risky) source of return than current income.

INTEREST-ON-INTEREST Question: When does an 8% investment end up yielding only 5%? Answer: Probably more often than you think! Of course, it can happen when investment performance fails to live up to expectations. But it can also happen even when everything goes right. For example, say an investor buys an 8% U.S. Treasury bond and holds it to maturity, a period of 20 years. Each year the bondholder receives $80 in interest, and at maturity, the $1,000 in principal is repaid. There is no loss in capital, no default; everything is paid right on time. Yet this sure-fire investment ends up yielding only 5%. Why? Because the investor failed to reinvest the profits. By not plowing back all the investment earnings, the bondholder failed to earn any *interest-on-interest*.

Consider, for example, the accompanying graph. It shows the elements of return for the 8% 20-year Treasury bond; observe that since the bond was originally bought at par ($1,000), you start off with an 8% investment. Where you end up depends on

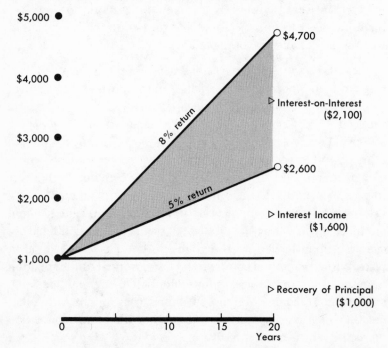

what you do with the profits from this investment. If you don't reinvest the interest income, you'll end up on the 5% line, with about the same rate of return as your neighbors who do little more than put their money into passbook savings accounts.

To move to the 8% line, you have to earn interest-on-interest from your investments. Specifically, since you started with an 8% investment, that's the rate of return you have to earn when reinvesting your income. The rate of return you start with, in effect, is the required, or minimum, reinvestment rate. Put your investment profits to work at this rate and you'll earn the rate of return you set out to; fail to do so and your return will decline accordingly. And keep in mind that even though we used a bond in our graph, this same principle applies to any type of investment vehicle. It's just as relevant to common stocks, mutual funds, or T-bills as it is to long-term bond instruments. So long as periodic investment income is involved, the reinvestment of that income and interest-on-interest are matters you're going to have to deal with.

The graph shows that interest-on-interest amounts to nearly half of the total return. This is by no means out of the ordinary; interest-on-interest can amount to as much as 70% to 75% of total return on some long-term high-yielding investments. In fact, interest-on-interest is a particularly important element of return for investment programs that involve a lot of current income. This is so because, in contrast to capital gains, current income has to be reinvested by the individual investor. (With capital gains, the investment vehicle itself is doing the reinvesting, all automatically—fortunately, this same principle of automatic compounding also applies to most forms of savings, such as passbook savings accounts, Series EE savings bonds, and money funds.) It follows, therefore, that if your investment program tends to lean toward income-oriented securities (as many safety-conscious investment programs do), then interest-on-interest—and the continual reinvestment of income—will play an important role in defining the amount of investment success you have.

Measuring Your Return

Rate of return can be measured in three ways: (1) by computing current yield, (2) by determining holding period return, and (3) by finding approximate yield. Each of these methods captures some element of return, and as such, is a measure of investment performance. In contrast, *nominal yield* is another indication of return, but it's not a measure of investment performance. Rather, nominal yield is nothing more than the stated rate of return on an investment. For example, a bond that carries a 10% coupon has a nominal yield of, you guessed it: 10%. Of course, the stated rate of return is one thing; what you actually earn may be another matter altogether.

CURRENT YIELD This, the most basic measure of return, recognizes only one source of income: the amount of current income generated annually from interest and dividend payments. Current yield is easy to measure: just divide annual interest (or dividend) income by the current market price of the security. For example, if you hold a bond that pays $80 a year in interest, and if that bond is currently priced at $900, then you're earning a current yield of 8.9% by holding the issue—that is, $80/$900. In a similar fashion, if you held stock that paid $2 a share in annual dividends, and if the stock was currently trading at $35.50 a share, you'd be earning a current yield of 5.6%.

Current yield is used mostly with long-term securities, since there's usually very little difference between the current and nominal yields of short-term savings/investment vehicles. If you're an investor looking for income, then current yield is a measure of return that you should follow very closely. Indeed, the higher the current yield from your investments, the more current income you'll earn annually.

HOLDING PERIOD RETURN A performance measure that recognizes not only current income, but also capital gains, is holding period return (HPR). It looks at the return from these two sources of income over a given period of time (known as a holding period, or investment horizon). The procedure for finding holding period return is pretty simple:

1. Add up all the dividend (or interest) income you've received over the holding period in question.
2. Figure out how much capital gains you've made over the same period of time (you do this by taking the difference between the beginning and ending price of the security).
3. Add the dividend (or interest) income to your capital gains.
4. Divide the total income (found in step 3) by the beginning price of the security, and you have HPR.

HPR can be used with just about any holding period—3 months or 3 years, it makes no difference. Consider, for example, a stock that you bought, say, 3 years ago for $70 a share. Here's what you do to find HPR:

1. If it paid $4 a share annually in dividends, you've made $12 per share in dividends over the past 3 years.
2. If the stock is currently trading at $110 a share, then you've made $40 a share in capital gains—which is the difference between the beginning ($70) and the ending ($110) price of the stock.
3. Therefore, you've made a total of $52 on this stock ($12 in dividends and $40 in capital gains).
4. Now for the final step—divide total income ($52) by the beginning price of the stock ($70) and you have its HPR of 74.3%.

While this is a fairly substantial return, keep in mind that HPR is *not* a measure of annual return. Instead, it measures performance over a given period of time that may or may not equal a year (as in the example above, which covered a 3-year period of time). Don't be tempted to divide holding period return by the number of years in the holding period to get an average annual return, since that will only overstate return performance. Rather, use the approximate yield measure to correctly introduce the annual compounding effects of interest-on-interest.

APPROXIMATE YIELD The best way to measure return performance over an extended period of time is with a technique that
considers not only current income and capital gains, but interest-
on-interest as well. Such a measure is available and, in fact, is
widely used by seasoned investors to evaluate long-term return
performance. Although finding the exact fully compounded rate
of return involves a highly complex mathematical procedure, you
can come up with a figure that's reasonably close by using the
approximate yield measure. Here's all you have to do:

1. Find the amount of *average annual dividend (or interest) income* that you've received from your investment over the holding period in question.
2. Next, find the *average annual capital gains* you've made over
   the holding period by taking the difference between the beginning and ending price of the security, and then divide that
   amount by the number of years in your holding period.
3. Now, determine the *average investment* by adding the beginning and ending price of the security, and divide that amount
   by 2.
4. Add the average annual dividend (or interest) income from
   step 1 to the average annual capital gains from step 2, and
   divide this total amount by the average investment (as found
   in step 3). What you get is the approximate yield.

Consider, for example, the 3-year investment we looked at
above. Recall: the stock was purchased 3 years ago at $70, it paid
$4 a share in annual dividends, and was currently trading at $110.
Using the procedure outlined above, you can find the approximate yield on this investment as follows:

1. Since the stock has paid $4 a share in annual dividends over
   each of the past 3 years, you can use that amount ($4) for your
   average annual dividends.
2. Now, if the stock moved from $70 to $110 a share, you've
   obviously made $40 a share in capital gains; however, because
   it took 3 years to earn this money, your average annual capital
   gains amounts to only $13.33 (that is, $40/3 = $13.33).

3. Next, to find the average amount of the investment, just add the beginning ($70) and ending ($110) prices together and divide by 2; that results in an average investment of $90 ($70 + $110 = $180/2 = $90).
4. Put it all together and you have approximate yield. Add the average annual dividend income (of $4.00) to the average annual capital gains (of $13.33), and you have $17.33. Divide this amount by the average investment (of $90.00) and you're left with an approximate yield of 19.25%—that is, $4.00 + $13.33 = $17.33/$90.00 = .1925.

This figure of 19.25% represents an annual rate of return that's been earned, on average, over the 3-year investment period. The reason it's a lot lower than the holding period return (of 74.3%) is because it's an annual rate, rather than an overall measure for the whole investment horizon. In addition, the compounding effects of interest-on-interest are fully integrated into the approximate yield measure but are totally ignored in HPR. Of the two, approximate yield is a far superior measure of return and should be used whenever you're evaluating long-term investments. In such cases, it'll give you the truest measure of investment performance.

Are You Getting a Satisfactory Return?

Whenever you calculate return—particularly holding period return and approximate yield—what you end up with is an absolute measure of performance. In other words, the figure gives no indication of whether that amount of return is good or bad. So, you really don't know if you're getting a *satisfactory* rate of return. To find out, you need a benchmark, or standard of performance. In investments, that standard is the desired, or minimum, rate of return you feel you should earn on a particular investment *in light of the amount of risk you have to assume.* We saw earlier that there should be a trade-off between risk and return—if you have to take on more risk, you should expect to earn more return. The desired rate of return is simply the vehicle through which you put this risk-return principle into practice.

It's a good idea to have a minimum rate of return in mind before you make an investment. In this way, you can bring your desired rate directly into your investment decision and, in so doing, take the steps to see to it that you are being adequately compensated for risk. Probably the easiest way to come up with such a rate is to start with the returns on U.S. Treasury securities. For example, if the returns on long-term government bonds are, say, 9%, then you should expect at least another 2 or 3 points if you're investing in high-quality stocks. Under such conditions, a good blue chip stock should generate a return of around 11% or 12%. In contrast, if you're thinking about putting money into a short-term vehicle, you might be satisfied with a rate of return that's a lot lower—say, 6% or 7%. Remember: *an investment is acceptable only if it promises to generate a rate of return that meets or exceeds your desired rate of return!*

How to Keep It Safe and Still Get a Good Return on Your Money

The whole idea of a safe investment program is that you do not have to take unnecessary risks in order to earn a decent rate of return. Start by identifying, in general terms, a tolerable level of risk, and then select those savings/investment vehicles that are not only within your tolerance for risk, but also promise a rate of return that fully compensates you for any risks you have to bear. In other words, get the kind of risk-return trade-off you want by looking for savings/investment outlets that offer preservation of capital as well as a satisfactory return on your capital. In addition, no matter what kind of savings/investment vehicles you choose, be sure you get as much as you can out of them. That is, make sure you're using the securities in such a way that you're gaining the most benefits—don't pass up any added returns that are there for the taking. Finally, to get the most over the long haul, be sure to put the concept of compound interest to work for you.

In short, when investing for safety's sake, keep these four
be's in mind:

- Be Safe
- Be Comfortable
- Be Consistent
- Be Patient

Be Safe

Safe investing means you shouldn't have to take any unnecessary
risks. Therefore, one of the first things to look for in an investment is *preservation of capital*—if not absolute preservation, at
least adequate protection against loss. Also, when selecting an
investment, make sure you consider each of the four major types
of risk: business/financial, market, purchasing power, and liquidity. Keeping these risks in check is the best way of reaching the
level of safety you're looking for. The bottom line if you want to
be safe is to stick to investments that don't involve a lot of risk.

Be Comfortable

Every investor has a particular tolerance for risk. Moreover, tolerance for risk tends to change over time as individuals go through
different stages in their lives—for example, people in their late 20s
or early 30s are often more tolerant of risk than those in their late
50s or early 60s. Given your station in life, your investment goals,
and so forth, you alone are the best judge of your tolerance for
risk. If you haven't already done so, take the time to think carefully about how you react to uncertainty and respond to losses,
and then try to get an idea of your own tolerance for risk. Be
honest with yourself. Don't make the mistake of letting an unreal-
istic (or far-fetched) investment goal be the principal factor in
setting your tolerance for risk.

Once you've specified your risk tolerance, use it as a guide
in selecting investments. If you have very low tolerance for risk,
you belong in very low-risk securities—perhaps nothing more

exciting than money funds or savings bonds. There's absolutely nothing wrong with that! If you employ these securities in an intelligent manner, you can still end up with a tidy profit down the road. If, however, you're willing to tolerate a bit more risk, then give some thought to moving some of your money to investment-grade bonds, blue chip stocks, and/or high-quality mutual funds. But in doing so, make sure that the investments you select offer returns that will fully compensate you for the added risks. In this way, you can *be comfortable* not only with the risks you have to bear, but also with the returns you're able to obtain.

Be Consistent

One of the ingredients found in most successful investment programs is consistency. Such investors develop an investment program and stick with it. They're consistent in the types of securities they invest in, their tolerance for risk, and in the financial commitments they make to their investment programs. This latter point is particularly important, since one of the best ways of building up a sizable amount of capital is to systematically add funds to your investment program over time. Decide on an amount of money that you can readily afford and put that amount in on a regular basis. By so doing, your capital will grow not only because of the success of your investment program, but also because of the regular contributions you make to it. It's as if you and your investment program are partners: you provide the capital and your investment program provides the performance. The importance of making regular contributions to your investment program cannot be overstated—it ranks right up there with compound interest. Thus, for best results, *be consistent* in your approach to investing and in adding funds to your investment pool.

Be Patient

The idea here is two-fold: get into your investments for the long run, and don't panic when things don't quite work out as expected in the short run. Make a long-term commitment to your investment program, a minimum of 5 to 7 years, preferably longer. That's not only the best way to get the most from your investments and from compound interest, it also gives you greater flexibility in deciding when to get out of an investment. But by all means, if you can't make a long-term commitment, then stick to the shorter-term securities. This may be the best way of avoiding a lot of potentially serious problems down the road.

Making a long-term commitment also means plowing back your profits. And it means sticking with your investment decisions for the duration. Don't bail out the first time the price drops or something goes wrong—if you can't take a little price volatility, then it's clear you're not comfortable with that security, and you probably should go back and reevaluate your tolerance for risk. More often than not, so long as you're careful in selecting your investments to begin with, things will work themselves out if you're just willing to *be patient.*

Some Investment Don'ts

In addition to those basic investment guidelines, here are a couple of investment don'ts that you should keep in mind when pursuing a safe investment program:

DON'T PUT ALL YOUR EGGS IN ONE BASKET In a word: *diversify.* Because in so doing, you'll be able to reduce your exposure to risk even more, and do it in such a way that you won't jeopardize your potential for profits. Allocate your capital to several different investments so that you're able to build a diversified portfolio of securities. (Asset allocation and portfolio management are discussed in chapter 8.) By holding a diversified portfolio of securities, you won't expose all your capital to loss in case things don't work out as expected with one of your investments. For example, if you had all your money in long-term government bonds, then a sharp rise in interest rates would hurt everything you owned. Portfolio diversification is an easy and effective way to avoid that kind of loss. If you do it right, it doesn't take a lot of money and a lot of different investments to achieve a well-balanced portfolio.

DON'T TRY TO TIME THE MARKET Boy, it sure sounds great: you buy at the bottom and sell out at the top! This is, after all, what investing is all about—"buy low, sell high." The trouble is, it usually doesn't work that way. The market is too efficient—or if you like, too fickle—for that kind of activity to occur with any degree of regularity. The fact is it's very difficult, if not impossible, to consistently out-perform the market by picking market highs and lows. Now, obviously, had you known for certain on Friday, October 16th, 1987, that come Monday, October 19th, the market was in for its biggest fall in history, you would have been foolish not to get out of stocks and into cash and bonds. But few, if any, people have such foresight. Professionals can't do it, so there's no reason to suspect that amateurs can do an even better job. Granted, there are financial planners and money managers who charge hefty fees to help you "time the market." But check their records and you'll find that all but a handful of them can't even keep up with the market, as they tend to sell well before the market tops and buy back in long after it's bottomed out. More often than not, when you try to time the market, you only end up making your broker and the IRS happy! Thus, for best results, get into the market for the long haul and learn to ride out those occasional market swings. That's what most successful investors do.

3

Getting Started—
It's Easier Than You Think

Contrary to what some people may believe, there is really nothing
mystical about the topic of investing. In fact, it's quite easy to get
started in investing and to expand your investment horizons beyond passbook savings accounts and bank CDs. Granted, the
terminology may seem a bit baffling at times, but don't let that
mislead you into thinking there's no room for someone who wants
to pursue a safe investment program. Nothing could be farther
from the truth.

To get started, you obviously need some money. But before
you rush out to withdraw all your savings, keep in mind that this
is investment capital we're talking about here—this is money
you've accumulated above and beyond your savings. That is, before you embark on a full-scale investment program, make sure
you have some savings put away for emergencies and other purposes, and that you have adequate insurance coverage to protect
you and your family against the unexpected. Indeed, having the
savings and insurance to meet life's emergencies are two investment prerequisites that are absolutely essential to the development of a successful investment program.

In addition to money, you need knowledge. Even though
investing for safety's sake means keeping it simple and basic, you
still need a fundamental grasp of the market and the different

types of securities. In most cases, the cornerstone of a successful investment program is not luck but know-how. Start following the market by becoming a regular reader of publications like *Money, Changing Times, The Wall Street Journal, Barron's, Forbes,* and *Fortune.* Sooner or later, you'll need a way to invest—more specifically, you'll need a broker, the party through whom you'll be buying (and selling) stocks, bonds, and other securities. If a friend or relative of yours has a broker that they like and trust, get an introduction. Alternatively, go to some of the free investment seminars that are put on by brokerage firms in your area; or visit several of the brokerage firms in your community. Talk to one of their account executives about your investment needs. You'll find that opening an account at a brokerage house is as easy as opening a checking account at a bank. Then, before you know it, you'll be on your way.

Knowing Where You Want to Go Is Half the Battle

Just where do you want to go with your investment program; what do you realistically want to accomplish? The most successful investment programs are those that have a purpose, a sense of direction—these investors know what they want to achieve and how they intend to get there. So, too, should you have a well-developed investment plan.

Where you want to go will depend on where you are. Your age, income level, and tax bracket, the ages of your children, your general health and that of your family, and of course, your tolerance for risk are all very important personal characteristics that play a critical role in defining the type of investment program you're likely to follow. For example, a young unmarried person is likely to be more aggressive in his or her investment program than a middle-aged homeowner with a mortgage and three kids to get through college. Deciding on a course of action to follow requires careful thought.

What Are Your Investment Objectives?

Some people buy securities for the protection they provide from taxes (that's what tax shelters are all about). Others want to have money put aside for that proverbial rainy day or, perhaps, to build up a nice retirement nest egg. Your goals tend to set the tone for your investment program, and play a major role in determining how conservative (or aggressive) you're likely to be in making investment decisions. In a very real way, they provide a purpose to your investments.

Given that you have adequate savings to cover any emergencies, the most frequent investment objectives are to: (1) enhance current income, (2) save for a major purchase, (3) fund your retirement, and (4) shelter income from taxes. Not surprisingly, investing for safety's sake is an approach that can be and, in our opinion, should be used with each and every one of these objectives.

ENHANCE CURRENT INCOME The idea here is to put your money into investments that will enable you to supplement your income. In other words, it's for people who want to live off their investment income. There's no compounding here; the income is gone shortly after it's received. A secure source of high current income, from dividends or interest, is obviously the principal concern of such investors. Retired people, for example, often choose investments offering high current income—at low risk. Another common reason for seeking supplemental income is that a family member requires extended costly medical care. Even after insurance, such recurring costs can heavily burden a family budget without this vital income supplement.

SAVE FOR A MAJOR PURCHASE People often put money aside, sometimes for years, in order to save up enough to make just one major expenditure. These savings might cover the down payment on a home or vacation property, the money for a child's college education, the capital to start a business, or the purchase of a very special car or boat. Whatever your goal, the idea is to set your sights on something and then go about building your capital with that objective in mind. It sure makes the whole act of investing a lot more pleasurable. Once you have a handle on approximately how much money you're going to need to attain one or more of these goals, you can specify the types of investment vehicles you intend to use. For example, you might decide to follow a low-risk approach by making a single lump-sum investment in a bond that matures in the year you need the funds; or you could follow a strategy that calls for investing a set amount of money over time in something like a high-quality mutual fund. For some major purchases, you will probably want to accept a lot less risk than for others. For example, the down payment on a home or a child's education should not be jeopardized in any way by the types of investment vehicles you choose.

FUNDING YOUR RETIREMENT Accumulating funds for retirement is easily the biggest and usually most important reason for investing. Too often, though, retirement planning occupies only a small amount of our time, since we tend to rely heavily on our employers and Social Security to meet our retirement needs. As many people learn all too late in life, this can be a costly mistake. A better approach is to review the amounts of income you can realistically expect to receive from Social Security and your employee pension plan and then decide, based on your own retirement goals, whether or not these sources will be adequate to meet your needs. Chances are they won't be, in which case you'll have to supplement them through your personal investments. Often this is done through some type of tax-sheltered arrangement, such as an IRA or Keogh account. These are largely self-administered programs and as such, they're ideally suited to the safe investment vehicles and strategies discussed in the coming chapters.

SHELTER INCOME FROM TAXES The federal and most state income tax codes do not treat all sources of income equally. For example, the interest income from most municipal bonds is considered to be *tax-free*, while the interest income on Series EE savings bonds is *tax-deferred*—that is, taxes aren't due until the bonds are cashed in. The goal of sheltering income from taxes was made considerably more difficult with the Tax Reform Act of 1986. Even so, such a goal for some investors still goes hand in hand with the goal of saving for a major purchase or for retirement. If you can avoid or defer paying taxes on your investment income, all other things being equal, you have more funds available for reinvestment during the period and so end up with more money at the end of your investment horizon.

You Need a Savings Plan

Once you have one or more investment objectives in mind, it's time to go about deciding how you intend to reach those goals. This is where a savings plan comes into play. Let's assume that you want to accumulate, say, $250,000 in capital over the next 20 years. Part of this will go toward building up a retirement nest egg that can be used to supplement your employer-sponsored pension plan, and the rest will be used to buy a mountain retreat. You now have a well-defined, specific financial goal. But how do you reach that goal?

The first thing you must decide is where the money will come from. Part of it, of course, will come from the return (profit) on your investments, but you'll still have to come up with the *investment capital* to start with. Most experts agree that the best way to accumulate funds is through some type of systematic savings plan. In this regard, saving should not be relegated to a random event that occurs whenever income happens to exceed expenditures. Rather, it should be a deliberate, well-thought-out activity designed not only to accumulate funds systematically over time, but also to preserve value, insure liquidity, and earn a decent rate of return.

So, just how do you go about meeting your goal of accumulating $250,000 over the next 20 years? If you're starting from scratch, then it's probably best to rely on a savings plan where you systematically add a set amount each year to your investment capital. Since you need $250,000 in 20 years, you might be tempted to simply divide your $250,000 goal by the 20-year time period: $250,000/20 = $12,500. Unfortunately, this procedure would fail to take into account the fact that the money can earn a positive rate of return over time. Because of this, the amount you need to save each year is considerably less than $12,500.

Actually, there are three things you need to know to find out how much you're going to have to save over time: the first is the targeted amount of money you want to accumulate ($250,000); the second is the period of time over which you're going to accumulate the money (20 years); and the third is the average rate of return you feel you can earn on your money. Clearly, the more you can earn on your savings, the less you'll have to save each year.

Given these three pieces of information, the correct way to find the amount of annual savings is to divide the amount you want to accumulate over time by what is known as an *annuity factor*. An annuity factor basically takes into consideration both the time period you're working with and the rate of return you think you can make on your money. To make the annual savings calculation, you need a table of annuity factors, such as the one reproduced here. To locate an annuity factor on the table, first find the time period to the left of the table that corresponds with the amount of time you have to meet your goal; then look across the top of the table for the interest rate that you estimate your investments will earn. The point where the interest rate column intersects with the time period row is the annuity factor. (*Note:* If you're using a time period or rate of return that's not on the

Annuity Factors

Years	Interest Rates				
	5%	8%	10%	12%	15%
3	3.15	3.25	3.31	3.37	3.47
5	5.53	5.87	6.10	6.35	6.74
7	8.14	8.92	9.49	10.10	11.10
10	12.60	14.50	15.90	17.50	20.30
15	21.60	27.20	31.80	37.30	47.60
20	33.10	45.70	57.30	72.10	102.00
25	47.70	73.10	98.30	133.00	212.00

table, just "eyeball" it—take an average, as that'll provide you with a sufficiently close approximation of the annuity factor you're looking for.)

For the purposes of our example, let's say you feel reasonably sure you can earn an average return of around 8% over the next 20 years. Using the table to locate the value that lies at the intersection of an 8% rate of return and 20 years tells you the annuity factor is 45.7. Now, to find out how much you'll have to save each year, just divide your target amount by this annuity factor: $250,000/45.7 = $5,470 per year. So long as you can earn 8% on your money, that's the amount you'll have to invest each year for the next 20 years in order to end up with a $250,000 retirement nest egg. The only assumption you're making here is that you'll be able to earn an average rate of return of 8% on your investments. In this case, you'll have to provide a total of about $110,000 in investment capital: the rest—nearly $140,000— comes from the 8% earnings on your investments. You now have a specific savings plan you can follow to achieve the specific investment objective you've set. Using this yearly savings formula, you can easily find the amount you'll need to set aside each year to accumulate any sum of money.

An Investment Plan Provides Direction

How you save $5,470 a year is up to you. Perhaps you'll put away $450 a month, or use part of your quarterly bonus checks to add $1,375 to your savings every 3 months. Whatever procedure you follow, keep in mind that all you're doing is accumulating the required investment capital. You still have to put that money to work in some kind of investment program, and that's where an investment plan comes into the picture. An *investment plan* is nothing more than a simple, preferably written, statement that lays out how your accumulated investment capital will be invested for the purpose of reaching the goals you've set. The target date— the date in the future when you want the money to be available—

should be clearly specified, along with the amount of risk you're willing to assume.

In the example we've been using, your savings plan set an average 8% rate of return as a target you felt you could achieve. Now you have to come up with a way of attaining that 8% on your money. Should you fall short of that goal, you won't make it to $250,000 in 20 years without more investment capital. Now, you won't earn 8% on your money by just putting it in a passbook savings account. So you have to specify, in general terms at least, the kinds of investment vehicles you intend to use, and the general asset allocation plan you propose to follow. When complete, your investment plan is a way of translating an abstract investment target (in this case, an 8% return) into a specific investment program.

Developing Investor Know-How

Face it: some people are more knowledgeable about investing than others. As a result, investment vehicles or tactics that hold appeal for some investors may not even be in the vocabulary of others. Investor know-how, in short, defines the playing field and helps determine how you'll go about meeting the investment objective you've set for yourself. Being knowledgeable about investments is particularly important to safety-conscious investors since one of the key elements in investing for safety's sake is *knowing how to achieve decent rates of return without taking unnecessary risks.*

There's no substitute for being informed when it comes to making investment decisions. While it can't guarantee success, it can help you avoid unnecessary losses—like the ones that seem to happen all too often when people put their money into savings and investment vehicles they don't fully understand. Such results aren't too surprising, since these investors violate the first rule of investing, which is: *Never start an investment program, or buy an investment vehicle, unless you're thoroughly familiar with what you're getting into.* If you don't understand it, then stay away from it!

Well, just what kind of information do you need to follow? Not a whole lot, really, and certainly not so much that it'll take up a lot of your time. If you stick to the basics and keep it simple, as most safe investors do, then it really doesn't take a great deal of time and effort to become an informed investor. There are four basic types of investment information that you should try to stay abreast of:

- *Economic developments and current events*—you need a way to evaluate the underlying investment environment.
- *Alternative investment vehicles*—so that you can stay abreast of market developments.
- *Current interest rates and price quotations*—both to monitor your investments, and to stay alert for developing investment opportunities.
- *Personal investment strategies*—so that you can hone your skills and watch for new techniques as they develop.

There's more discussion about staying informed in the Appendix, including a list of some useful, reader-friendly sources of investment information.

Working with a Broker

If you choose to follow a safe investment program that's confined to bank CDs, money market deposit accounts, and Series EE savings bonds, then you'll be able to make all your transactions through your local friendly banker. But when you expand your investment horizon beyond Main Street and start looking to Wall Street for stocks, bonds, and mutual funds, you'll also have to start working with a broker. Just as it's important to find a banker that you can work with, it's also important to find a broker you're comfortable with.

Try to select a broker, or account executive as they're also called, who understands your investment objectives and who can effectively assist you in pursuing them. If you choose a broker whose own disposition toward investing is similar to yours, you should be able to avoid conflict and establish a solid working relationship. It is probably best to ask friends or business associates to recommend stockbrokers. It is not important—and often even inadvisable—to know your stockbroker personally since most, if not all, of your orders are placed by phone anyway. In addition, a strict business relationship eliminates the possibility of social concerns interfering with the achievement of your investment objectives. This does not mean, of course, that your broker's sole interest should be commissions. Indeed, a broker should be far more than just a salesperson, for a good broker is someone who's more interested in your investments than in commissions. Should you find you're dealing with someone who's always trying to push new products or investments on you, then by all means, dump that broker and find a new one!

The Services Provided by a Broker

In addition to carrying out purchase and sale transactions, stockbrokers offer their clients a variety of other services. For this reason, selecting a good brokerage house is just as important as choosing a good broker, since the brokerage house will have a bearing on the types of services available to you. Not all brokerage firms provide the same services. Thus, you should try to select a broker who is affiliated with a firm that provides the types of services you are looking for. Many brokerage firms provide a wide array of free information, ranging from stock and bond guides to research reports on specific securities or industries. Brokerage houses often have research staffs that periodically issue analyses of economic, market, industry, or company behavior and events, and relate them to recommendations for buying or selling certain securities. As a client of a large brokerage firm, you can usually expect to receive monthly bulletins discussing market activity and possibly even a recommended investment list. You will also receive a statement describing all of your transactions for the month, commission charges, interest charges, dividends and interest received, and your account balance.

Another valuable service is that most major brokerage firms will automatically invest any surplus cash left in a customer's account in one of its money funds, thereby allowing the customer to earn a reasonable rate of return on these balances. Such arrangements help the investor to manage cash more effectively and earn as much as possible on temporarily idle funds. Brokerage houses will also hold your securities for you, as protection against their loss; the securities kept in this way are said to be held in *street name.* As a client, you are protected against the loss of securities or cash held by your broker by the Securities Investor Protection Corporation (SIPC), an agency of the federal government that insures each customer's account against the financial failure of the brokerage firm. SIPC insurance covers each account for up to $500,000 (of which up to $100,000 may be in cash balances held by the firm). If your securities are worth more than $500,000, split them up into more than one account so that you can get full coverage for each account. Note, however, that SIPC insurance does not guarantee that the dollar value of the securities will be recovered. It only insures that the securities themselves will be returned.

If all you want to do is make security transactions and aren't all that interested in obtaining any of the other brokerage services then you should probably consider using a *discount broker.* Such brokers do little more than execute orders for customers—they provide little or no research information or investment advice. Transactions are initiated by calling a toll-free telephone number. The discount brokerage firm then executes your order at the best possible price and confirms the details of the transaction by mail. Discount brokers are becoming so popular that many banks and savings and loans are making discount brokerage services available to their customers. Listed below are some of the major discount and full-service brokerage houses.

Discount Brokers

Brown & Company
Bull & Bear Securities
Charles Schwab
Fidelity Brokerage Services
Muriel Siebert & Company
Quick & Reilly
Rose & Company
Stock & Trade
Vanguard Discount Brokers
Waterhouse Securities

Full-Service Brokers

A. G. Edwards & Sons
Dean Witter
Drexel Burnham Lambert
Kidder, Peabody
Merrill Lynch
Paine Webber
Prudential-Bache Securities
Shearson Lehman Hutton
Smith Barney, Harris Upham
Thomson McKinnon Securities

Coping with Commissions

As a rule, there are no commissions to pay when you invest in bank products like CDs and money market deposit accounts. You may, of course, be assessed a service charge if your account drops below a certain level, or be faced with a penalty if you withdraw funds prior to maturity, but at least you don't have to pay a commission when you buy or cash in these things. Not so with stocks, bonds, and a large number of other investment vehicles. Take mutual funds, for example. They can be sold either as no-load funds, in which case there is no commission, or as load funds, in which case you pay a commission equal to a certain percentage of your initial investment—which may be as high as 8½%. You also pay a commission with stocks or bonds, both when you buy and when you sell the securities. To get a feel for commission costs, let's take a look at what you might expect to pay when buying (or selling) stocks and bonds.

THE COST OF BUYING AND SELLING STOCKS Common stocks can be bought (or sold) in round or odd lots. A *round lot* is 100 shares, or increments of 100 shares of stock; an *odd lot* is any transaction of less than 100 shares. The sale of 400 shares of stock would be considered a round lot transaction, but the purchase of 75 shares would be an odd lot transaction; trading 250 shares of stock would involve a combination of two round lots and an odd lot. The cost of executing common stock transactions has risen dramatically since the introduction in 1975 of negotiated, as opposed to fixed, commissions. In practice, most brokerage firms have fixed fee schedules that are applied to small transactions, while negotiated commissions usually kick in at transaction levels of around $25,000 or more. As a result, while negotiated commissions are fine for large institutional investors and individuals of substantial means, they have not proven to be so beneficial for more modest investors.

Basically, an investor incurs two types of transaction costs when buying or selling stock. The major one is the brokerage fee paid at the time of transaction. As a rule, brokerage fees equal between 1 and 3 percent of most transactions. The other component of the transaction cost is the transfer fee and tax levied on the seller of the securities. Fortunately, these charges are modest compared with the brokerage commission.

The accompanying table shows a commission schedule used by one major brokerage house. Not surprisingly, the amount of the commission increases with the number and price of shares traded. Thus, the cost of selling 50 shares of stock trading at $35 per share amounts to $45.79, whereas the cost of trading 200 shares of a $75 stock is $175.97. Although the dollar cost increases with the size of the transaction, on a relative basis, it actually declines. For instance, the brokerage fees for the 50-share transaction amount to 2.6 percent of the transaction, whereas those for the 200-share trade represent a cost of only 1.1 percent.

The Cost to Buy or Sell Common Stock

Share Price	Number of Shares						
	5	10	25	50	100	200	500
$ 1	$ 1.66	$ 2.24	$ 4.00	$ 6.94	$12.82	$ 24.57	$ 59.81
5	3.79	6.52	12.65	16.09	22.98	44.90	101.13
10	6.46	11.86	15.83	22.45	33.92	66.77	129.73
25	12.43	15.66	25.36	37.52	58.71	103.63	225.03
35	13.71	18.21	31.06	45.79	70.15	132.11	284.83
50	15.61	22.02	37.26	58.18	84.77	168.00	354.60
75	18.79	28.38	47.58	72.48	88.52	175.97	434.33
100	21.97	32.96	57.91	84.23	88.52	175.97	438.33
125	25.15	37.10	65.06	87.99	88.52	175.97	438.33
150	28.32	41.22	72.21	87.99	88.52	175.97	438.33

Source: A major full-service brokerage house.

As you can see, dealing in odd lots quickly adds to the cost of a stock transaction. This is because all transactions made on the floor of major stock exchanges are in round lots, and so the purchase or sale of odd lots requires the assistance of a specialist. This usually results in an odd lot differential charge of 12.5 to 25 cents per share at the times of both purchase and sale.

The commission schedule shown above is that used by a

Full-Service vs. Discount Broker Stock Commissions

Type of Broker	Size of Stock Transaction				
	$3,000 (100 shs. at $30)	$5,000 (500 shs. at $10)	$10,000 (1,000 shs. at $10)	$15,000 (300 shs. at $50)	$25,000 (500 shs. at $50)
Typical full-service broker	$65	$130	$240	$235	$355
Typical discount broker	$30	$50	$80	$60	$80
Discount broker commissions as % of full-service broker commissions	46%	38%	33%	25%	22%

full-service brokerage firm. You could, of course, do your trading through a discount broker and, very likely, reduce your transaction costs substantially. In order to discourage small orders, most discounters charge a minimum transaction fee of $18 to $35. Normally, depending on the size of the transaction, discount brokers can save investors from 30% to 80% of the commissions charged by full-service brokers. A brief comparison of full-service versus discount brokerage commissions is provided in the next table.

THE COST OF BUYING AND SELLING BONDS Aside from transfer and sales taxes, which are minimal, the major expense in bond transactions is the brokerage fee paid when bonds are bought and sold. The advent of negotiated commissions has also done away with standard commission tables for bonds, but you can gain an idea of what kind of commission costs you're likely to encounter with bonds by referring to the accompanying table.

Bond Commissions

CORPORATES	Brokerage Fee
First 5 bonds, or $5,000 par value	$10 each bond, or per $1,000 of par value
Next 20 bonds, or $20,000 par value	$7.50 each bond, or per $1,000 of par value
For everything above 25 bonds, or $25,000 par value	$5 each bond, or per $1,000 of par value
TREASURIES	
For transactions involving par value of $50,000 or less	Net bid or ask price* plus $20 odd lot charge (per trade)
For transactions involving par value of $50,000 or more	Net bid or ask price*

* The net bid or ask price differs from the bid or ask price quotations by the amount of the brokerage fee charged on the transaction.

Source: A major brokerage house.

The cost of executing small transactions is fairly high—*$10 to $25 per bond* is not an unusual fee to pay for transactions involving 4 or 5 bonds or less. However, as with stocks, the relative cost declines quickly as the size of the transaction increases. Consider, for example, the cost of acquiring 40 corporate bonds:

For the first 5 bonds	5 × $10.00	=	$ 50.00
For the next 20 bonds	20 × $7.50	=	$150.00
For the next 15 bonds	15 × $5.00	=	$ 75.00
Total commissions			$275.00

In relation to the $40,000 worth of bonds being purchased, commission costs amount to less than 1 percent. In fact, compared to most other types of securities, bond transaction costs are definitely on the low side.

This chapter has looked at investment planning, sources of investment information, and dealing with brokers. These are all essential ingredients in developing a sound investment program; and they're the things you ought to have a good handle on before setting out in the world of investments. Once you've selected a broker, opened an account, and have other preliminaries out of the way, you're ready to start putting your money to work, which means finding investment vehicles that meet your needs. That's where the next four chapters come in—they discuss in detail the four basic types of safe investment vehicles: short-term securities, high-grade bonds, blue chip stocks, and quality mutual funds.

PART TWO

MANAGING YOUR INVESTMENTS

4

Saving and Investing for Liquidity and Return

It's been estimated that more than 75% of all American households have some money put away in savings—and, incredibly, of those households that do save, over half have more than $10,000 socked away! Clearly, to a lot of people, saving money is not just a matter of putting loose change into a piggy bank. It's serious business.

Savings should first and foremost be held as a cushion, or safety valve, to meet those "rainy day" emergencies. They should be the vehicle for accumulating funds that will be readily available when and if the need arises. While opinions differ on how much to hold for such purposes, the general consensus seems to be that 3 to 6 months' worth of after-tax income is best for most families. Now, if your employer has a strong salary continuation program and/or if you have access to a sizable line of credit, then the lower figure is probably suitable. But if you lack one or both of these, the more you should have in savings.

In addition to their *savings* function, short-term securities can also be held as part of an *investment* portfolio. Indeed, most investment experts recommend that in addition to the 3 to 6 months' holding of liquid reserves, you should also hold at least 10% to 25% of your investment portfolio in savings-type instruments. Under these conditions, short-term securities are used not only because of their liquidity, but also because of the return they offer. Some investors may, as a matter of practice, devote all or most of their portfolio to such securities. They feel these investments provide the best return for the risk—a course of action that's totally appropriate for a very conservative investor, who can't (or doesn't want to) tolerate much risk.

Perusing the Menu

Over the past decade or so, there has been a tremendous proliferation in the kinds of savings and short-term investment vehicles available to individual investors. Saving and investing in short-term securities is no longer the simple task it once was, when the decision for most people boiled down to whether funds should be placed in passbook savings accounts or Series E bonds. Today, in a time when even checking accounts pay interest, investors can choose from a full menu of savings and investment vehicles. For in addition to the basic passbook savings account, individual investors can also select from certificates of deposit (CDs) of all stripes and colors, several different kinds of money funds, money market deposit accounts, Series EE savings bonds, and U.S. Treasury bills.

Very briefly, here's a rundown of those securities:

• **Passbook Savings Account** This is the traditional savings account you open at banks, savings and loans (S&Ls), and other thrift institutions. It pays a set, very low, rate of interest; can be opened with very little money; and funds can be deposited and withdrawn at any time.

• **Certificates of Deposit** Better known simply as CDs, these truly are time deposits in that when you put funds into these securities, they're supposed to remain on deposit for the life of the CD—there's usually a penalty for early withdrawal. CDs are convenient to buy and hold, and they offer attractive and highly competitive yields.

• **Money Market Mutual Funds** More commonly called money

funds, they pool the resources of many small investors and purchase highly liquid, short-term securities offered by the U.S. Treasury, major corporations, large commercial banks, and various government organizations. In effect, with a money fund, you're buying a professionally managed portfolio of short-term securities that offers highly competitive rates of return.

• **Money Market Deposit Account** These are accounts that are meant to look and act like money funds, but really aren't. Available at banks, S&Ls, and other thrifts, there is no portfolio of securities that's being managed for your benefit; rather, the bank merely pays a rate of interest that it feels will be competitive with money market returns. And as with a money fund, you can get in and out whenever you like.

• **Series EE Savings Bonds** These are the well-known savings bonds that have been around since World War II; issued by the U.S. Treasury, they are sold on a discount basis in denominations of $50 through $10,000. Though normally viewed as a form of savings, these really are investments that should be held for the long term, since there's a severe interest penalty if they're redeemed within the first five years.

• **U.S. Treasury Bills** Known as T-bills for short, these issues are backed by the full faith and credit of the U.S. government; they are short-term securities (3- and 6-month maturities are the most common), sold on a discount basis in minimum denominations of $10,000. T-bills carry no stated rate of interest but rather, the difference between what you pay for the bill and what you receive at maturity is your interest.

These are the short-term securities most popular with individual investors. We'll look at each of them in more detail later in the chapter.

Ranking the Returns . . . and the Risks

Keeping some of your money in short-term securities makes sense both for the diversification and for the steady, dependable returns they offer. Granted, over the long haul you'll probably earn more from high-grade bonds or blue chip stock funds, but only if you can stomach the wide market swings that have become so common in the last few years. Actually, the returns on short-term securities have not been all that bad. Over the quarter century from 1963 to 1987, such securities out-performed the stock market in no less than 10 of the 25 years, or about 40% of the time.

There's a whole spectrum of short-term interest rates, and just like the rest of the market, you do have some risks to contend with. The table ranks the returns on short-term securities, along with their exposure to the four major types of risk.

SHORT-TERM RETURNS Looking first at return, it's clear that the worst place to keep your money is in a passbook savings account. Not only is the return very low, but it's also a relatively fixed rate that's almost totally insensitive to other market yields. Money market deposit accounts are also on the low side, primarily because their returns are artificially set by banks and thrifts. Unlike passbook savings accounts, however, the yields paid on money market deposit accounts do tend to reflect current market rates fairly closely. The problem is that, all too often, the rates tend to be just under the market, and while they usually go up a lot more slowly than the market, rate cuts are incredibly up-to-the-minute! The returns on T-bills and money funds, in contrast, are fully responsive to prevailing market forces, and for that reason, they tend to yield more than the bank products. Not surprisingly, the

Short-Term Securities	Representative Returns (as of Early Spring 1988)
Passbook savings account	5.0%
Money market deposit account	5.8
6-month T-bill	6.3
Money market mutual fund	6.5
6-month CD	7.2
Series EE savings bond	7.4

best returns come with the least liquid securities: Series EE savings bonds (where the stated return requires a minimum 5-year investment) and 6-month CDs, that are subject to penalty for early withdrawal.

SHORT-TERM RISKS As far as risk is concerned, you get almost perfect preservation of capital with all of these securities, as there's really no risk that you'll ever lose your money, either through default or through adverse price behavior. In addition, notice that none of these securities is subject to any real *business/ financial risk*. The T-bills and savings bonds are issued by the U.S. Treasury, so there's no risk there; and the savings accounts, money market deposit accounts, and CDs can all be obtained at banks and thrifts that are federally insured up to $100,000. Even the money funds are rated as risk-free because of their extensive diversification and professional money management.

Likewise, none of these securities is subject to any *market risk* to speak of, since there's really no exposure to capital loss when interest rates rise. However, because short-term interest rates are so volatile, the returns to investors do suffer when rates drop. In essence, it's not your capital that's at risk here, but your earnings. For with the possible exception of long-term CDs, it's hard to lock in high yields for any length of time, since the maturities are so short. While falling rates have a negative impact on short-term securities, quite the opposite is true when rates rise. Unless you're

Risk (Risk is measured numerically: the lower the number, the lower the risk.)			
Business, Financial	Market Risk/ Interest Rate Risk	Purchasing Power	Liquidity
0	0 / 5	4	1
0	0 / 3	2	1
0	0 / 2	1	2
0	0 / 3	2	1
0	0 / 2	1	3
0	0 / 3	1	4

in a passbook savings account or long-term CD, you'll reap the benefits of higher interest income as market rates move up over time. Indeed, this is one of the positive and very attractive features of short-term investment vehicles.

This ability to move up with market interest rates has another positive side as well. For note that, except for passbook savings accounts, exposure to *purchasing power risk* is also on the low side for these securities. Interest rates rise with inflation, and because the returns on most short-term securities rise with market rates, these securities at least let you keep up with inflation. Finally, *liquidity risk* is seen to be the biggest problem with the longest-term securities and with those where there's a penalty for early withdrawals. In contrast, it's very easy to get money out of savings accounts, money market deposit accounts, and money funds—as simple and as convenient as using an automatic teller machine (ATM) and/or writing a check. T-bills are also highly liquid, but they're not as convenient, since you have to execute the trade through your banker or broker and then wait for several days before you receive your cash.

Those Interest Earnings Aren't Always What They Seem

Basically, interest from short-term investments can be earned in one of two ways. First, some securities—U.S. Treasury bills and Series EE savings bonds, to be specific—are sold on a *discount basis.* This means that the security is sold for less than its redemption (or face) value, and the difference between its selling price and redemption value is the amount of interest earned. Thus, the lower the price of the T-bill, the more you're going to earn in interest. The other way to earn interest is by *direct payment,* which is the procedure used with passbook savings accounts, money market deposit accounts, CDs, and money funds. You invest a certain sum, and the amount of money you make is figured relative to the amount of money invested—the more you have invested, the more you're going to earn in interest.

Although it should be a relatively simple process, there is one major complication that you should be aware of whenever you're dealing with products sold by banks, S&Ls, and other thrifts. That complication pertains to the rate of interest being used to figure earnings on savings accounts, money market deposit accounts, and CDs. Unfortunately, a 7% rate at one place may not be nearly as much as a 7% rate somewhere else. The reason: it's all in the way the interest is compounded. The more often the interest is compounded during the year, the greater the effective rate of interest and as such, the more you're going to earn. Don't be misled by advertised rates; instead, ask your banker to tell you specifically not only the quoted rate, but also the *effective annual yield* you'll be earning on your money.

The table shows how the effective rate of return steadily increases along with the frequency of compounding. Regardless of the quoted rate, the highest effective return always occurs with daily compounding—meaning that interest is credited to your account every day of the year. For example, notice that with a 10% quoted rate, daily compounding adds more than half a point to your total return. Now, while this may appear to be a trivial amount, the fact is that over an extended period of time the difference can be substantial. For example, over a 10-year period, the difference between earning 10% and 10.52% on a $10,000 investment amounts to $1,252! All this added income just from getting 10% compounded daily rather than 10% compounded

Quoted Rate	Effective Rate with Different Compounding Periods				
	Annually	Semiannually	Quarterly	Monthly	Daily
4%	4.00%	4.04%	4.06%	4.07%	4.08%
5	5.00	5.06	5.09	5.12	5.13
6	6.00	6.09	6.14	6.17	6.18
7	7.00	7.12	7.19	7.23	7.25
8	8.00	8.16	8.24	8.30	8.33
9	9.00	9.20	8.31	9.38	9.42
10	10.00	10.25	10.38	10.47	10.52
11	11.00	11.30	11.46	11.57	11.62
12	12.00	12.36	12.55	12.68	12.74

annually! Clearly, it pays to shop around for both attractive rates *and* frequent compounding.

Caution: A Savings Account May Be Hazardous to Your Financial Health

How would you like to put your money into something that pays a *very low* rate of return and keeps that very low rate, regardless of how high market interest rates go? It doesn't make any difference whether market rates are 7% or 17%, you'll still get 5% on your money. Obviously, this doesn't sound like a very good deal. Yet this is precisely what you get from a *passbook savings account.* With so many more attractive ways to save, you might think that no one uses passbook saving accounts any more. Well, think again. For, as incredible as it may seem, there's still over *$300 billion* held in such accounts. There's actually as much money in these accounts as there is in money market mutual funds.

Passbook savings accounts are offered by banks, S&Ls, and other thrift institutions. Such accounts have been the traditional savings vehicle for millions of Americans, and they're still popular with a lot of savers. Though the term *passbook* continues to be used with these accounts, computerized bank statements are rapidly replacing the passbooks (which, in the old days, served as the ledger of account activity). Generally, there are no minimum balance requirements on these accounts, though many banks do impose monthly maintenance (or service) charges if the balance drops below a certain amount (say, $500). And you can make as many withdrawals as you like, though again, there's usually a fee for excess withdrawals. In spite of the fact that interest rate ceilings on these accounts were eliminated in 1986, they continue to pay very low rates of interest: typically around 4½% to 5½%. The rates are artificially set by the deposit institution—and, indeed, as long as billions of dollars continue to flow into these accounts, the financial institutions will have little motivation to set more competitive rates.

Here's a simple test you can take to find out if a savings account is right for you:

Are you *under* 19 years of age? `YES` `NO`

Do you have *less* than $1,000 in your savings? `YES` `NO`

If you answered *yes* to one or both of these questions, a passbook savings account may be okay for you. However, if you answered *no* to both questions, put your money someplace else! Passbook accounts are fine for young savers: they're an ideal way to teach your child about savings, and most institutions will waive all maintenance charges for young depositors. In addition, they're usually about the only way you can accumulate a savings stake, since most other forms of savings require minimum deposits of $500 to $1,000. But once you've met this minimum, there's no reason to leave your money in a passbook account. You'll get just as much safety and convenience from a money market deposit account, *and* a lot better return.

The Good Points:

- *Very safe* if kept in federally insured institutions.
- *Convenient*—easy to open, and with ATMs, deposits and withdrawals can be made at just about any time.
- *Automatic compounding* so you don't have to reinvest your earnings.
- Excellent for instilling valuable *savings habits* in a young person.

And the Bad:

- *Intolerably low rate of interest*—the lowest of any savings or short-term investment vehicle.
- *Fees and hidden charges* can eat you alive and reduce your yield to zero (or less).

In short, while passbook accounts are generally viewed as a convenient savings vehicle (appropriate, perhaps, for accumulating basic emergency funds), they have *no* place in an investment program. With so many other, more attractive short-term investment outlets to choose from, keeping anything more than $1,000, or so, in a passbook savings account is simply too high a price to pay for safety and convenience.

Socking It Away in CDs

Individual savers and investors put more money into certificates of deposit (CDs) than into any other kind of short-term security—indeed, they hold roughly $1 *trillion* worth of these instruments. CDs appeal to investors because they're safe and they offer higher yields than T-bills or money funds. But they're also less liquid; for unlike a money fund or savings account, the money put into a CD is supposed to stay on deposit for a given period of time, as specified by the term (or life) of the CD. Although it is possible to withdraw funds prior to maturity, an interest penalty, usually in the form of a severely reduced rate of interest, makes withdrawal fairly costly.

CDs are sold by banks, S&Ls, and other thrifts (for safety's sake, make sure they're federally insured); they can also be purchased from brokerage houses. You'll probably need $500 to $1,000 to buy a CD from a bank or thrift, and a minimum of $1,000 to buy a brokered CD. Certificates of deposit usually pay a fixed rate of interest for the life of the security, and most institutions have tiered rates that pay higher yields for larger deposits. If your bank or thrift has tiered rates, find out where the cutoffs are, since you may be able to raise your return a bit with just a slight increase in the amount of your investment.

Also, before buying a CD, check out the frequency of compounding, as well as the quoted rate of interest. And, if you're a long-term investor, you might want to look into *rolling over* your CDs as they mature. It's a simple and effective way of keeping your money fully invested. Here's how it works: at the time you purchase your CD, have it set up so the bank or thrift automatically puts the money from your maturing CD into a new one (usually of the same maturity). By continually rolling over your CDs in this way, you don't have to worry about renewing your investment each time it matures. It'll all be taken care of for you.

Certificates of deposit are issued with maturities from as short as 7 days to 5 years or longer. The most popular maturities are 7 days, 30 days, 3 months, 6 months, 1 year, 2½ years, and 5 years. As demonstrated in the table, you can get higher yields from longer CDs.

CD Maturities	Representative Yields from Federally Insured Banks and S&Ls, Spring 1988
7 days	6.46%
30 days	6.61
3 months	6.78
6 months	7.17
1 year	7.51
2½ years	7.96
5 years	8.49

These representative yields are annualized, fully compounded rates of return. This is a fairly standard way of quoting yields in the financial marketplace. But keep in mind that for the shorter maturities (of less than a year), these figures assume that you will stay invested in CDs for the full year *and* at the rate of return that existed at the beginning of the year. For example, the yield on the 3-month CD doesn't mean that's what you'll earn in 3 months—cash out after 3 months and you'll only earn about a fourth of that amount. Likewise, if you leave your money in, the rates that you actually get when you roll over your CD will play a key role in determining the kind of annualized yield you actually realize on your investment: get a higher rate than what you started with and you'll end up with a higher annual yield. Most important, understand that with standard CDs, the bank makes no guarantees as to what the rate will be when you roll your CD over—*you*, not the bank, assume the reinvestment risk in this case.

The Good Points:

- *Very safe* if kept in federally insured institutions, assuming the amount invested doesn't exceed the $100,000 insurance limit.
- *Yields highly competitive* with other short-term securities.
- *Relatively low minimum deposit requirement,* so these investments are within the reach of most households.
- *Convenient and flexible,* since once you meet the minimum, you can invest just about any amount you want, for just about any period of time you want.
- *Taxes can be deferred* for up to a year, since there's no tax liability until the interest is actually paid or credited to your account.
- *Automatic compounding* for CDs with maturities of more than a year.
- *Current income,* if you arrange to have the issuing institution pay you your interest every month, or every quarter.

And the Bad:

- *Lack of liquidity,* since you're supposed to commit your money for the term of the issue.
- *Interest penalty,* and usually a fairly substantial one, for cashing in prior to maturity.
- *Reinvestment risk*—with short maturities, if rates drop so does your annualized yield; with long maturities, if rates rise you miss out on a better return.

The Growing List of New CDs

They're turning out new lines of CDs about as fast as the market can absorb them. No longer content to issue just the standard, plain vanilla brand, CDs now have all sorts of sexy, macadamia-nut kickers. If you're tired of old faithful and want to try something new, then you might want to consider CDs that are linked to major sporting events (such as a football game, where the bigger the beating that your team gives the opponent, the more interest you earn on your CD!), or CDs that are tied to the price of gold, or the stock market. While there's a whole herd of these things out there, here's a brief run-down of a few of the more popular ones.

• **Brokered CDs** These are simply certificates of deposit that are sold by stockbrokers. The brokerage house looks around the country for the best deal—highest yield—it can get, and then sells these CDs to its customers. In essence, a bank or S&L issues the CDs, and the brokerage house merely sells (or places) them with the investing public. The minimum denomination is usually only $1,000, so they are affordable, and there's no commission to pay since the broker earns its commission from the issuing bank or S&L.

If you're a serious CD investor, you ought to look into brokered CDs. They're attractive for two reasons: *First,* you can sell them prior to maturity without incurring a penalty, since the brokerage firms maintain active secondary markets; therefore, you can improve your liquidity. But remember, there are no guarantees here—the market prevails, so if rates go up, the relative value of your CD falls and you don't end up earning the rate you started out with. *Second,* you may be able to get higher yields from brokered CDs than from your local bank or thrift. For example, look at the average yield differentials that existed in late 1987:

	6-Month CD	1-Year CD	5-Year CD
Average bank or S&L	7.09%	7.49%	8.46%
Average brokerage house	7.36	7.97	9.25

As these figures reveal, you could have picked up ¼ to ¾ of a point by dealing with a broker. But be careful. The broker can always get higher yields by selling CDs issued by troubled banks or S&Ls. Therefore, *never buy a brokered CD unless it's from a federally insured institution*—ask your broker, just to be sure.

• **Bump-up CDs** This is a CD where the rate of interest keeps getting higher and higher over time. In essence, you sign up to buy a series of 6-month CDs, but you also have the option of getting out if you want. Here's how a typical bump-up CD works: you buy a 6-month CD that's renewable every 6 months for a period of 2 or 3 years, and every time you renew (or roll over) your CD, the rate of interest goes up by a set amount (say, ¼ of a percentage point). Thus, you start out by earning, say, 6% for the first 6 months, then 6¼% for the next 6 months, then 6½%, and so on. But there's more. Every time the CD comes up for renewal, you have the option of getting out—withdrawing your funds without any penalty. There is a downside to all this, and that is the beginning rate is usually set well below the rates on standard 6-month CDs. So you better carefully consider whether the benefits of a bump-up CD are worth the costs. Chances are they're not, since the most attractive attribute of this CD is its ability to lock in a high rate for an extended period of time, which is something that can be done with far greater return by simply buying a 2- or 3-year CD to begin with.

A variation of the bump-up CD is the *variable-rate CD*, which is simply a long CD (they usually have maturities of 1 year or more) whose interest rate floats up and down with a certain market rate. Thus, rather than a fixed rate of interest on your CD, you have a floating, or variable rate.

• **Stock Market CDs** These are the sexiest of the new CDs, and they offer not only the highest potential performance, but also the greatest potential for disappointment. In essence, the interest earnings on these securities are pegged to the performance of the stock market. They generally work something like this: You buy a CD (with a maturity of, let's say, 1 year) that's pegged to the Standard & Poor's 500 Stock Index. If the stock market goes up in a year, you earn 60% to 70% of the index's annualized appreciation; if, however, it goes down, you simply get your money back. Rather than striking out all together, you can get a small, guaranteed yield if you're willing to take a smaller piece of the action when the market goes up. Stock market CDs come in *bull* flavors and in *bear* flavors (which you buy if you think the market is going to drop). You can also buy CDs that are pegged to other financial markets—like the price of gold, for inflation-conscious investors. Most experts agree that these are *not* very good investments. After all, if you want to play the stock market, you can go out and buy stocks. There's no need to do it with a safe, secure investment like a CD.

Getting the Most from Your CD Investments

Putting some of your money into CDs makes a lot of sense if you're trying to invest for safety's sake. The reason: it's a safe, secure way to invest and you can still earn a decent rate of return on your money. Indeed, as we saw earlier in this chapter, when compared to other short-term securities, CD yields rank at, or near, the top. But there are a few things you can do to improve your returns even more. And all of them are pretty simple.

SHOPPING FOR TERMS For one thing, you can shop around for the best terms—make sure you're getting competitive returns, the best compounding, and that the withdrawal penalty isn't out of line. You might even consider a brokered CD if the yield differential is wide enough. Now please understand, this does *not* mean you should move from one place to another every time you can pick up a little more return—that would very likely be more trouble than it's worth. But when you initially invest in a CD, and periodically thereafter, just take the time to evaluate the terms—in effect, consider your alternatives—so that you know you're getting top dollar for your money (or at least a highly competitive yield).

Also, unless you're trying to lock in an abnormally high return (such as the substantial double-digit yields we had in 1980–81), there's usually no reason to select a 5-year CD over a 2½-year CD. In most cases, all you're going to get is another ½ point or so in added return. Big deal! So you can get 8½% from a 5-year CD versus 8% from a 2½-year CD. That translates into another ½ a point in return for another 2½ years of your time. When the added compensation is that small (and it usually is), don't lock your money up for any more than a 2½-year period; there's just too much added risk and not enough added return.

FOLLOW THE LADDER Ideally, you should try to put your money into long-term CDs (maturities of 2 to 3 years or more) when rates start falling, and short CDs (those with 3- to 6-month maturities) when rates start heading up. That way, you can lock in high yields before they fall and move up with them as they rise. Now granted, it makes a lot of sense to go long or short with your investments depending on what you think is going to happen to interest rates, but what if you have little confidence in, or aren't very comfortable with, your ability to predict market rates? What do you do then? The answer is to follow a simple yet highly effective technique known as the *laddered* approach to investing.

There are two ways to set up a ladder of CDs. One technique is to spread your money over several different maturities; say, 6 months, 1 year, and 2½ years. Put one-third of your money into each of the maturities and then just keep rolling the CDs over as they mature. In this way, you're covered no matter what happens: you can ride the market up with the short maturities and lock in the high yields with the long CDs. You may not do as well as you could if you were able to predict interest rates accurately, but even so, over the long haul, you'll probably be able to generate a very respectable rate of return.

Some would argue that you'd be able to earn an even better return by following another type of ladder. This technique is based on going after the higher yields that exist with the longer maturities. Here's how this CD ladder works: rather than put your money into three different maturities, pick one long maturity and then stagger the expiration dates. For example, if you want to invest in, say, 2½-year CDs, put one-third of your money into a 2½-year CD, one-third into an 18-month CD, and one-third into a 6-month CD. Now, when the 6-month issue matures, roll it over into a new 2½-year CD; do the same thing when the 18-month issue matures. From that point on, you'll have all your money invested in a staggered ladder of 2½-year CDs and every time one of them matures, you roll it over into a new one. In this way, by not putting all your eggs in one basket, you'll be able to ride the market and still reap the higher yields associated with the longer maturities.

Investing in Money Funds and Money Market Deposit Accounts

For an investment vehicle that started out so inauspiciously, the money market mutual fund has had an absolutely remarkable impact on our system of financial markets. Started in November 1972, with only $100,000 in total assets, this simple product helped usher in a whole new era in financial services. Actually, money funds weren't all that innovative. All they really did was apply the notion of a mutual fund to the buying and selling of short-term money market instruments, such as jumbo CDs, commercial paper, bankers acceptances, Treasury and agency securities, and the like. But now, for the first time, individual investors of modest means had access to a market where many securities require *minimum* investments of $100,000 or more. These investments became immensely popular with savers and investors, and in time, banks and thrifts were allowed to offer a competitive product: the money market deposit account (or MMDA, for short).

Money funds and MMDAs are high in liquidity, and very low in risk—indeed, they are virtually immune to any kind of capital loss. And their yields, which are a bit on the low side relative to some short-term securities, tend to follow general market conditions. As such, the returns are subject to the ups and downs of the marketplace. From a *savings* perspective, money funds and MMDAs are an excellent way to build up a pool of emergency funds. They pay more than a passbook account and they're just as liquid.

They're also popular as an *investment* vehicle, as they offer a convenient, safe, and profitable way to accumulate capital and temporarily store idle funds. However, because of their generally lower yields, don't put too much of your money into them. Granted, every investment portfolio needs something in money funds or MMDAs, but when the account starts to build up (to more than, say, 10% to 20% of your portfolio), you really should consider putting some of that money into other, higher-yielding short-term securities—like 3- to 6-month CDs, for instance.

Money Market Mutual Funds

A money fund simply pools the capital of many individual investors and uses it to build and manage a portfolio of short-term debt securities. Most require a minimum investment of $1,000 or so (though $2,500 to $5,000 minimum requirements are not uncommon). Just about every major brokerage firm has at least one or two money funds of its own, and another 250 or so are sold by independent fund distributors. Thus, if you've got an account with a brokerage firm, you can buy one of the house funds by simply phoning your order into your broker; or if you want to buy one of the unaffiliated funds, all you do is phone a toll-free number, request a prospectus and application, and then follow a few simple instructions. All but a few of these funds are sold as *no-loads*, which means there's no commission to pay when you buy (or sell) the fund. And once a money fund account is open, it's a simple matter to add more to your account.

The returns on money funds amount to whatever the fund managers are able to earn from their investment activities—net, of course, of any management fees levied for running the portfolio. All earnings are credited to your account daily, so your money's earning a rate of return that's also compounded daily. Money funds are closely followed by the financial media, and the latest net returns of the larger funds are reported regularly in *The Wall Street Journal, Barron's,* and other major newspapers. In addition, popular publications like *Money* magazine, *Changing Times,* and *Sylvia Porter's Personal Finance* periodically list the top-performing money funds.

Actually, there are several different kinds of money market mutual funds:

• **General Purpose Money Funds** Essentially, these funds invest in any and all types of money market investment vehicles, from Treasury bills and bank CDs to corporate commercial paper. The vast majority of money funds are of this type: they invest their money wherever they can find attractive short-term yields.

• **Government Securities Money Funds** These funds were established as a way to meet investor concerns for safety. They effectively eliminate any risk of default by confining their investments to Treasury bills and other short-term securities of the U.S. government or its agencies (such as the Federal Farm Credit System, the Federal Home Loan Mortgage Corporation, and the Federal National Mortgage Association).

• **Tax-exempt Money Funds** These are funds that limit their investing to very short (30- to 90-day) tax-exempt municipal securities. Since their income is free from federal income tax, they appeal predominately to investors in high tax brackets. The yields on these funds are about 25% to 35% *below* the returns on other types of money funds, so you need to be in a high enough tax bracket to produce a competitive after-tax return. Some tax-exempt funds confine their investing to the securities of a single state, so that residents of these high-tax states can enjoy income that's free from both federal and state tax.

Provided in the table are some of the bigger, more popular, and better-performing funds in each of the three categories. To give you an idea of the kind of return you can expect from money funds, we've computed the fully compounded annual yields on our sample of funds over the 5-year period 1983–87. While such returns are highly sensitive to prevailing market conditions, the yield patterns shown in the table are fairly typical. That is, the general purpose funds normally provide slightly better returns than the government securities funds, with the tax-exempt issues having the lowest yields because they're after-tax returns (as a point of reference, you would have to have been in the 39% tax bracket from 1983 to 1987 to make up for the big yield give-up

Fund Name	Minimum Initial Investment	5-Year (1983–87) Avg. Annual Return	Telephone Number
GENERAL PURPOSE FUNDS			
American Capital Reserve Fund	$1,000	7.90%	1-800-231-3638
Cash Mgmt. Trust of Amer.	5,000	8.06	1-800-421-9900
Dreyfus Liquid Assets	2,500	8.03	1-800-645-6561
Fidelity Cash Reserves	1,000	7.96	1-800-544-6666
Kemper Money Market Fund	1,000	8.23	1-800-621-1048
Paine Webber Cashfund	5,000	7.94	1-800-544-9300
Transamerica Cash Reserves	1,000	8.17	1-800-527-0727
T. Rowe Price Prime Reserve	1,000	8.01	1-800-638-5660
USAA Mutual—Money Market	1,000	7.93	1-800-531-8000
Vanguard MM Reserves—Prime	1,000	8.15	1-800-662-7447
Average		8.04%	
GOVERNMENT SECURITIES FUNDS			
Benham Capital Preservation Fund	$1,000	7.48%	1-800-227-8380
Cardinal Govt. Secs. Trust	1,000	7.98	1-800-848-7734
Carnegie Govt. Secs.—Money Market	1,000	7.59	1-800-321-2322
Dreyfus MM Instruments—Govt. Secs.	2,500	7.85	1-800-645-6561
Fidelity U.S. Govt. Reserves	1,000	7.71	1-800-544-6666
Mariner Government Fund	1,000	7.90	1-800-845-8406
Merrill Lynch Govt. Fund	5,000	7.76	1-800-637-3863
Pru-Bache Money Mkt. Assets	1,000	8.05	1-800-872-7787
Seligman Cash Management—Govt.	2,000	7.46	1-800-221-2450
Shearson Govt. & Agencies	2,500	7.83	1-212-321-7155
Average		7.76%*	
TAX-EXEMPT FUNDS			
Calvert Tax-free Reserves	$2,000	5.20%	1-800-368-2748
Delaware Tax-free Money Fund	5,000	4.72	1-800-523-4640
Dreyfus Tax-exempt Money Market	5,000	4.83	1-800-645-6561
Fidelity Tax-exempt Money Market	2,500	4.95	1-800-544-6666
Franklin Tax-exempt Money Fund	500	4.84	1-800-632-2350
Reich & Tang Daily Tax-free Income	5,000	4.92	1-800-221-3079
Shearson Daily Tax-free Dividend	2,500	4.68	Not available
Smith Barney Tax-free Money Fund	5,000	4.73	1-800-221-8806
T. Rowe Price Tax-exempt Money Fund	1,000	5.01	1-800-638-5660
Vanguard Muni Money Market	3,000	5.08	1-800-662-7447
Average		4.90% *	

* Return figures for the tax-exempt funds are *after-tax* yields, and so they will be less than the other reported returns.

Sources: Basic issue and performance data were obtained from *Donoghue's Mutual Funds Almanac* and *Forbes*; 5-year return figures are fully compounded yields, given reinvestment of all interest income.

between the average tax-exempt fund and the average general purpose fund).

One concern that many investors have pertains to the question of safety. Since money funds are not federally insured, you could argue that they will always be less secure than deposits in federally insured institutions. Indeed, banks and thrifts underscore this theme in a good deal of their advertising. However, the fact is that the default risk of money funds is almost zero, since the securities the funds purchase are very low in risk to begin with, and diversification by the funds lowers risk even more. Despite a remarkable record of safety, it is impossible to say with certainty that money funds are as risk-free as federally insured deposits—and in the event of a massive financial crisis, they probably are not. On the other hand, the amount of extra risk might be viewed as so minimal as to be easily offset by a slightly higher yield. This is a choice individual investors must make within their own risk-return framework.

Money Market Deposit Accounts

These investment vehicles were created for one simple reason: to give banks and thrifts the ability to compete with the enormously popular money market mutual funds. Unlike money funds, there's no portfolio of marketable securities to determine the rate of return being paid. Instead, the bank (or thrift) merely sets a rate that it feels is competitive with general money market yields (especially the returns being paid on money funds) and which it feels is sufficient to attract and hold deposits. Now, since the rate of return on an MMDA is set by the issuing institution, this also means that the frequency of compounding is unilaterally set as well—so read the fine print to make sure you're not being short-changed when it comes to effective yield. You also have to watch out for the tiered structure of rates that many banks and thrifts use with their MMDAs. To illustrate: You may be eligible for the full quoted rate only if you keep, say, $2,500 or more in your account; let it drop below $2,500 and the rate of interest also drops (usually to the rate paid on passbook accounts). Even worse, let your balance drop below, say, $1,000 and you may also be hit with a $5 to $10 monthly maintenance fee. This is in sharp contrast to money funds, which have no such minimum balance requirements—your balance can drop to 50 bucks and you'll still earn the same rate of return as everybody else.

MMDAs can be opened at just about any bank or S&L with a minimum initial deposit that usually ranges from about $1,500 to $2,500. (But watch out: a few institutions have minimum initial deposit requirements that are less than their minimum balance requirements, so it's possible to start off by earning less than the quoted rate.) MMDAs are federally insured up to a maximum of $100,000 by the FDIC or FSLIC. *Never* open one of these accounts at an institution that's not federally insured. Depositors have access to their money through check-writing privileges or through ATMs, though the number of free withdrawals is usually limited.

One final point about MMDAs: a lot of people like these accounts because they're so convenient. These people would rather deal with their friendly banker than with a broker or some impersonal voice at a faraway mutual fund office. They're just more comfortable doing business that way. And, of course, this is one of the major attributes of a MMDA. However, keep in mind that while convenience and comfort are fine, you're also very likely taking a hit on yield. For on average, money funds tend to pay about ¼ to ½ a percentage point *more* than MMDAs. Now if you normally keep less than $4,000 or $5,000 in a money account, it's probably not going to make a great deal of difference. But if it's more than that, then you, as an investor, ought to decide if the convenience of an MMDA is worth that kind of sacrifice in yield. Since there's virtually no difference in liquidity and safety between the two investment vehicles, you may find the yield give-up is just too much to take. In which case, you should use a money fund to maintain the liquidity needs of your investment portfolio.

The Good Points:

- *Easy and convenient* way to earn *competitive rates of return.*
- *No transaction costs or commissions.*
- *Automatic compounding of all interest earnings* so your investments grow at fully compounded rates.
- *Safe.* You don't have to worry about losing your capital, either through adverse price behavior or default. MMDAs are federally insured, and although money funds are not, they are so well diversified that the risk of default is virtually nonexistent.
- *Highly liquid.* You have access to your money at any time by simply writing a check. With MMDAs, you can also use ATMs.

And the Bad:

- *Fluctuating returns,* varying with the market, which is a distinct disadvantage when rates fall.
- *Substantial minimum initial deposit requirements.* It could be $1,000 to $1,500 or more for both money funds and MMDAs; in addition, most MMDAs have minimum balance requirements that you must maintain to earn the full quoted rate of return.
- *Checks must be written for a minimum amount,* typically $500 or more in a money fund, while MMDAs normally *restrict the number of free withdrawals.*
- *Yield sacrifice,* since higher rates are normally available from short-term CDs and occasionally from longer-term (6- to 12-month) T-bills.

Taxes:

Interest earnings are taxed as ordinary income in the year they're earned unless you hold tax-exempt money funds.

Treasury Bills and Savings Bonds—It Can't Get Any Safer

Looking for the ultimate safe haven for your investments? Well, there's no need to look any further than *U.S. Treasury bills.* Indeed, T-bills are viewed by market professionals as risk-free investment vehicles, and for this reason, they're often used as a benchmark in assessing the risk-return behavior of other securities. There's no risk of default here, nor is there much risk that you'll lose any of your money from adverse price behavior—these securities are just too short to be exposed to any real market risk. Another U.S. Treasury security that's considered equally safe is the *Series EE savings bond.* Even though it is a long-term savings/investment vehicle, it is totally immune to any capital loss. Though a lot of people look down their noses at the Series EE bond, it actually makes an interesting investment and should definitely be considered by safety-conscious investors.

U.S. Treasury Bills

T-bills are obligations of the U.S. Treasury and, as such, are backed by the full faith and credit of the U.S. government. They are sold on a discount basis in minimum denominations of $10,000, followed by $5,000 increments after that. Being sold on a discount basis means that the bills are sold for less than their face value, with the difference between what you pay for the security and what it's worth at maturity being the amount of your interest earnings. Thus, pay $9,750 for a $10,000 bill and you'll earn $250 in interest. T-bills are issued with 3-month (13-week), 6-month (26-week), and 1-year maturities. The 3- and 6-month bills are auctioned off every week and the 1-year bills roughly every 4 weeks or so.

INVESTING IN T-BILLS You can purchase T-bills from your banker or broker. However, if you buy through them, you'll have to pay a commission, or service fee. You can also purchase T-bills directly from the Treasury Department (or any Federal Reserve Bank), in which case there's no commission to pay. Doing this is really very simple, and it should be used by any serious T-bill investor. Simply contact the Bureau of Public Debt, Securities Transaction Branch, Main Treasury Building, Washington, D.C. 20239, or call 202-287-4113. They'll send you the necessary tender form and easy-to-follow instructions. The form requires little more than your name, address, Social Security number, amount of purchase, and whether you're submitting a competitive or noncompetitive bid. Unless you're a real pro, the safest and best thing to do is to submit a *noncompetitive* bid. In essence, all noncompetitive tender offers are awarded T-bills at a price equal to the average of all the accepted competitive bids. Thus, the investor is assured of being able to buy bills in the quantity desired while obtaining the benefit of an open auction system.

When you mail in your completed tender form, include a cashier's check or certified personal check, *in the amount of the T-bills you want to purchase.* For example, to buy a $15,000 bill, send in a $15,000 check—the full maturity value of the bill, not what you think you're going to pay for it. Shortly after the auction is completed, you'll receive a computer-generated receipt (statement) of your purchase, along with a refund check for the difference between what you actually paid for the bill and what you sent in with your tender. Then, when the bill matures (in 3, 6, or 12 months), you'll receive another check from the Treasury for the full maturity value of the security. You can also request that the proceeds from your T-bill be reinvested at maturity into another bill of the same maturity. You can do this for a period of up to 2 years; thus, you can invest in up to eight consecutive 13-week bills, or four 26-week bills, or two 1-year bills.

T-bills are highly liquid investments, since they can be readily sold (in a very active secondary market) without any interest penalty. However, you won't be able to do this by yourself, but will have to use a bank or broker and therefore pay the customary commission. Though all our discussion above has dealt with new bills, it should be pointed out that, just as you can sell bills in the secondary market, so too can you purchase outstanding T-bills in this same market (through banks or dealers). The biggest advantage of this approach is that you have a much wider selection of maturities to choose from, ranging from less than a week to as long as a year.

T-BILL RETURNS The yields on T-bills are widely quoted in *The Wall Street Journal* and other major newspapers and financial media. In addition, auction results (including the yields awarded on the noncompetitive bids) are reported weekly, on Tuesdays. Because T-bills offer almost total safety, along with fairly attractive yields, they make excellent short-term investments. In fact, because they're virtually free from capital loss, T-bills can also provide highly competitive returns over the long haul. Of course, the safety doesn't come free. For except for passbook savings accounts, T-bills are generally the lowest yielding of all investments. Investors are going to have to decide for themselves whether the yield give-up is worth the added safety.

A particularly attractive, though often overlooked, feature of these securities is that their interest income is *exempt from state and local taxes.* In addition, there are no federal taxes to pay until the interest is actually received at maturity or sale. Thus, it's possible to defer taxes (for up to a year) by buying bills that mature after the end of the year.

The Good Points:

- *Completely safe*—indeed, the safety feature is about the best possible.
- *Highly liquid.* There's an active secondary market, so these securities can be readily sold should the need ever arise.
- *Easily purchased* directly from the government, so you can save (avoid) commissions.
- *Automatic roll-over* available as your investment matures.
- *Yields rise as market interest rates rise.*
- Interest income is *exempt from state and local taxes.*

And the Bad:

- *Yields drop as market interest rates fall.* There's not much you can do to lock in rates of return for more than 6 months to a year.
- *No automatic compounding.* Even if you arrange to roll your bills over, your interest income is not reinvested.
- *Lowest yielding of all investments,* except passbook savings accounts.

Taxes:

Interest income is exempt from all state and local taxes but subject to federal income tax in the year it's received (which offers some tax deferment possibilities if you invest in bills with maturities that extend into the next calendar year).

Series EE Savings Bonds

These are the well-known savings bonds that have been around for half a century or so (they were first issued in 1941 and used to be called Series E bonds). Issued by the U.S. Treasury, Series EE bonds are backed by the full faith and credit of the U.S. government, and can be replaced, without charge, in case of loss, theft, or destruction. They can be purchased with no commission or sales charge at banks and thrifts or through payroll deduction plans.

Savings bonds are issued in denominations of $50 through $10,000, with the purchase price of all denominations being half of the face amount. Specifically, savings bonds come in the following denominations (face values):

Face Values	Purchase Prices
$ 50.00	$ 25.00
75.00	37.50
100.00	50.00
200.00	100.00
500.00	250.00
5,000.00	2,500.00
10,000.00	5,000.00

There is a $30,000 (face value) limit on the amount that can be purchased in any one calendar year.

As with T-bills, the interest on Series EE bonds is also *exempt from state and local taxes,* and they are also sold on a discount basis. In essence, they are *accrual-type securities,* in that the interest is paid when the bond is cashed in, on or before maturity, rather than periodically over the life of the issue. If held 5 years or longer, the bonds pay a *variable rate of return,* which is set every 6 months, in May and November, at 85% of the average return on 5-year Treasury securities. In mid-1988, this amounted to 6.90%. However, there's also a safety net in place; for at the present time, the rate of interest on EE bonds cannot fall below a guaranteed minimum of 6%. Your banker should be able to give you the latest rates on Series EE bonds, or you can call 1-800-USBONDS for current rates.

Even though you should hold these bonds for their duration, you can cash them in any time you want *after the first 6 months.* But if you do, you'll earn a yield of less than 6%. Redeem your bond after the 5 years is up and you'll earn the full rate of return that existed over the period you held the issue. By the way, if you ever do have to cash in one of these bonds before maturity, try to time the redemption so you don't lose any interest: after the first 2½ years, interest is credited to your bond every 6 months, so if you cash your bond in just before the interest is credited, you stand to lose up to 6 months of earnings.

Actually, because these issues pay a variable rate of interest, you don't know in advance just how long you're going to have to wait until the bond matures—the term to maturity will vary with the rate of return. The higher the overall rate of return, the less time it takes for the bond to double in value. At a 6% rate, one of these bonds will mature in 12 years; but if you can earn an average of, say, 7%, that same bond will mature in just over 10 years.

INVESTING IN SAVINGS BONDS Series EE bonds have a lot to offer to the serious, safety-conscious investor. For one thing, they're a very safe, secure form of investment. And since the Treasury converted them from fixed to variable rate securities, their holding period returns have become highly competitive with other investment vehicles: because their returns are pegged to Treasury yields, you're essentially getting a 5-year rate on your funds, which is usually comfortably above what you can get on other short-term securities. Remember also that since they are accrual-type securities, these are *fully compounded* rates of return—all earnings are automatically reinvested at the prevailing semiannual compound rate of return. On top of all this, the return *of* your capital is absolutely guaranteed, regardless of what happens to interest rates—a feature you don't have on *any other* long-term investment vehicle.

There are also some very attractive tax features. For in addition to being exempt from state and local taxes, you don't even have to report the interest on your federal tax return until the bonds actually mature, or you cash them in. This, of course, can take as long as 10 to 12 years, over which time your money will be earning an after-tax rate of no less than the guaranteed 6%— and probably more. In fact, it's even possible to defer this tax shelter for another 10 years beyond the maturity date of your EE bond if, instead of cashing in your bond at maturity, you *exchange it for a Series HH bond.* By doing this, you won't have to pay taxes on your EE interest earnings until the HH bond reaches maturity, or you cash it in. Series HH bonds are sold in $500, $1,000, $5,000, and $10,000 denominations; they're issued at full face value, with 10-year maturities, and pay interest at the current fixed rate of 6%.

The Good Points:

- *Safety of principal.* Highly competitive 5-year yields, which tend to move up with market interest rates.
- *Convenient to buy.* The bonds are available in amounts as small as $25.
- *No brokerage fee or sales charge.*
- *Replaced free if lost, stolen, or destroyed.*

- *Fully compounded rates of return*—all accrued interest earnings are automatically reinvested.
- Interest *exempt from state and local taxes.*

And the Bad:

- *Lack of liquidity.* They cannot be cashed in for the first 6 months and must be held for at least 5 years to earn the full rate of return.
- *Variable rate of interest,* so your earnings stand to fall if interest rates drop (though the rate of return cannot drop below 6%).

Taxes:

Interest income is subject to federal income tax, but not until the bond is cashed in or redeemed at maturity, so these taxes can be deferred for a number of years; also, all interest earnings are exempt from state and local taxes.

One Final Point about Short-Term Investments

Throughout this chapter, we've devoted our attention exclusively to savings and short-term investment vehicles. One point that should be clear is that, if you're so inclined, *there's no reason you can't build a whole portfolio of nothing but short-term securities.* While this probably wouldn't be appropriate for everyone, it may be just the ticket for some safety-conscious investors—especially those who have real trouble handling risk.

But if you fall into this category, whatever you do, don't just sink your money into a savings or money market account and let it go at that. Instead, consider putting a part of your capital into several CDs, say with 6-month, 1-year, and 2½-year maturities, and maybe some into Series EE savings bonds. In this way, you can stretch your maturities out a bit and, in the process, pick up a good deal *more return* without jeopardizing the overall safety of your money. If you stick to federally insured institutions (and abide by the insurance limits), there's really no way of losing money with any of these investments.

Even after you discard passbook savings accounts, there are still plenty of perfectly safe short-term investments to choose from—investments that offer respectable and at times highly attractive rates of return, particularly in light of the very low risks involved. And remember that you can do all this without ever having to use a broker. You can buy money market accounts, CDs, and Series EE bonds from your favorite bank or thrift, while T-bills can be purchased directly from the government and money funds directly from the fund distributors. Thus, with these securities, you truly can have hassle-free investing.

5

Bonds:
The Next Closest Thing

Buy bonds! That's the message you used to get from those posters of Uncle Sam. And that's still the message a lot of investors get when they're looking for a good, safe place to put their money. Rightly so, too, because bonds are a safe form of investing, and they can produce attractive returns to boot. Big deal, you say. You can get that from T-bills and CDs, so why should you consider bonds? The answer: try bonds if you'd like to get a bit more bang from your investment dollar. The price? To get the bigger return, you're also going to have to deal with a bit more risk. But as we'll see in this chapter, if you're careful about how you use bonds, the added risks are easily manageable. In fact, by following just a few simple rules, most of the risks can be avoided altogether.

Bonds offer some truly interesting investment opportunities, as they are ideally suited to meet the current income and long-term return objectives of safety-conscious investors. Bonds are often referred to in the marketplace as *fixed income securities*, because the payoff from a bond is fixed for the life of the issue. Buy a bond and you'll receive a fixed amount of interest every year, and be repaid a fixed amount of principal at maturity. The *coupon* on a bond tells you how much interest you'll receive, generally in the form of semiannual payments. In a similar fashion, the principal amount of a bond—also known as *par value*—defines the amount of money you'll receive at maturity.

Of course, just because a bond has a stated principal value

doesn't mean it'll always be priced at that amount! Indeed, bonds usually trade at prices that are above or below their stated par values. This occurs because of changes in market interest rates, which lead to differences between the coupon that a bond carries and the prevailing market rate of interest. When that happens, the price of the issue changes until its yield is compatible with the prevailing market yield. Such behavior explains why an 8% bond carries a market price of $750 in a 10% market: the drop in price (from its par value of $1,000) is necessary in order to raise its yield from 8% to 10%. Think about it. Would you pay full price for an 8% bond when you could get exactly the same thing from an issue that pays 10%?

A Bond Is Just a Long-Term I.O.U.

In many ways, bonds are like the short-term securities we looked at in the previous chapter—they're like first cousins in that they're both forms of debt. For example, invest in something like a CD and what you're really buying is a short-term I.O.U. (a promise from the bank that you'll get your money back, plus a stated rate of interest for as long as you hold the security). In a similar fashion, that's what you get when you buy a bond, except the I.O.U. covers a longer period of time.

So What Do Bonds Have to Offer?

Bonds have a lot to offer safety-conscious investors. For one thing, they provide a generous amount of current income. And because they're long-term investment vehicles, you can lock in these cash flow streams for extended periods of time, perhaps for as long as 25 to 30 years or more. Do that, and no matter what happens in the market, so long as the bond isn't called in for retirement, you can count on collecting that coupon income every 6 months— year in, year out until the bond matures. What's more, you can usually earn a lot more interest on bonds than on short-term securities. For example, in mid-1988, while 6-month securities were yielding in the neighborhood of 6% to 7%, high-quality, long-term bonds were posting returns of around 9½%.

In addition to yield, bonds also offer safety. Because of this, they're often used for the preservation and long-term accumulation of capital. But you have to use a little care here, because not all bonds are alike. To be on the safe side, *be sure to always buy quality.* If you do so, there's little, if any, risk that you'll end up with an issue that goes into default. With quality issues, not only do you have a high degree of assurance that you'll get your money back at maturity, but the stream of interest income is also highly dependable.

Granted you do have to contend with occasional swings in bond prices, but if you're in the investment for the long haul (and don't need to sell on short notice), such price swings should not concern you, since in no way can they affect your stream of income. Just because the price of your bond drops doesn't mean your interest income's going to fall, or that the return of your capital is in jeopardy. True, it's not exactly pleasant to see the price of your bond drop, but it's not the end of the world either, *since the price of a high-quality bond is always going to return to its full par value at maturity.*

There Are Some Risks

Earlier we identified four basic types of risks that are found, to one degree or another, in different types of securities. Let's see the extent to which you're exposed to these risks when you invest in bonds.

• **Business and Financial Risk** This is basically the risk that the issuer will default on interest and/or principal payments. With bonds, it's a risk that either doesn't exist at all—as in the case of Treasury and agency bonds—or can be easily avoided, by buying only investment-grade corporate or municipal bonds. Clearly, this is a risk you don't have to put up with: just remember to buy quality!

• **Market Risk** Unfortunately, you're not so lucky here, as even the highest quality long-term debt securities are subject to a full dose of market risk. In the case of bonds, this translates into *interest rates:* when they rise, bond prices fall, and vice versa. Even Treasury securities are subject to this type of price volatility. The best way to reduce it is to invest in shorter bonds—for example, a 5- to 7-year issue is subject to considerably less price volatility than a 25-year bond. On the other hand, one consolation of rising interest rates is that if you're holding an issue to its maturity, then at least you'll be able to reinvest the coupon income at the higher rates and thereby enjoy a higher rate of return than what you set out with.

• **Purchasing Power Risk** This is what you get when you have inflation. During periods of mild inflation, bonds do pretty well, as their returns tend to outstrip inflation rates. Purchasing power risk really heats up, however, when inflation takes off the way it did in the late 70s; then, bond yields start to lag behind inflation rates. Remember, you're dealing with *fixed income* securities. You have a fixed coupon rate on your bond—so even though market yields are rising with inflation, your return is locked in for the long haul. In essence, while an 8% return may look good when inflation is running at 3% or 4%, it doesn't look so good when inflation jumps to 10% or 12%. Now, while you might be tempted to simply sell out when inflation goes way up, think again! Because when inflation shoots up, so do bond yields. And when that happens, bond *prices* tumble, so the only way you're going to be able to sell out is by taking a big loss in capital. If you feel very strongly that inflation is about to take off in a big way, then stay away from long-term bonds. If you must invest in bonds, do it in the short maturities of 5 to 7 years, *or less*. On the other hand, if you don't anticipate anything worse than mild inflation, then purchasing power risk shouldn't be much of a problem and there's no reason to avoid these securities.

• **Liquidity Risk** Except for Treasury and agency issues, long-term bonds are sometimes difficult to sell in the secondary market. As such, these issues are subject to a fair amount of liquidity risk.

Many corporate and municipal bonds just are not actively traded, so if you ever do have to sell one of these issues before it matures, you may be faced with a long wait, or even worse, you may have to take a big hit in price in order to move it. You can, of course, avoid, or at least minimize, this kind of liquidity risk by confining your investments to widely traded Treasury or agency issues. In addition, you should always try, as best you can, to match bond maturities with your investment horizons—in essence, don't buy 20-year bonds if you only want to invest for a period of 10 years.

There's a Full Lineup to Choose From

The bond market is chiefly over-the-counter in nature, and in comparison to the stock market, prices are far less volatile. Granted, market interest rates—and therefore bond prices—do move up and down over time, but when bond price activity is measured on a daily basis, it is remarkably stable. Which, of course, is one reason they're so well liked by safety-conscious investors.

There are basically four major issuers of bonds: the U.S. Treasury, federal agencies, states and municipalities, and corporations.

• **U.S. Treasury** These bonds are a dominant force in the market and, if not the most popular type of bond, they certainly are the best known. In addition to T-bills, the U.S. Treasury also issues notes and bonds. Treasury *notes* have maturities of 10 years or less; Treasury *bonds* have maturities that extend out as far as 25 years or more. These securities are of the highest quality (they're backed by the full faith and credit of the U.S. government), and this feature, along with their liquidity, makes them very popular with individual investors.

• **Federal Agencies** Various agencies and organizations of the *U.S. government* are frequent issuers of debt securities. Actually, there are two types of agency issuers—government-sponsored organizations and federal agencies—though as a general rule, the generic term *agency* is used with both types. There are over two

dozen issuers of agency obligations, including the Federal Home
Loan Bank, the Tennessee Valley Authority, the U.S. Postal
Service, the Federal Housing Administration, and the Federal
National Mortgage Association. These are political subdivisions
of the U.S. government; they should *not* be viewed in the same
way as the Treasury. While a few of these bonds are backed by
the full faith and credit of the U.S. government, they all are moral
obligations of the government, so it's highly unlikely that Congress would ever allow one to default. Yet even though there's
very little difference in risk between these and Treasury securities,
agency bonds normally provide yields that are comfortably above
those on Treasuries.
• **States and Municipalities** Municipal bonds are issued by
states, counties, cities, and other political subdivisions, like school
districts and public power authorities. They are often referred to
as tax-free bonds, because their interest income is exempt from
federal income tax. Municipals can come out either as *general
obligation (G.O.) bonds* or as *revenue issues.* G.O.s are backed by
the full faith and credit (and taxing power) of the issuer, whereas
revenue bonds are serviced by the income generated from specific
income-producing projects (like toll roads, for example). Be careful when buying municipals, because the distinction between a
G.O. and a revenue is an important one. The issuer of a revenue
bond—unlike that of a G.O.—is legally obligated to pay principal
and interest *only if a sufficient level of revenue is generated.* If the
funds aren't there, the issuer does not have to make payments on
the bond. Thus, as an investor, you're subject to a lot more risk
with a revenue bond than you are with a G.O.
• **Corporations** Business firms and corporations are the only significant nongovernmental issuers of publicly traded bonds. Corporate bonds are issued as either *secured* or *unsecured* debt. Collateral trust bonds, equipment trust certificates, first and
refunding bonds, and first mortgage bonds are all examples of
secured bonds. Capital notes, debentures, and subordinated debentures are all forms of unsecured bonds. A secured bond is
considered the senior form of security, since it's backed by a

specific piece of collateral such as a plant or some other piece of real estate, a piece of rolling stock, like a railroad car, or even marketable securities. As the holder of a secured bond, you have a legal position that gives you a prior claim to certain assets of the company in case of default. On the other hand, an unsecured issue is said to be a junior bond, since your position as a bond-holder is secondary to all forms of secured debt. When you buy a junior bond, all you get is the word of the issuer that you'll get your interest and principal in a prompt and timely fashion. While junior bonds are generally considered to be more risky than senior securities, *don't ever let the question of collateral be the major factor in your investment decision.* After all, what matters is the ability of the issuer to repay the debt, not the amount of collateral behind the issue.

Call Features: Let the Buyer Beware!

Consider the following situation: you've just made an investment in a great, high-yielding, 25-year bond. Now all you have to do is sit back and let the cash flow in, right? Well, perhaps. Certainly, that'll happen for the first several years; but if market interest rates drop off, it's also very likely that you'll be hit with a notice from the issuer that the bond is being *called*. This means that the whole issue is being retired before its time, and there's nothing you can do but turn in your bond and invest your money else-where. How can this happen? Well, so long as the bond is *calla-ble,* it can be prematurely retired any time the issuer cares to. It's all perfectly legal and it happens all the time. But there are things you can do to prevent—or at least reduce—the chance of this happening to you.

A provision that's found on any bond is one which stipulates the conditions under which the bond can be called in for retire-ment prior to maturity; this provision is known as a *call feature.* Basically, there are three types of call features:

■ *Freely callable,* which means that the issuer can prematurely retire the bond at any time

- *Noncallable,* which means that the issuer is prohibited from retiring the bond prior to maturity
- *Deferred call,* which means that the issue cannot be called until after a certain length of time has passed from the date of issue—in essence, the issue is noncallable during the deferment period and then becomes freely callable

As a rule, you'll find that short- to intermediate-term issues (notes that originally come out with maturities of 10 years or less) are usually noncallable—and this applies to corporate and municipal issues as well as Treasuries and agencies. Also, most long-term Treasury and agency securities are either noncallable, or they carry very long call deferment periods; in contrast, long municipal and corporate bonds normally come out as deferred callable, with deferment periods today running for about 5 to 7 years. The exact provisions of a bond's call feature are spelled out in detail in the issue's prospectus, or offering memorandum. Summary information pertaining to a bond's call feature can also be found in several Moody's and Standard & Poor's publications, or ask your broker to get the information for you.

As a substitute for call features, some bonds may contain a specific *refunding* provision, which is exactly like a call feature except that it prohibits just one thing: the premature retirement of an issue from proceeds of a lower-coupon refunding bond. This distinction is important, since it means that a nonrefunding or deferred refunding issue *can still be called and prematurely retired for any reason other than refunding.* For example, you could face a call on a high-yielding (nonrefundable) issue if the issuer has the cash to prematurely retire the bond.

SEEKING PROTECTION FROM CALLS How can you protect yourself against the threat of a call? The best way to avoid trouble is to *find out exactly what kind of call feature a bond has before you invest in it.* The adage Buyer Beware certainly applies in this case. If you want to lock in a high rate of return for an extended period of time, then stick with issues that are either noncallable or have very lengthy call deferment periods, like Treasury securities or agency bonds. If you want the added return of corporates, or the tax-free income of municipals, then stick with 7- to 10-year notes, or look for bonds with long deferment periods (though 5 to 7 years is probably about as good as you're going to get). In essence, find a bond with the kind of call feature you like, and then you'll be in the driver's seat.

SINKING FUND CALLS Bonds can also be called for sinking fund purposes. Sinking funds are found on many, though certainly not all, corporate bonds. They're also found on some term bonds issued by municipalities. Such a provision specifies how a bond will be paid off over time—it's like an annual repayment schedule that the corporation must follow. Sinking fund calls aren't nearly as big a problem as calls for refunding purposes. First of all, rather than retiring the whole issue all at once, only a small fraction of the issue is retired at a time. And then, a lot of sinking fund requirements are met by open market purchases rather than calls, so the chance of your bond being called for sinking fund purposes is actually pretty low. Still, if you want absolute protection from a sinking fund call, don't invest in sinking fund bonds. Information about sinking fund provisions can also be found in the bond's prospectus, or in Moody's and Standard & Poor's publications.

What's in a Rating?

When you buy a Treasury security, you have the assurance that you're buying a high-quality issue that's backed by the full faith and credit of the U.S. government. Likewise, when you buy an agency issue, you also know you're buying quality. There's virtually no chance these bonds will default. This is not the case, however, with corporate and municipal bonds. As a result, you need a way to assess the investment quality of these issues. Enter *bond ratings*. Bonds are rated for quality by several independent organizations, the two biggest and best-known being Moody's and Standard & Poor's.

Each time a large new issue comes to the market, it is analyzed to determine risk of default and investment quality.

Things like earnings records, debt burdens, liquidity position, and the like are thoroughly evaluated. The product of all this is a bond rating—a letter grade—that indicates the ability of the issuing organization to service its debt in a prompt and timely fashion. The easier it is for the firm to service its debt, the higher the rating. The table provides a summary of the bond ratings assigned by Moody's and Standard & Poor's.

If you're going to invest in corporate or municipal bonds, then you should pay careful attention to agency ratings. You can get up-to-date ratings from publications like *Moody's Bond Record* or *Standard & Poor's Bond Guide* or simply ask your broker about the rating of the bond you're interested in. *Never invest in a corporate or municipal bond unless you know its rating!* And if you're a safety-conscious investor, *don't invest in a bond if it's less*

Bond Ratings*

Moody's	S&P	Description
Aaa	AAA	*Prime-quality investment bonds*—This is the highest rating assigned, denoting extremely strong capacity to pay.
Aa A	AA A	*High-grade investment bonds*—These are also considered very safe bonds, though they're not quite as safe as Aaa/AAA issues; double-A-rated bonds are safer (have *less* risk of default) than single-A-rated issues.
Baa	BBB	*Medium-grade investment bonds*—These are the lowest of the investment grade issues; they're felt to lack certain protective elements against adverse economic conditions.
Ba B	BB B	*Junk bonds*—With little protection against default, these are viewed as highly *speculative* securities.
Caa Ca C	CCC CC C D	*Poor-quality bonds*—These are either in default or very close to it.

* Some ratings may be modified to show relative standing within a major rating category; for example, Moody's uses numerical modifiers (1, 2, 3), whereas S&P uses plus (+) or minus (−) signs.

than A-rated. Obviously, if you want as much protection as you can get, stick with triple-A-rated issues. But if you want a bit more return from your money, you might want to consider moving down to double-A- or single-A-rated bonds. Generally speaking, you can expect to find a difference of about ¼ of a point or so between triple-A- and double-A-rated bonds, and another ¼ to ½ point between double-A- and single-A-rated issues. Thus, if a triple-A bond is yielding something like 9¾%, you'll probably be able to get 10½% or so from an A-rated issue.

Bond ratings serve to relieve individual investors from the drudgery of evaluating the investment quality of an issue on their own. The rating agencies have a good record of performance, and you can use bond ratings with confidence. There's a final point you should keep in mind, however: bond ratings are intended as a measure of an issue's default risk only. A bond rating has no bearing whatsoever on an issue's exposure to market risk, or price volatility. Just because a bond is highly rated doesn't mean it's immune to interest rate risk or that its price won't respond to rising rates. High-quality bonds are still subject to capital losses as market interest rates rise.

Getting a Grip on Bond Yields and Prices

Bond yields are important since they define the amount of return you'll make. Likewise, bond prices are important since they too can have a bearing on your return. Whether you're looking at bond yields or bond prices, there's one variable that stands out: *market interest rates.* Through their impact on both bond yields and prices, market interest rates determine the amount of current income you'll make and the amount of capital gains (or loss) you'll incur. Make no mistake about it, the bond market is driven by interest rates.

The Structure of Interest Rates

Just as there is no single bond market, but a series of different market sectors, so too there is no single interest rate applicable to all segments of the market. Rather, each segment has its own, somewhat unique, level of interest rates. Granted, the various rates tend to drift in the same direction and to follow the same general pattern of behavior, but it's also common for *yield spreads*, or interest-rate differentials, to exist in the various market sectors. Some of the more important market yield spreads include the following:

- Municipal bonds usually carry the lowest market rates because of their tax-exempt features. As a rule, their yields are about 15% to 30% lower than corporates; accordingly, before you invest in a municipal, make sure you're in a high enough tax bracket to offset the lower yield on the bond.
- In the so-called taxable sector of the market, you'll find that Treasuries have the lowest yield (because they have the least risk), followed by agencies, and then corporates; thus, if you want a bit more return, you might want to consider agency issues or high-grade corporates.
- Corporate and municipal bonds generally behave the same when it comes to bond ratings: the lower the rating, the higher the yield. Therefore, to get more return, buy, say, a double-A-rated bond rather than a triple-A. For safety's sake, though, never invest in anything lower than an A-rated issue.
- Also expect to find a direct relationship between the coupon that a bond carries and its yield—that is, discount (low-coupon) bonds generally yield less than premium (high-coupon) bonds; thus, if all you want to do is maximize current income, then go for the high coupons (but keep in mind, high-coupon bonds are a lot more susceptible to call than lower-coupon issues).

All these yield spreads are fairly common in the market and tend to occur with regularity. As indicated, these are also features that you can use to improve the return on your bond holdings. Best of all, you can pick up the added yield without having to do a bunch of fancy trading, and without having to take on any more measurable risk. Just pay attention to the prevailing yield spreads and use a little care when you select a bond. For example, you may be able to pick up a full percentage point or so by doing nothing more sophisticated than buying a triple-A-rated public utility issue rather than a Treasury bond. Clearly, just knowing where to find the extra yield can make a world of difference in how much you earn over the long haul; and in this regard, the above list should at least point you in the right direction.

Two Measures of Yield

Yield is the single most important measure in the bond market, and it's used in a variety of ways. For instance, it serves to trace the behavior of the market in general, as well as to measure the return of a single issue. In addition, yield is the mechanism that's used to price bonds in the marketplace. Two basic types of yield are widely used in the bond market: current yield and promised yield.

CURRENT YIELD This is the simplest of the two measures and has the most limited application. It simply measures the amount of current income that a bond provides relative to its prevailing market price. For example, an 8% bond would pay $80 per year in interest for every $1,000 of principal. However, if the bond were priced at $800, it would have a current yield of 10% ($80/$800 = .10). Current yield would be of interest to you if you're seeking high levels of interest income: you'll get high annual interest income by investing in bonds with high current yields. But a drawback of current yield is that it ignores capital gains (or losses), and it assumes that the semiannual interest payments are consumed, rather than plowed back into your investment program—there's no compounding here.

PROMISED YIELD The most important and widely used bond valuation measure, *promised yield* evaluates both interest income and price appreciation over the life of an issue. Also known as *yield to maturity*, it indicates the fully compounded rate of return available to an investor, assuming the bond is held to maturity. Other things being equal, the higher the promised yield of an issue, the more attractive it is. This is the yield figure that's used to describe the return on most types of long-term bonds. When your broker tells you she has some bonds that are yielding 8½%, she's talking about promised yield. In a similar fashion, the terms *market rate of return* and *market yield* are also referring to promised yield.

The easiest way to find a bond's promised yield to maturity is to use the approximate yield procedure, first introduced in chapter 2. Here's what you do: take the annual interest income, add that to the *average* annual capital gains you'll make from the bond (given you hold it to maturity), and divide it all by the *average* amount of the investment. The net result of all this is a close approximation of a bond's promised yield.

As an example, consider a 7½% bond with a par value of $1,000 that has 18 years to maturity and is currently priced at $825. To begin with, the annual interest income on this bond is 7½% of $1,000, or $75. The capital gains is the difference between its current price of $825 and its par value of $1,000—or $175. Now, over the 18 years remaining to maturity, that'll translate into an average capital gain of $9.72 a year ($175/18). Finally, the average investment is simply the sum of the beginning price ($825) and ending par value ($1,000), all of which is divided by 2—($825 + $1,000)/2 = $1,825/2 = $912.50. Believe it or not, when you put this all together you have promised yield. First, add annual interest income to average annual capital gains: $75 + $9.72 = $84.72. Now divide this by the average investment ($912.50) and you have the approximate promised yield: $84.72/$912.50 = 9.28%. That's the rate of return you'll earn if you buy this bond today at $825 and hold on to it for the next 18 years until it matures. Note that even though the bond carries a 7½% coupon, the only return that's relevant is the 9.28%. *The coupon defines the amount of annual interest income you'll receive, but the yield defines your return.*

There are two very important assumptions imbedded in promised yield. For not only does it assume that you'll hold the bond to maturity, it also assumes that you'll reinvest all the interest income at a rate of return *equal to or greater than* the promised yield. This is because the calculated approximate yield figure is only the return promised so long as the issuer meets all interest and principal obligations on a timely basis, *and* so long as you, the investor, reinvest all coupon income at an average rate equal to or greater than the computed promised yield (9.28% in our example). Failure to do so will result in an actual yield of less than the 9.28% promised. This is a very important concept of bond return and, in fact, applies to just about any type of long-term investment program. Reinvesting periodic investment income is every bit as important with stocks and mutual funds as it is with bonds.

Getting Acquainted with Bond Prices

When a bond is first issued, it is usually sold to the public at a price that equals, or is very close to, par value. Likewise, when the bond matures—some 15, 20, or 30 years later—it will once again be priced at its par value. But what happens to the price of the bond in between is dependent largely on the behavior of market interest rates. Now, while bond prices can just as easily fall as rise, as a conservative investor you shouldn't become overly alarmed about a drop in bond prices. Granted, watching the price of your bond fall isn't the greatest experience in the world, but if you've stuck to quality issues, *the price of the bond will recover as the issue approaches maturity.* No matter what happens to interest rates, the bond will still be priced at $1,000 when it matures.

For example, consider a 15-year 8% issue. If market yields are at 10%, this bond will be worth about $850. Now, even if interest rates stay right at the 10% mark, this same issue will be priced at $950 some 12 years later—when it has 3 years left to maturity. In other words, as a bond gets closer to its maturity, it also inches closer to its par value. This is an important behavioral trait, and is one of the main reasons that safety-conscious investors are so attracted to high-quality bonds: they know that *in time, the market price of their bonds will recover.*

SHORTEN MATURITIES TO REDUCE BOND PRICE VOLATILITY While it's true that bond prices are responsive to market interest rates, there's a bit more to it than that. For the price volatility of a bond also varies according to the coupon and maturity of the issue. In particular, bond price volatility *increases* with lower coupons and longer maturities. Thus, when interest rates change, bonds with the lowest coupons and the longest maturities will undergo the biggest change in price.

Actually, of the two variables, the maturity of an issue has by far the most impact on price volatility. For example, look what happens to the price of an 8% bond when market interest rates rise by 1, 2, or 3 percentage points:

Bond Maturity	Change in the price of an 8% bond when interest rates rise by:		
	1 percentage pt.	2 percentage pts.	3 percentage pts.
5 years	− 4.0%	− 7.7%	−12.5%
25 years	−10.9	−18.2	−33.7

Clearly, the shorter (5-year) bond offers a lot more price stability. Such a behavioral trait is universal with all fixed income securities and is important to you as a safety-conscious investor because it means that if you want to reduce your exposure to capital loss, or more to the point, if you want to lower the amount of price volatility in your bond holdings, then just *shorten your maturities.*

Obviously, one way to eliminate the possibility of capital loss is to stick with short-term investments like CDs and money funds. And if you simply cannot tolerate any price volatility, then that certainly is an appropriate—indeed, a highly recommended— course of action. If you find that a bit too extreme, however, then you might want to consider a variation of this basic investment theme. That is, rather than buy long-term bonds (with maturities of, say, 25 to 30 years), confine your investing to securities that have only 5 to 10 years to go to maturity. In other words, stick with notes and shorter-term bonds. By doing so, you'll be able to sharply reduce your exposure to capital loss and yet experience very little drop in yield.

Historically, longer-term bonds generally do yield more than

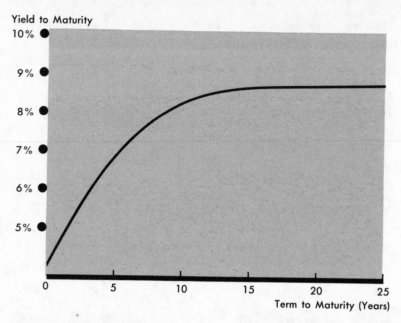

shorter issues, but the *yield curve*—a graph that shows the relationship between yield to maturity and term to maturity—tends to flatten out after the first 7 to 10 years or so. In essence, most yield curves look something like the accompanying graph. As you can see, there's not much difference between a 7- to 10-year issue and a 25- to 30-year bond. And that's fairly typical: For example, in mid-1988, 7-year Treasury notes were yielding around 9.0%, while 25-year Treasury bonds were selling at yields of 9.4%. That's a yield give-up of less than half a percentage point, not a lot considering the big drop in price volatility you're getting in return. Really, about the only thing you give up is the ability to lock in high yields for extended periods of time—but that's a small price to pay for preservation of capital and peace of mind.

Putting Your Money to Work in the Bond Market

Investing in fixed income securities can be a safe, rewarding experience. Indeed, it's often viewed as such a secure place to invest that many people buy these securities without really knowing what they're getting into. These are the investors who are shocked to see their Treasury bonds drop in price, or surprised to find that their high-yielding corporate issue can be called out from under them. Don't let this happen to you; know the vehicle you're buying—its call feature, agency rating, and exposure to price volatility.

Even though bonds are a very simple investment vehicle, you still have to know the product, because those seemingly innocuous features can have a dramatic effect on your holding period return. Getting the information is no big deal: it's widely available and easy to obtain. It's really just a matter of knowing what to look for. Knowing how to use bonds is also important in getting the most from your investment dollar. The trick, of course, is being able to pick up a point or two here and there, without violating your tolerance for risk. Doing that can make a big difference in what you earn over the long haul. Let's look now at some safe investment strategies that you can follow when investing in bonds.

Buying Treasury and Agency Issues

Because both Treasury and agency securities are issued by various organizations of the U.S. government, they are generally referred to as *government bonds*—or simply governments, for short. The main appeal they hold for individual investors is, of course, the safety and peace of mind they offer. So long as you can hold the bond to maturity, there's no doubt you'll get your money back. And while you're holding the bonds, you'll earn a nice return to boot. In addition, all Treasury securities and most agency obligations are exempt from state and local income taxes. This means that if you live in a state that has a state and/or local income tax—and chances are you do—your return is even higher than the quoted promised yield.

Government bonds come in a full range of coupons and maturities, so no matter what your needs or wants, you'll probably find a number of issues to fit your fancy. Among debt securities, they are by far the most actively traded, and as such, they offer much better liquidity than either municipals or corporates. Thus, if liquidity—the ability to sell out your position in a hurry—is important to you, then you'd probably be better off sticking with governments, and especially Treasuries, which have a slightly better after-market than agencies.

USE CALL PROTECTION TO LOCK IN YIELDS One of the real attractions of government securities is the call features they carry. In particular, most Treasury and agency issues are noncallable for life. And even if they are callable, they usually carry very long call deferment periods. *You can put such call protection to work for you as a way to lock in high yields.* If you think interest rates have peaked and are about to head down, there's no better way to lock in those high yields than through a lengthy prohibition against call. So don't overlook the call protection offered by government notes and bonds, because being able to lock in high yields can mean substantial improvements in what you earn over the long haul.

TRY THE LADDERED APPROACH Treasury and agency issues can also be used in laddered investment programs (for that matter, so can corporates and municipals). As we saw with CDs in chapter 4, following a *laddered approach to investing* is an effective way of reducing your exposure to interest rate risk and bond price volatility, without jeopardizing return. It's a highly recommended approach for serious safety-conscious investors who want to be in bonds.

Here's an illustration of how it might work. For purposes of this illustration, we'll assume you're investing in Treasury securities, though we could just as easily have used agencies. While maturity preferences are irrelevant with this approach, let's say you want to stick with maturities of 10 years or less. You could set up the ladder by investing in equal amounts of, say, 3-, 5-, 7-, and 10-year issues (needless to say, all of the securities should be noncallable). Then, when the 3-year issue matures, you put the money from it, along with any new capital you want to invest, in a new 10-year note. The process would continue like this every time one of your bonds matured. Actually, the laddered approach is followed by a lot of professional money managers, because it's a safe, simple, and almost automatic way of investing. Once the program's set up, it's followed in a fairly routine manner.

THE NEED TO REINVEST One of the things we've touched on repeatedly in this book is the need to reinvest investment income—if you want to reap the long-term benefits of a fully compounded rate of return, then you have to plow back your earnings. This applies just as much to Treasury and agency securities as it does to any other type of investment vehicle. Getting absolute call protection or putting an issue into a ladder of investments in no way reduces the need to reinvest income. But this is a real problem for many investors because of the relatively small amounts of money involved. Face it, when your semiannual interest income is only $300 or $400, it's hard to reinvest that amount in anything but a deep discount bond issue. So what's an investor to do? Well, to begin with, keep in mind that the key issue here is to *keep the money invested*—in any viable investment vehicle. Put the money in a short-term (6- to 12-month) CD or a money fund, at least until you can find a better, more permanent place for it.

As it turns out, one of the nice by-products of the laddered approach is that it enables you to systematically reinvest your accumulated earnings. Here's what you do: As you receive interest income semiannually from your laddered bond holdings, put those earnings into a separate CD or money market deposit account, and let your reinvested interest earnings accumulate over time. (It's important to note that you put the interest earnings from all your laddered bonds into this one account—don't set up one account for, say, the 3-year bonds, another for the 5-year issues, and so on. . . .) Now, every 2 to 3 years, when you roll over into a new 10-year issue, simply clean out the short-term account and add the accumulated interest earnings to the amount you're putting into the new 10-year security. Doing this is a simple yet highly effective way of earning a fully compounded rate of return on your money. And over the long haul, it can have an enormous impact on how much you make from your investments.

LOOK TO AGENCIES FOR HIGHER YIELDS One way to get a bit more return from your money is to invest in agency issues. These obligations consistently provide better yields than Treasury securities—indeed, the yield spread between these two types of securities regularly runs from ¼ to ½ a percentage point, and it's not uncommon for the differential to exceed a full point. This is easy money, too, since there's really little or no difference in risk between a Treasury and agency issue. Granted, many agency issues aren't backed by the full faith and credit of the U.S. government, but the general consensus is that there's no way the federal government would allow any of these issues to go into default. So, what you have is the implied backing of the government—the next best thing to its full faith and credit.

There's a full menu of agency securities to choose from. While maturities of 25 to 30 years are common, many agencies also carry maturities of 10 to 15 years or less, so you can stick with the shorter maturities if you choose. Minimum denominations of $1,000 to $5,000 are widely used with agencies, so you don't need to be a Rockefeller to buy these things. This isn't true of all agencies, however; some have minimum denominations of $50,000 or more. The accompanying table provides a small sample of some of the literally hundreds of agency issues that are actively traded every day. The table lists the issuing agency, along with specific securities, including coupon, maturity, call feature, minimum denomination, and current and promised yields. This list is not a recommendation, but is meant to illustrate the types of issues and yields that are available to the general public (all of these issues are regularly quoted in such publications as *The Wall Street Journal*). Also, keep in mind that this list was prepared in mid-1988; many new issues have come to the market since then. Call your broker or dealer to get the latest on available issues and yields.

A Representative List of Agency Issues

Issuing Agency—Coupon and Maturity	Minimum Denomination	Call Feature*	Current Yield**	Promised Yield**
Federal Farm Credit Banks—14.10s '91	$ 1,000	NC	12.42 %	8.63 %
Federal Farm Credit Banks—11.90s '97	1,000	NC	10.48	9.62
Federal Home Loan Banks—9.20s '97	10,000	NC	9.36	9.46
Federal Land Banks—7.95s '91	1,000	NC	8.09	8.55
Federal Land Banks—7.35s '97	1,000	NC	8.47	9.61
FNMA (Capital Debentures)—8s '96	5,000	NC	8.62	9.31
Inter-Amer. Development Bank—7.50s '96	1,000	NC	8.42	9.50
Private Export Funding Corporation—11¼s '95	1,000	NC	11.07	10.92
Student Loan Marketing Association—9¼s '92	10,000	NC	9.20	8.85
Student Loan Marketing Association—9½s '97	10,000	NC	9.60	9.61
Tennessee Valley Authority—7.30s '96	1,000	DC('95)	8.20	9.20
Tennessee Valley Authority—7.70s '98	1,000	DC('97)	8.75	9.54
U.S. Postal Service—6⅞s '97	10,000	FC	8.09	9.37
World Bank—9.35s '00	1,000	NC	9.54	9.72

* Call provisions are designated as follows: NC = noncallable; FC = freely callable; DC('year) = deferred call feature, with the year in which the issue becomes freely callable in parentheses.

**Current and promised yields are as of mid-1988.

Sources: Issue features and basic performance data were obtained from *Moody's Government Manual, Moody's Bond Record,* and *The Wall Street Journal.*

WHAT ABOUT MORTGAGE-BACKED BONDS? Simply put, a mortgage-backed bond is a debt issue that's secured by a pool of insured mortgages. An issuer, such as the Government National Mortgage Association (GNMA), puts together a pool of mortgages and then issues securities in the amount of the total mortgage pool. These securities, known as *pass-through securities,* or *participation certificates,* are sold in minimum denominations of $25,000. Though their maturities can go out as far as 25 to 30 years, the average life of one of these issues is generally much shorter (perhaps as short as 10 to 12 years), because so many of the pooled mortgages are paid off early. Pass-through securities are issued primarily by three federal agencies. Although there are some state and private issuers—mainly big banks and S&Ls—agency issues dominate the market and account for 90% to 95% of the activity. The major agency issuers of pass-through securities include the following:

Agency	Nickname	Description
Government National Mortgage Association (GNMA)	Ginnie Mae	The first and largest pass-through issuer. These issues are backed by the full faith and credit of the U.S. government.
Federal Home Loan Mortgage Association (FHLMC)	Freddie Mac	Second largest. First to offer pools containing conventional mortgages; the major issuer of Participation Certificates (PCs). Government-sponsored but no government guarantees.
Federal National Mortgage Association (FNMA)	Fannie Mae	Offers a pass-through security similar to Participation Certificates. Privately owned corporation with government sponsorship but no government guarantees. Leader in the purchase of "older" mortgages with low coupon rates.

As an investor in one of these securities, you hold an undivided interest in the pool of mortgages. Thus, when a homeowner makes a monthly mortgage payment, that payment is essentially passed through to you, the bondholder, to pay off the mortgage-backed bond that you hold. While these securities come with normal coupons, the interest is paid monthly, rather than semiannually. The monthly payments you receive are, like mortgage payments, made up of both principal and interest, with only the interest portion being subject to taxes (since the principal part of the payment represents return of capital). Actually, nearly all mortgage-backed securities today are issued to the public either as CMOs (*C*ollateralized *M*ortgage *O*bligations) or as REMICs (*R*eal *E*state *M*ortgage *I*nvestment *C*onduits). All these amount to are different ways of packaging standard pass-through securities for resale to the investing public. The nice thing about them is that they provide investors with fairly well-defined maturity dates, something you *don't* get with regular pass-throughs, which was a real source of problems.

Mortgage-backed securities have some interesting investment attributes. They're certainly a safe form of investment, and they offer highly competitive, attractive rates of return. What's more, there's a well-developed after-market, so it's relatively easy to buy and sell the bonds in the open market. Plus, these securities enable you to earn a monthly stream of income—indeed, if that's important to you, then mortgage-backed pass-through securities could be just the ticket.

These securities aren't without their problems, however. The most noteworthy, perhaps, involves the monthly cash flow. In particular, if you're a serious long-term investor with no need for the current income, you might want to think twice about buying pass-through securities. The reason: the monthly cash flow, including the return of principal, only magnifies your reinvestment problems, making it all that much more difficult to achieve a fully compounded rate of return. Also, these are long-term debt securities and, like any long-term bond, they too are subject to wide price swings when interest rates shoot up or down. Just because they're secured with a pool of mortgages doesn't make these securities immune to normal bond price volatility. Finally, it's important to keep in mind that these securities are essentially self-liquidating, since part of the monthly cash flow to the investor is the principal originally invested in the issue. Thus, the investor is always receiving back part of the original investment capital, so there is no big principal payment at maturity. Indeed, some uninformed investors are shocked to find so little left of their original capital.

Earning Tax-free Income from Municipal Bonds

Without a doubt, the one thing that draws investors to municipal securities is the fact that their interest income is free of federal taxes. (Note, however, that in contrast to interest income, capital gains are fully subject to taxes.) It's very likely that your interest earnings are also exempt from state and local taxes, so long as you hold an in-state bond. Thus, if you live in a state that has an income tax, you might be able to obtain even better after-tax returns by holding in-state bonds. The accompanying table provides a complete rundown of the exposure of municipal bond interest earnings to state income taxes.

How the States Treat Municipal Bonds

State	Interest on In-State Bonds	Interest on Out-of-State Bonds
Alabama	Exempt	Taxable
Alaska	No income tax	No income tax
Arizona	Exempt	Taxable
Arkansas	Exempt	Taxable
California	Exempt	Taxable
Colorado	Exempt (exceptions)	Taxable
Connecticut	Exempt	Taxable
Delaware	Exempt	Taxable
D.C.	Exempt	Exempt
Florida	No income tax	No income tax
Georgia	Exempt	Taxable
Hawaii	Exempt	Taxable
Idaho	Exempt	Taxable
Illinois	Taxable (limited exceptions)	Taxable

State	Interest on In-State Bonds	Interest on Out-of-State Bonds
Indiana	Exempt	Exempt
Iowa	Taxable (limited exceptions)	Taxable
Kansas	Specified issues exempt	Taxable
Kentucky	Exempt	Taxable
Louisiana	Exempt	Taxable
Maine	Exempt	Taxable
Maryland	Exempt	Taxable
Massachusetts	Exempt	Taxable
Michigan	Exempt	Taxable
Minnesota	Exempt	Taxable
Mississippi	Exempt	Taxable
Missouri	Exempt	Taxable
Montana	Exempt	Taxable
Nebraska	Exempt	Exempt
Nevada	No income tax	No income tax
New Hampshire	Exempt	Taxable
New Jersey	Exempt	Taxable
New Mexico	Exempt	Exempt
New York	Exempt	Taxable
North Carolina	Exempt	Taxable
North Dakota	Exempt	Taxable
Ohio	Exempt	Taxable
Oklahoma	Specified issues exempt	Taxable
Oregon	Exempt	Taxable
Pennsylvania	Exempt	Taxable
Rhode Island	Exempt	Taxable
South Carolina	Exempt	Taxable
South Dakota	No income tax	No income tax
Tennessee	Exempt	Taxable
Texas	No income tax	No income tax
Utah	Exempt	Exempt
Vermont	Exempt	Exempt
Virginia	Exempt	Taxable
Washington	No income tax	No income tax
West Virginia	Exempt	Taxable
Wisconsin	Taxable	Taxable
Wyoming	No income tax	No income tax

While tax-free return may sound good, make sure it's right for you before you invest. After all, just because it's tax-free doesn't mean it will automatically provide you with the best after-tax return. Indeed, there are some investors holding municipal bonds who simply should not be doing so; the reason: it's costing them money. Tax-exempt securities generally yield less than fully taxable obligations, and because of that, *you have to be in a sufficiently high tax bracket to make up for the yield short-fall.* Look at the table; it shows what a fully taxable bond would have to yield to equal the return on a tax-free municipal issue.

Federal Tax Bracket	To match a tax-free yield of				
	5%	6%	7%	8%	9%
	you must earn this yield on a taxable investment:				
15%	5.88%	7.06%	8.24%	9.41%	10.59%
28	6.94	8.33	9.72	11.11	12.50
33	7.46	8.96	10.45	11.94	13.43

Federal Tax Bracket	To match a tax-free yield of				
	10%	11%	12%	13%	14%
	you must earn this yield on a taxable investment:				
15%	11.76%	12.94%	14.12%	15.29%	16.47%
28	13.89	15.28	16.67	18.06	19.44
33	14.92	16.42	17.91	19.40	20.90

For instance, if you're in the 28% tax bracket, a fully taxable bond would have to yield at least 11.11% in order to give you the same after-tax return as an 8% tax-exempt security. Obviously, if you can't find an 11% taxable issue, then stick with the municipal bond. Of course, when you're making such comparisons, make sure you're looking at comparable issues—the taxable and tax-free bonds under consideration should have comparable maturities, quality ratings, and so on. Otherwise, you'll bias the selection one way or the other. Generally speaking, an investor has to be in the 28% or 33% tax bracket in order for municipal bonds to offer yields competitive with fully taxable issues. For unless the tax effect is sufficient to raise the yield on a municipal to a figure that equals or surpasses taxable rates, it doesn't make any sense to buy municipals.

In addition to yields, pay attention to bond maturities, as a very poor after-market exists for many municipal issues. Because liquidity is such a problem, try to match issue maturity with your anticipated investment horizon. If you want to invest for 7 to 10 years, then select bonds with comparable maturities—or consider staggering maturities over your desired investment horizon through the use of a ladder. By doing so, you can eliminate (or at least greatly reduce) any liquidity risk by simply eliminating (or reducing) your need to sell a bond before it matures.

Because so many municipals come out in serial form—in a serial bond, the issue is broken into a series of smaller bonds, each with its own unique maturity date and coupon—it's fairly easy to pick and choose the maturities you want. As the list on the next page indicates, there's certainly no shortage of attractive high-grade municipal bonds to choose from; and this is just a tiny fraction of the recent new issues. Notice that our list contains basically two types of issues—G.O.s and guaranteed revenue bonds. The reason for this is that, as a safety-conscious investor, you ought to confine your investing to either general obligation bonds or revenue issues that carry municipal bond guarantees (described below). As with the agency obligations, this list is only meant to be representative of the kinds of issues available to individual investors—call your broker or dealer for a rundown of current offerings and rates, particularly for the latest on available in-state bonds. Also, when investing in munis, remember to check out agency ratings and call features; and if you want to avoid a lot of price volatility, then stick to intermediate-term (7- to 10-year) issues.

LOOK FOR BOND GUARANTEES An unusual aspect of the municipal market is the widespread use of *bond guarantees*. These guarantees are like an insurance policy in that they provide the bondholder with the assurance of a party other than the issuer that principal and interest payments will be made in a prompt and timely manner. As a result, bond quality is improved. The third party, in essence, provides an additional source of collateral in the form of insurance placed on the bond, at the date of issue, which is nonrevocable over the life of the obligation.

Several states and four private organizations provide munici-

A Representative List of Municipal Bonds

Issuer and Type of Issue
City of Albuquerque, NM, Gen. Purpose (G.O.) Bonds
New Jersey Health Care Facilities Financing Authority Revenue Bonds
Ocean County, NJ, Gen. Obligation Bonds
State of Arkansas Water Resources (G.O.) Bonds
Duval County, FL, School District G.O. Bonds
Osseo, MN, Independent School District Building (G.O.) Bonds
City of Beaumont, TX, Refunding Bonds
Clark County, NV, G.O. Bonds
Colorado Health Facilities Authority Revenue Bonds
Erie City, PA, School District G.O. Bonds
City of Mesa, AZ, Various Purpose (G.O.) Bonds
State of Nevada G.O. Bonds
North Carolina Medical Care Community Hospital Revenue Bonds
City of Birmingham, AL, G.O. Refunding Bonds
City of High Point, NC, G.O. Bonds
Kent County, MI, Refuse Disposal System (G.O.) Bonds
Nashville & Davidson Counties, TN, Energy Production Revenue Bonds
Riverside, CA, Sewer Revenue Bonds
Washington Township, NJ, Board of Education G.O. Bonds
Chicago Park District Museum (G.O.) Bonds
State of Florida Public Education Capital Outlay (G.O.) Bonds
State of Mississippi G.O. Bonds
Prince George's County, MD, Consolidated Public Improvement (G.O.) Bonds
New York City Municipal Assistance Corporation (G.O.) Bonds
Lake County, OH, Hospital Facilities Revenue Bonds

Source: Basic issue information was obtained from *S&P CreditWeek.*

pal bond guarantees. The four private insurers are the Municipal Bond Insurance Association (MBIA), the American Municipal Bond Assurance Corporation (AMBAC), Bond Investors Guaranty Insurance Company (BIG), and the Financial Guaranty Investment Corporation (FGIC). Each one of these organizations is actually a consortium of some of the biggest and best-

When Issued	Size of Issue (in Millions of Dollars)	Bond Guarantee Provided By	S&P Rating
Aug. 1986	$ 19.5	—	AA
Aug. 1987	52.8	BIG	AAA
Oct. 1987	21.0	—	A
Sept. 1987	15.0	—	AA
Oct. 1987	101.5	—	AA
Oct. 1987	15.1	—	A
Aug. 1987	55.6	FGIC	AAA
Oct. 1987	40.0	—	A
July 1987	14.9	MBIA	AAA
Oct. 1987	11.4	—	A
Oct. 1987	86.0	—	AA
Oct. 1987	11.5	—	AA
Aug. 1987	25.7	AMBAC	AAA
Sept. 1987	118.2	—	AA
Aug. 1987	26.0	—	AA
Oct. 1987	90.0	—	AAA
July 1987	42.0	BIG	AAA
Aug. 1987	60.0	AMBAC	AAA
Sept. 1987	19.4	—	AA
Sept. 1987	15.0	—	AA
June 1987	220.0	—	AA
Aug. 1987	35.1	—	AA
Sept. 1987	52.4	—	AA
July 1987	79.5	—	A
June 1987	28.1	AMBAC	AAA

known insurance companies in the world—firms like Aetna, Travelers, Kemper, and Allstate. Accordingly, the quality of the insurance coverage is first-rate in every respect. (A variation of the municipal bond insurance concept that's becoming increasingly popular is the use of a bank *letter of credit* [**LOC**]; in essence, an LOC from a major commercial bank is added as collateral to the municipal bond and so the quality of the bond, and its agency rating, are improved accordingly. An LOC is a lot like a bond guarantee in that the bank stands ready to make principal and interest payments in case the municipality falters.)

All four of the private guarantors will insure any general obligation or revenue bond as long as it carries an S&P rating of triple-B or better. Municipal bond insurance results in higher ratings (up to triple-A) and improved liquidity, as these bonds are generally more actively traded in the secondary markets. Guaranteed municipal bonds are especially common in the revenue market and, as such, put a whole new light on these issues. That is, whereas an uninsured revenue bond lacks certainty of payment, a guaranteed issue is very much like a G.O. bond in that you know the principal and interest payments will be made on time. Guaranteed bonds provide you with a way of getting into the higher-yielding revenue market, without jeopardizing your standards for safety. Indeed, safety-conscious investors shouldn't even give revenue bonds a second look *unless* they carry some kind of municipal bond guarantee.

WATCH OUT FOR TAXABLE MUNIS The 1986 Tax Reform Act had far-reaching effects on the municipal bond market. For one thing, the greatly reduced tax rates had a chilling effect on tax-exempt securities: i.e., lower tax rates mean investors have less incentive to hold tax-exempt municipal bonds. For another, the 1986 law changed the status of municipal bonds used to finance nonessential projects so that their interest income is no longer exempt from federal taxes. As a result, some municipal bonds are now tax-exempt and others are not. Those that are not are known as *taxable munis,* and they offer yields that are considerably higher than normal tax-exempt securities. Expected eventually to account for 20% or so of the municipal market, the vast majority of these issues will be revenue bonds. Buy a taxable muni and you'll end up holding a bond whose interest income is fully taxable by the federal government. At this writing it is not clear how the states will handle taxing these bonds. Some will probably continue to exempt all their munis from state tax, while others, following the lead of the IRS, will subject some of their own munis to state taxes. The bottom line is *be careful in the selection process.* If you come across an issue that has an abnormally high yield, make sure it's not because the issue's a taxable muni.

Investing in High-Grade Corporates

With so many Treasury and agency securities to choose from, why would any safety-conscious investor ever want to buy corporate bonds? Why should you take on the additional risk that comes with corporates? The answer to both of these questions, of course, is to pick up the added returns that corporate bonds offer. As a rule, the spread between a Treasury and a double-A-rated corporate amounts to a full percentage point or so; the differential is a bit less with triple-A-rated corporates and a bit more with single-A-rated issues. But even from a risk-return perspective, many market observers would argue that the added return from high-grade corporates is more than adequate compensation for the very slight (virtually unnoticeable) increase in risk.

In the corporate market, there's no doubt that you do have business and financial risk to contend with, and the bonds don't have the same liquidity as Treasuries or agencies. *But,* if you're careful in the selection process, much of that kind of risk exposure can be eliminated, or at least minimized. How? Simply by confining your investments to one of the top two or three rating categories and by matching bond maturities with your anticipated investment horizon. If you're willing to assume a little more risk, then you ought to consider corporate bonds a viable investment vehicle. Just make sure you're fully compensated for the added risk you have to bear. In other words, don't select a corporate over a Treasury issue unless you're satisfied with the added return you'll receive.

Now, if you tend to be extra-conservative, then don't buy anything rated lower than double-A. And if you really have trouble dealing with risk, stick with Treasuries or agencies—chances are the added return from a corporate issue won't be enough to offset the mental turmoil you'll go through. If, however, you do decide to make corporates a part of your investment program, make sure to watch out for call features and sinking fund provisions. If a bond has a call and/or sinking fund feature that you don't like, go with something else. Whenever you're considering a corporate over a Treasury or agency, be sure you're not making a big sacrifice in call protection for a bit more in yield. Over the long run, the added call protection may be worth its weight in gold if market rates drop.

You can buy corporate bonds through your broker, either when they come out as new issues or in the secondary market. If you decide to invest in a corporate, have your broker look up the call feature and the bond's rating to make sure it meets your requirements; or look it up yourself in publications like *Moody's Bond Record* or *S&P Bond Guide*. There are plenty of high-grade corporate bonds to choose from, so finding one to fit your needs should be no problem. The table provides a brief sample of the wide variety of corporate bonds available to the investing public. Note that the table lists information like coupon, maturity, promised yield, agency rating, and call features. This is the kind of information you, too, should have whenever you're making a corporate bond investment decision.

Because there's such a diversity of issues available, you can follow just about any type of investment approach you want when investing in corporates. For example, you can stick to the shorter, often noncallable, maturities of 7 to 10 years to avoid wild price volatility without incurring a big loss in yield; and/or, if you like, you can always stagger the maturities to obtain a ladder of bonds.

WHAT ABOUT CONVERTIBLES? A convertible debenture is a type of corporate bond that gives you, the bondholder, the right to convert your bond into a certain number of shares of the issuing company's common stock. (Preferred stocks can also be issued as convertibles, though our discussion here concentrates on convertible bonds; our comments, however, apply as much to convertible

A Representative List of Corporate Bonds

Company—Coupon and Maturity	Current Yield*	Promised Yield*	Call Feature**	S&P Rating
Aetna Life & Casualty—8⅛s '07	9.34%	9.60%	FC	AAA
Ashland Oil—11⅛s '17	10.72	10.70	DC('97)	A
AT&T—8⅝s '07	9.50	9.70	FC	AA
AVCO Financial—9⅜s '92	9.37	9.37	NC	A
Borden Company—9⅞s '97	9.62	9.45	FC	A
Burlington Northern—10s '97	9.96	9.93	DC('94)	AA
CBS, Inc.—10⅞s '95	10.26	9.70	DC('92)	A
Chesebrough-Pond's—10⅝s '95	10.07	9.59	DC('92)	AAA
Consolidated Edison—7.9s '02	9.21	9.79	FC	AA
Emerson Electric—8s '90	8.04	8.20	NC	AAA
Exxon Corporation—6½s '98	7.84	9.11	FC	AAA
Ford Motor Credit Company—9⅞s '97	9.67	9.53	DC('92)	AA
General Electric—7s '92	7.40	8.67	NC	AAA
GTE—10¾s '17	10.48	10.46	DC('97)	A
Honeywell, Inc.—8⅝s '06	9.66	9.92	NC	A
Household Finance—9⅝s '92	9.53	9.33	NC	AA
IBM Corporation—10¼s '95	9.62	9.03	DC('92)	AAA
Johnson & Johnson—9⅛s '92	8.97	8.63	DC('91)	AAA
Marriott Corporation—9⅞s '97	9.75	9.67	DC('94)	A
Morgan (J.P.) & Company—8s '96	8.61	9.29	DC('93)	AAA
New York Telephone—4⅝s '04	7.63	9.50	FC	AA
Sears, Roebuck—12s '94	10.60	8.98	NC	AA
Times Mirror—8⅜s '91	8.43	8.62	DC('90)	A
Whirlpool Corporation—9⅛s '16	9.90	9.96	DC('96)	AA

* Current and promised yields are as of mid-1988.

** Call provisions are designated as follows: NC = noncallable; FC = freely callable; DC('year) = deferred call feature, with the year in which the issue becomes freely callable in parentheses.

Source: Basic performance data were obtained from *S&P Bond Guide.*

preferreds as they do to convertible bonds.) Most investors buy convertibles not because of their attractive yields but because of the potential price performance offered by the stock side of the issue. Thus, it's the *equity kicker* that makes these bonds so popular.

Should you invest in convertibles if you are following a safe investment program? *Probably not.* There are several reasons for this. One is the complicated nature of convertible securities; because they combine elements of both stocks and bonds, these securities are difficult to evaluate. And as we've maintained all along, if you don't fully understand an issue, you should stay away from it. In addition, even though convertibles are a form of fixed income security, they often involve a big give-up in yield. Relative to comparable straight debt securities, they start off offering very low yields and it just gets worse over time as the price of the stock—and the convertible—goes up. Substantial yield give-ups run contrary to the whole notion of investing for safety's sake. Finally, there's the matter of risk. Not only is most of the return from these securities based on the highly uncertain component of capital gains, as derived from the equity kicker, but most of these securities are fairly low rated—there just aren't many high-grade, investment-quality convertibles.

The Special Case of Zero-Coupon Bonds

As the name implies, zero-coupon bonds have no coupons. Rather, these securities are sold at a deep discount from their par value and then increase in value over time at a compound rate of return, so that at maturity they're worth their full par value. Other things being equal, the cheaper the bond, the greater your return. For example, a 10% bond might cost $239, while an issue with a 15% yield costs only $123. Because they don't have coupons, these bonds do not pay interest semiannually, and in fact pay nothing to the investor until the issue matures. As strange as it might seem, this is the main attraction of zero-coupon bonds. That is, since there are no interest payments, investors do not have to worry about reinvesting coupon income twice a year. Instead, the fully compounded rate of return on a zero-coupon bond is virtually guaranteed at the stated rate that exists when the issue is purchased. For example, in early 1988, high-grade zero-coupon bonds with 20-year maturities were available at yields of around 8%; so for just $200 you could buy a bond that would be worth five times that amount, or $1,000, at maturity in 20 years. Best of all, you would be locking in an 8% fully compounded rate of return on your investment capital for the full 20-year life of the issue. We have stressed throughout the importance of generating a fully compounded rate of return in a safe investment program. Well, zero coupons do precisely that—all automatically—and they do it over just about any holding period you want. Accordingly, zero coupons merit serious consideration if you're investing for safety's sake, particularly if you have a long-term investment goal. Zeros are a simple way to reach a long-range goal, since all you have to do is set a target terminal value you want to achieve and then buy enough zeros to meet that objective. But be careful, since not all zero-coupon bonds are high-grade issues; there are plenty of junk zero-coupon bonds on the market. Because quality is so important, don't buy anything that's less than triple- or possibly double-A-rated. A default with one of these means you lose everything, so stick with quality.

The foregoing advantages notwithstanding, there are some disadvantages you should be aware of. One is that if rates move up over time, you won't be able to participate in the higher return because you'll have no coupon income to reinvest. In addition, zero-coupon bonds are subject to tremendous price volatility; thus, if market rates climb, you'll experience a sizable capital loss as the prices of long-term zero coupons plunge. You can greatly reduce your exposure to market risk by carefully matching bond maturity with your anticipated investment horizon—in other words, invest for the duration. Finally, the IRS has ruled that zero-coupon bondholders must report interest on an accrual basis, even though no interest is actually received—not a very good deal! For this reason, most fully taxable zero-coupon bonds should either be placed in tax sheltered investments, like individual retirement accounts (IRAs), or possibly given to some minor children, who are taxed at the lowest rate if at all. Zeros are issued by corporations, municipalities, federal agencies, and the U.S. Treasury. In addition, many of the major brokerage houses package U.S. Treasury securities as zeros and sell them to the investing public in the form of investment trusts, which are marketed under such names as TIGRS, CATS, and LIONS.

The Good Points:

- *Steady and attractive stream of current income,* except for zero-coupon bonds.
- *Lock in high yields* by selecting bonds that offer extended protection against call.
- *Safety and preservation of capital,* as long as you can hold high-quality bonds to maturity. Regardless of what happens to interest rates, the issues return to their par values at maturity.
- *Match just about any investment horizon.* A wide range of maturities are available from short- (3 to 5 years) to intermediate- (7 to 10 years) to long-term (15 to 20 years or more).
- *Well secured* for prime grade issues involving little if any risk of default.
- *Active secondary market* exists for Treasuries and agencies, as well as a number of corporate issues. These securities are fairly liquid and relatively easy to sell should the need ever arise.
- *Attractive tax features* with a number of Treasury, agency, and municipal bonds.

And the Bad:

- *Subject to swings in price,* no matter how high the quality, as interest rates change; and the longer the issue, the greater the price volatility.
- *Miss out on rising yields* because the coupons are normally set for life. When market rates move up over time, you can't take full advantage of rising rates; this is an especially serious problem with long-term issues.
- *Can be called,* so if you hold notes and bonds that face premature retirement, your ability to lock in high yields is severely limited.
- *Possibility of default,* and no matter how small it may be, it tends to increase as you go to longer and longer issues.

- *Substantial commitment of capital needed,* usually $1,000 for corporates, $5,000 for municipals, $1,000 to $5,000 for Treasury notes and bonds, and as much as $10,000 to $25,000 for some agency issues.
- *Lack liquidity.* Some types of bonds, notably municipals and some corporates, don't have much of an after-market.

Taxes:

The interest income and capital gains earned on *corporate bonds* are fully taxable at the federal level and in most states, too.

The interest income from most *municipal bonds* is tax-free at the federal level and normally at the state level, too, if it's an in-state issue; capital gains, in contrast, are fully taxable at the state and federal levels. However, some municipals (taxable munis) are *not* tax-exempt at the federal level; further, having income from some municipal bonds may subject you to the alternative minimum tax (AMT), depending upon your level of income and other specifics surrounding your return—check with your tax adviser for details.

The interest income from *Treasury* securities and some *agency* issues is subject to normal federal tax but is exempt from state income tax; capital gains are fully taxable at both the federal and state levels.

Regardless of the type of bond held, if interest income is taxable, it's taxable *as received* in the case of coupon bonds, and *as accrued* in the case of zero coupons. Taxes on capital gains, in contrast, are payable only when the gain is *actually realized*— when the security is sold, or when it matures.

6

For a Bigger Bang from the Buck, Try Stocks

A not-so-funny thing happened on the way to the market in October of 1987. The stock market "crashed"; it experienced a "major correction"; it went through a "melt-down." No matter how you care to describe it, the events of October 19, 1987, certainly weren't very pleasant, as the market lost over 500 points on volume of over 600 million shares. The incredible bull market that had begun some 5 years earlier was over. It was now the bears' turn to have the run of Wall Street.

Welcome to the world of common stocks. Actually, this is a highly distorted view of the stock market. For it's not all risk and wild price volatility. There are also some pretty attractive rewards. Consider the fact that even though the last quarter of 1987 was a wild and woolly one, the market still ended the year on the plus side—if only up by a meager 2%. In a similar fashion, if you look at the 5 plus years from August 1982 through December 1987, you'll find a market that went up over 150%—and that's *after* factoring in the impact of the October crash.

Now, all this doesn't mean that stocks are right for everyone. Quite the contrary. There's a major segment of the investing public that simply does not belong in the stock market, if for no other reason than they just don't have the risk tolerance for it. But if you can put up with a bit more risk, there just might be a segment of the stock market that you should look into. Let's understand going in that not all stocks are speculative high flyers. Rather, there are some good-quality, high-grade stocks that make good, safe investments. We're talking, for the most part, about stocks issued by rock solid companies like Abbott Labs, IBM, Bordens, Merck, Coca-Cola, Raytheon, Minnesota Mining, RJR Nabisco, and others. The risk exposure with these stocks *may* be more than with high-quality bonds, but as a rule, so are the returns. Let's look now at common stocks and how you, as a safety-conscious investor, can use these securities to improve the return on your portfolio.

Earnings, Dividends, and Stock Prices

As an investment vehicle, a share of common stock is about as basic as it gets. You buy a share of common and you own a piece of the company: in a roundabout fashion, you supply capital to the firm, and as a part owner, you are entitled to a piece of the profits. When the company prospers, so do you; and when it falters, so do your returns. Ultimately, it's this claim on income that appeals to common stock investors. But this claim is not without its limitations, for common stockholders are really the *residual* owners of the company. That means, as a stockholder, you are entitled to dividend income and a prorated share of the company's earnings only *after* all the firm's other obligations have been met. Equally important, as residual owners, holders of common stock have no guarantee they will ever receive any return on their investment. Stocks aren't like bonds—there's no requirement to pay dividends, and there's no requirement to pay you your money back at some future date.

High-grade common stocks are generally used by safety-conscious investors in one of two ways:

1. *As a way to earn current income.* The thing that's important here is the dividend income that stocks produce. To these

investors, stocks are just another type of income security—
they like the attractive current yields that they can get from
high paying stocks, and the fact that the level of annual dividends tends to grow over time.

2. *As the basis for long-term wealth accumulation.* Here, it's not
only dividend income that's important, but also a steady dose
of capital gains. Nothing spectacular; just a nice, steady rate
of appreciation as the long-run well-being of the company
improves. These investors recognize that high-quality stocks
have a tendency to go up in price over the long term.

The Rewards and Risks of Investing in Stocks

Actually, high-grade stocks have a lot to offer. For one thing,
there's the opportunity for return. The fact is, over the long haul,
stocks generally do provide attractive, highly competitive returns.
This is so because, as *equity securities,* they are entitled to participate fully in the residual profits of the firm. The market price of
a share of stock ordinarily reflects the profit potential of the firm;
increasing corporate profits therefore translate into rising share
prices (capital gains) and are a critical component in producing
attractive investment returns. In addition, investors are drawn to
high-grade stocks for the current income they offer in the form
of dividends, especially now that the Tax Reform Act of 1986 has
effectively lowered taxes on dividends and raised them on capital
gains. Stocks are also highly liquid and easily transferable. They
are easy to buy and sell, and the transaction costs are modest.
Moreover, price and market information is widely disseminated
in the news and financial media. A final advantage of common
stock ownership is that the unit cost of a share of stock is usually
fairly low, well within the reach of most individual investors.
Unlike bonds, which carry minimum denominations of at least
$1,000, and some mutual funds that have fairly hefty minimum
requirements, common stocks present no such investment hur-
dles. Instead, most stocks today are priced at less than $50 per
share—and any number of shares, no matter how few, can be
bought or sold.

Unfortunately, there's also a down side. Without a doubt, the biggest problem with stocks is their *risk*. Even with investment-quality stocks, you still need some tolerance for risk, if only to be able to put up with the recurring swings in market prices. Here's how stocks stack up with regard to the four basic types of risk:

• **Business and Financial Risk** Because they are residual securities, all common stocks are subject to business and financial risk, to one degree or another. Such risk shows up in companies that have very volatile earnings, big operating losses, or just have trouble staying in business. You can avoid most of this kind of risk by sticking to high-quality, investment-grade stocks. These are the shares issued by big, solid, established firms that have strong earnings records and that are financially situated to weather any rough economic times. Stay with the blue chip stocks and you can keep business/financial risk to an absolute minimum. Indeed, you can almost reduce it to the point where such risk exposure really isn't much of an issue. Face it: if the IBMs and General Electrics of this world go belly-up, we've got *serious* economic problems!

• **Market Risk** If you confine your investment activities to high-quality stocks, the biggest risk you're likely to incur is market risk—that is, the volatility in the market price of your shares. The market's a pretty important force with stocks and generally has a substantial bearing on stock price behavior. Even the shares of IBM and AT&T go up and down in price as they respond to the market. Again, you can reduce such risk by sticking to stocks with *low betas*. (As a rule, a low beta means something less than 1.0—for example, a beta of 0.7 or 0.8 would be considered low.) In essence, low-beta stocks have less price volatility. Remember, however, that a low beta doesn't mean the stock will be totally immune from price volatility. It'll just be less volatile than the average stock. Betas on major stocks are widely published, so they're easy to keep track of. Ask your broker, or check in your library for publications like *Value Line*.

• **Purchasing Power Risk** Common stocks are like other financial assets in that they, too, are subject to the nasty side effects of inflation. However, it's generally felt that common stocks tend to do a better job than most other long-term securities in protecting your return against inflation. For except in times of abnormally high inflation, stocks customarily provide rates of return comfortably above the rate of inflation. So purchasing power risk shouldn't be much of a problem.

• **Liquidity Risk** So long as you stick to the major stocks (those traded on the NYSE, AMEX, or NASDAQ's national market), this type of risk simply won't be a concern. Indeed, the general liquidity of stocks is one of their positive attributes.

Types of Quality Stocks

High-quality, established stocks tend to fall into one of two categories: *blue chips* or *quality income stocks*. Actually, there's a bit of an overlap here, since blue chips can also be income stocks, and vice versa. There are all sorts of different types of stocks on the market, but as a safety-conscious investor, *you should confine your investing to these two categories only!* Quite frankly, all the other kinds of stock involve too much business and/or market risk.

BLUE CHIP STOCKS These are the high-grade, investment quality issues of major corporations, many of which are household names. They are the large, well-established, mature firms that have impeccable financial credentials. With a long and unbroken record of earnings and dividends, blue chips are unsurpassed in quality. Indeed, many of these companies haven't had losses in 30 or 40 years, and an even larger number haven't missed a dividend payment in 50 years or more! The companies hold important, if not leading, positions in their industries and frequently determine the standards by which other firms are measured. These are farsighted firms that have taken the steps to insure future growth without jeopardizing current earnings. Of course, they also have the advantage of size and can easily hold their own even in times of economic difficulty.

Not all blue chips are alike, however. Some provide consistently high dividend yields, while others are more growth oriented. Good examples of blue chip growth firms are Merck,

McDonalds, Bristol-Meyers, Philip Morris, H.J. Heinz, and R.R. Donnelly; some high-yielding blue chips include PNC Financial, Northern States Power, American Brands, Norstar Bancorp, Wisconsin Energy, and Consolidated Natural Gas. As a rule, quality-conscious investors are drawn to blue chips because they offer respectable dividend yields and moderate growth potential. In essence, these low risk stocks offer safety and stability, along with a way of obtaining modest but dependable rates of return.

QUALITY INCOME STOCKS Income stocks are appealing for one basic reason: because of the attractive dividend yields they pay. Technically, stocks are classified as income shares if they regularly pay higher-than-average dividend returns. But sometimes, firms pay abnormally high dividend yields not because they're so rich, but because they're high-risk/low-growth companies that have to pay high dividends to attract investors. Our interest here is with *quality income stocks*—those securities issued by financially sound firms that consistently pay high levels of dividends, over bad years as well as good.

In short, quality income stocks are characterized by a fairly stable stream of earnings and a long and sustained record of paying higher-than-average dividends. These features make them ideal for those who want a relatively safe and high level of current income from their investment capital. Unlike holders of bonds and preferred stock, however, holders of income stocks *can also expect the amount of dividends they receive to increase over time.* Take, for example, Texas Utilities: it paid $1.52 a share in dividends in 1978; 10 years later in 1987, it was paying $2.77 a share. That's a big jump in dividends—nearly 85%—and it's something that can have quite an impact on total return.

Many quality income stocks are found in the public utility and communications industries; they can also be found in the banking and financial services area and, to some extent, in the industrial sector of the market. This group of securities includes such public utilities as Central Illinois Public Service, San Diego Gas and Electric, and Southwestern Public Service, and such industrial and financial issues as General Motors, Mobil Oil, W.R. Grace, Bank of New York, and Boatman's Bancshares. Income shares are susceptible to interest rate risk, since their returns are usually judged relative to other income-oriented securities, like bonds.

Quality Stocks Have Quality Financials

As a conservative, safety-conscious investor, one thing you quickly learn is that in the stock market, there's no substitute for quality. Unlike bonds, common stocks don't have terminal values to hold up their prices. If the price of a stock falls, it can stay down for years, even decades. While you can't avoid this kind of thing altogether, you can sharply reduce its likelihood of occurring by confining your investments to high-quality stocks.

WHAT TO LOOK FOR In a general sense, quality companies have several things going for them:

- They're in an industry that has a future, and they're usually at the forefront of the industry; in fact, many of the best firms in the country are diversified into several promising industries.
- Their financial credentials are impeccable: they have plenty of liquidity, a manageable debt load, and a lot of net worth; equally important, they've invested their money wisely and so are able to get the most from their assets.
- They're able to experience growth while keeping operating results under control; in essence, they're able to maintain an almost constant growth in sales and still preserve attractive profit margins. The net result is a steady improvement in earnings.
- They share their successes with their stockholders in the form of cash dividends; and the level of dividends paid out to stockholders tends to increase over time in line with earnings growth.
- Finally, the stocks of quality companies tend to be less price-volatile than most other types of stock; indeed, many of them have betas of less than 1.0.

It's obvious from a brief rundown of this list that the vast majority of companies would fail to meet these criteria, and that's the way it should be! As a safety-conscious investor, you've eliminated most stocks from consideration because they're not high quality and therefore involve too much risk. Critics might argue that you're throwing the baby out with the bath water, because by being so restrictive, you're passing up stocks that are going to produce some fat returns in the future. And that may be. But, so long as risk is a key concern with you, that's something you can certainly live with. Furthermore, as a conservative investor, you want to be able to invest for the long haul, which is something that should be done only with high-quality stocks.

WHERE TO FIND THEM Now that you know what to look for, the next question is where do you find these stocks? To begin with, your broker can probably provide you with a list of attractive blue chips and quality income stocks. Most full-service brokerage firms keep tabs on the major companies and publish a list of recommended stocks. Just be sure to let your broker know that *you only want to look at quality.* If you're willing to do a little digging yourself, two of the best sources of information are *Value Line Investment Survey* and Standard & Poor's *Stock Reports.* Both of these publications are easy to use and are written for the lay investor, assuming nothing more than a basic understanding of stocks. Value Line reports are 1 page long; S&P's are 2 pages. Both provide quality ratings that can be used much the same way you use bond ratings.

Standard & Poor's assigns letter grades to stocks based on their assessment of the growth and stability of the company's earnings and dividends. If you want to stick to high quality, look for stocks that carry an A+ or A rating, or possibly even an occasional A— (as that's still an above-average rating).

Value Line's ratings are a bit more comprehensive, covering both the financial strength of the firm and the price stability of the stock. In assessing financial strength, Value Line looks at both the operating results and the financial condition of the firm. The financially strongest companies receive one of three A ratings (A,

A+, or A++), which is what you should stick with. The price stability of the stock is also statistically evaluated, with number grades being assigned. Generally, the least volatile stocks are graded 80 to 85 or better, with 100 being the highest score possible. The elements of price stability and financial strength are then combined into a single measure, which Value Line calls its *Safety Rank*. The safest, strongest stocks carry a ranking of 1. This is clearly the place to start looking for blue chips!

If you're relying on your broker for suggestions about blue chip stocks, let him/her know you'll consider the stocks only if they carry a safety rank of 1, a price stability score of, say, 80 or better, and a financial strength rating of, say, A or better. Should you want even more quality, set the standards higher still—say, 1, 90, and A+, respectively. If you want to find a quality income stock, you might want to consider an issue with a safety rank of 2, *so long as it still carries a financial strength rating of A or better, and a price stability score of 85 or better*. There's no doubt that such an issue would still be considered a high-quality security.

SOME KEY MEASURES OF PERFORMANCE Professional money managers and seasoned investors tend to use a variety of financial ratios and measures when making investment decisions, particularly where common stock is involved. Likewise, published stock reports (like those from S&P or Value Line) are replete with such ratios. So long as you're relying on quality ratings, like those of Value Line or S&P, there's no need for you to go through the rigors of an in-depth security analysis. Even so, there are a few key measures of performance you should keep track of if you're thinking about buying, or already have a position, in common stocks. Most or all of these can be found in published stock reports, so you don't have to actually compute the ratios.

• **Net Profit Margin** This ratio relates net profits of the firm to its sales, and provides an indication of how well the company is controlling its cost structure. The higher the net profit margin, the more money the company earns; look for a relatively stable, or even better, an increasing net profit margin.

- **Return on Equity (ROE)** ROE reflects the overall profitability of the firm. It captures, in a single ratio, the amount of success the firm is having in managing its assets, operations, and capital structure. Return on equity is important because it has a direct and significant impact on the profits, growth, and dividends of the firm. The better the ROE, the better the financial condition and competitive position of the firm: thus, look for a stable or increasing ROE; in contrast, watch out for a falling ROE, as it could spell trouble.
- **Earnings per Share (EPS)** Here, the net profits of the firm are converted to a per share figure. EPS is important because of its impact on dividends and share prices. Look for a steady rate of growth in EPS.
- **Dividends per Share** This ratio indicates the dollar amount of dividends paid to each share of stock; again, look for a steady increase over time in the level of dividends paid.
- **Dividend Payout Ratio** This indicates how much of the company's earnings are paid out in dividends. Well-managed companies have target payout ratios they try to maintain, so if earnings are going up, so will dividends. Income-oriented stocks (like public utilities) tend to have much higher payout ratios than growth-oriented securities; for example, income stocks could easily have ratios of 60% to 70%, compared to 30% to 40% for others.
- **Dividend Yield** By relating dividends received to the prevailing market price of the stock, this measure shows the kind of return you're getting from dividends; the higher the current yield, the better your return. As a rule, dividends account for a sizable portion of the total return to quality-conscious stockholders. Dividend yields can range from about 1% to 3% for growth-oriented blue chips to as much as 6% to 8% or more for quality income stocks. These standards aren't fixed for life, however, as dividend yields tend to move with the general level of market interest rates—higher rates lead to a generally higher level of yields.
- **Stock Beta** This measure is an indication of the stock's price volatility; it shows how the stock responds to the market in general. Look for low betas—preferably less than 1.0—if you're trying

to invest in relatively stable stocks. The lower the beta, the less volatile the stock. This also means that if you have a low-beta stock, you better plan on getting a big chunk of your return from dividends.

• **Price/Earnings Ratio** Also known as the P/E multiple, this measure relates the price of the stock to its earnings per share. A very important and widely followed market measure of performance, the P/E multiple reveals how aggressively the stock is being priced in the market; a relatively high P/E indicates that the stock is being highly priced by investors. Another thing: the higher the P/E, the greater the likelihood that the stock is being overpriced—that the market's putting too high a value on the company's earnings. P/E ratios are not static, but tend to move with the market: when the market is soft, a stock's P/E will be low, and when things heat up, so will the stock's P/E. As a rule, look for stocks that have P/E ratios of *no more* than 15 to 18 times earnings. Indeed, consider buying stocks with P/Es as high as 18 *only* if the market's doing well *and* the company's fundamentals are particularly strong. (By the way, if you already hold the stock, don't sell it just because the P/E goes over the 15 to 18 mark; if you're in for the long haul, it's not costing you anything. All you did was buy the stock before the market started more aggressively pricing the issue, which if anything, will just add to your return.)

Maybe Quality Stocks Do Have a Place in Your Portfolio?

It's probably no exaggeration to say that many—perhaps most—conservative, safety-conscious investors have never invested in common stocks, or any other form of equity security. To them, these securities just involve too much risk, especially when it comes to price volatility. You can minimize most of the other risks by following a rigid selection process, but aside from looking for low-beta stocks, there's little you can do to avoid the price volatility of even high-grade common stocks. And that, unfortunately, is a problem, because a lot of people just can't stomach that kind of instability.

Face it, stocks are a long-term investment vehicle and as such, they're naturally subject to price volatility. But common stocks—high-quality stocks in particular—also have their rewards. For one thing, there's the dividend yield. Plus, you're almost guaranteed that the level of dividends will steadily increase over time—which is a feature that you can't find in any other type of security. And on top of all this, there's the potential price appreciation that you can usually count on over the long haul. Stock prices may be a bit volatile over the short run, but over the long term, they usually do tend to go up in price.

Follow a Sound Investment Program

Maybe quality stocks do have something to offer? But to keep the risks down and still get the most out of these securities, you have to develop and follow some type of systematic investment program. Now, understand, this doesn't mean it has to be complicated or highly sophisticated. Indeed, more often than not, the simpler programs are the more successful. So let's keep it simple!

Perhaps more than any other type of investment vehicle, common stock investing requires discipline. And that's what our investment program should provide: a series of guidelines that we can follow to develop the discipline necessary for success. Of course, no investment program can guarantee success; all we can hope to do is (greatly) increase the odds of achieving a measure of success. Here, we define success as being able to earn a respectable rate of return on our money—something that fully compensates us for the risks we have to take, and hopefully, gives us a little extra to boot.

A sound, conservative investment program is one where you:

- Stick with good, solid stocks.
- Diversify your holdings.

- Invest for the long haul.
- Plow back your earnings.

Putting these elements to work should help you reach your objective of earning a satisfactory return on your money.

STICK WITH GOOD, SOLID STOCKS This should be the first rule of anybody who's investing for safety's sake. Relax the quality criterion and you move into the realm of speculation. There's no doubt that's one way to improve your chances of making a bigger return, but it's equally certain to lead to more risk as well. So stay with quality stocks, issued by companies that have long and sustained records of earnings and dividends. If the company's had even the smallest loss in the past 10 or 15 years, don't buy the stock. Also, don't buy it if dividends haven't steadily increased over time. They don't have to increase every year, but if they've been cut (or skipped) any time in the recent past, beware. Follow the Value Line and/or Standard & Poor's quality ratings. In short, go with stocks that offer value—as derived from a strong record of earnings, a solid capital structure, plenty of liquidity, and an ability to compete with the best of them.

DIVERSIFY YOUR HOLDINGS Whenever possible, try to diversify your holdings across three or four different stocks. This will reduce your exposure to risk, as it will lessen your susceptibility to loss if things don't work out as expected with a given security. Of course, if you don't have a lot of money to invest, you probably won't be able to do much diversifying. For example, if you have only $2,500 to invest, then you probably can't do much more than invest in one stock—under such circumstances, it makes no sense to hold three or four different issues, since you'll be hard hit with big commissions and odd-lot transaction costs. On the other hand, you can easily afford to hold three, four, or even five different stocks if you have, say, $25,000 to invest.

INVEST FOR THE LONG HAUL Before buying a single share of stock, force yourself to answer one question: are you reasonably sure that you can keep your money invested for 7 to 10 years? If the answer is no, then *don't* invest in common stock. You have to be able to ride out those occasional soft markets, and the greater the chance that you'll have to sell on short notice, the greater the chance that you'll have to sell into a depressed market. Thus, when you invest in stocks—even high-quality stocks—do so for the long haul. And whatever you do, don't get involved with market timing! Forget about trying to buy in and out of a stock as it goes up and down in price. Chances are, far more often than not, you'll come out on the short end of the stick. Market timing is not only enormously difficult, it's also very expensive—transaction costs alone can eat you alive.

In addition, once you've invested in a stock, learn to be patient with it. Unfortunately, stocks occasionally do go down in price, and sometimes in a fairly big way. But if it's a carefully selected high-quality issue, it'll be able to ride out those occasional soft spots in the market. The question is: can you? Just because an issue is experiencing some softness doesn't mean it's no longer a viable investment. If the stock remains fundamentally strong, it will probably recover. So don't run for the nearest exit the first time your stock experiences a drop in price. Most stocks have a pronounced tendency to go up in price over time, but to take advantage of that, you have to be patient.

PLOW BACK YOUR EARNINGS Unless you're living off the income, the basic investment objective with stocks is the same as it is with bonds or any other security: to earn an attractive fully compounded rate of return. That means you have to deal with the regular reinvestment of dividend income. Doing so is the only way you're going to keep your money fully invested and earn a fully compounded rate of return on your capital. The message is unmistakable: reinvest your dividends, don't spend them. If you get regular dividend checks mailed to your home, make it a habit to deposit them into something like a money market deposit account, where your capital can grow and be available for future investment purposes. On the other hand, if your account is set up so dividends are sent directly to your brokerage firm, you can arrange to have them automatically deposited into one of the firm's money funds, where it can earn a market rate of return while waiting to be put to use in another investment.

There is no better way to reinvest your dividends than through a *dividend reinvestment plan (DRP)*. The basic investment philosophy at work here is that if the company is good enough to invest in, it's good enough to reinvest in. In a dividend reinvestment plan, shareholders can sign up to have their cash dividends automatically reinvested in additional shares of the company's common stock—in essence, it's like taking your cash dividends in the form of more shares of common stock. The idea is to put your money to work by building up your investment in the stock. Such an approach can have a tremendous impact on your investment position over time, as shown by the figures in the table.

Today, over 1,000 companies (including most major corporations) have DRPs in existence, and each one provides investors with a convenient and inexpensive way to accumulate capital. Both Value Line and Standard & Poor's identify companies that have DRPs. Stocks in most DRPs are acquired free of any broker-

Cash or Reinvested Dividends

Situation: Buy 100 shares of stock at $25 a share (total investment $2,500); stock currently pays $1 a share in annual dividends. Price of the stock increases at 8% per year; dividends grow at 5% per year.

Investment Period	Number of Shares Held	Market Value of Stock Holdings	Total Cash Dividends Received
TAKE DIVIDENDS IN CASH			
5 years	100	$ 3,672	$ 552
10 years	100	5,397	1,258
15 years	100	7,930	2,158
20 years	100	11,652	3,307
PARTICIPATE IN DIVIDEND REINVESTMENT PLAN			
5 years	115.59	$ 4,245	$0
10 years	135.66	7,322	0
15 years	155.92	12,364	0
20 years	176.00	20,508	0

age commissions, and some plans even sell stocks to their DRP investors at below-market prices—usually at discounts of 3% to 5%. In addition, most plans credit fractional shares to the investor's account. Shareholders can join these plans by simply sending in a completed authorization form to the company. Generally, it takes 30 to 45 days for all the paperwork to be processed. Once in the plan, the number of shares held will begin to accumulate with each dividend date. DRPs really do serve an important function, and every safety-conscious investor who does not need the current income should use them.

When to Invest

The first step in investing is to know where to put your money; the second is to know when to make your moves. The first question is fairly straightforward, as it basically involves matching your risk and return objectives with the available investment vehicles. Unfortunately, the second question is not as easy to deal with.

We have stressed throughout this book that *a security should be considered a viable investment candidate only so long as it promises to generate a sufficiently attractive rate of return,* and in particular, one that fully compensates you for any risks you have to take. Thus, when considering an investment in stock, look at the return it offers and compare that to some benchmark, like the market yields available on high-grade corporate bonds. Say high-grade corporates (such as double-A-rated industrials) are presently yielding around 9%; if you can't get at least 2 to 3 percentage points more, or in this case 11% to 12%, then don't invest in the stock. The reason: stocks are riskier than bonds, so you deserve more return.

Before assessing return, let's identify a couple of conditions when investing in stocks just doesn't make any sense at all. In particular, *don't* invest in a stock if:

- You feel very strongly that the market is headed down in the short run. If you're absolutely certain the market's in for a big fall, then wait until the market drops and buy the stock when it's cheaper. But be careful. We're not advocating market timing here; all we're saying is that you should not be completely oblivious to market conditions. If you have good reason to believe the market's in for a big drop (or will continue to fall, if it's already doing so), then act accordingly. On the other hand, if you lack such conviction, then go ahead with the transaction.

- You feel very uncomfortable with the general tone of the market—it lacks direction, or there's way too much price volatility to suit you. This became a problem prior to and after the October crash, when program trading started taking over the market. The result was a stock market that behaved more like a commodities market, with an intolerable amount of price volatility. When this happens, fundamentals go out the window and the market simply becomes too risky. If you're uncomfortable with the market, then do what the pros do and wait it out on the sidelines.

Now, if neither one of these conditions exists, the time may be right to invest in stocks, so long as you can find one that provides the type of return you're looking for. If you're an income-oriented investor, use dividend yield to assess stocks. If you're looking for attractive total return over the long haul, use the approximate yield measure.

USE DIVIDEND YIELD IF YOU'RE LIVING OFF THE INCOME The basic investment objective of retired people and others living off their investments is very simple: to get as much as they can from interest and/or dividends. These investors look for good, sound, high-yielding securities. Quality income stocks are often used for such purposes, since they offer both a measure of safety and a fairly hefty level of dividends.

You can get a handle on return in these cases by determining the dividend yield of the stock. Dividend yield is easy to find: just divide the latest annual dividends per share by the current market price of the stock. Other things being equal, the higher the yield, the more attractive the stock—high dividend yield translates into increased dividend income. Take the case of Texas Utilities, a quality income stock traded on the NYSE. Texas Utilities is fairly price-stable (it has a beta of only 0.7); it pay out about 60% of its earnings in dividends; and over the 7 years from 1981 to 1987, its dividend yield ranged from 8% to 10%. Indeed, in 1987, the company paid a dividend of $2.77 a share, and based on a year-end price of $27 a share, was offering a dividend yield of 10.3% ($2.77/$27 = .103). Most income-oriented investors would probably find this yield fairly attractive, and especially so in light of the fact that Texas Utilities dividends have grown at the rate of about 7% a year since 1981. Thus, here's a quality stock that pays a highly attractive dividend yield of 10.3%; *plus*, the company's had a tendency to steadily increase its dividends over time. If you think such a combination stacks up well, then this might be a stock to consider.

USE APPROXIMATE YIELD IF YOU'RE AFTER TOTAL RETURN While dividends are a major concern to individuals living off their investment income, it's total return over the long haul that's important to many other investors. Dividends are important here, too, but so are capital gains and the ability to earn interest-on-interest. In essence, it's fully compounded rate of return that matters. Under such circumstances, the best way to gauge return is with the approximate yield procedure—a measure we first introduced in chapter 2, and which we used in the last chapter to find the promised yield to maturity on a bond.

To determine the approximate yield of a stock, you find the average annual dividend income, add that to the average annual capital gains, and divide it all by the average amount of the investment. While this is a great way of measuring the promised yield on a bond or the historical performance of a stock (where, in both cases, all the input variables are known), it's a lot tougher to use when you're trying to get a handle on the expected (or future) return performance of a stock. The main reason this is so tough is that you really don't know what the future price of the stock is going to be. One way to get around this difficulty is to start with dividends and then sort of back into future price performance. In other words, you find the kind of price performance that's necessary to give you the approximate yield you're looking for. Here's what you have to do:

1. Make an estimate of what *future dividends* are likely to be. It's often helpful, particularly with blue chips and income stocks, to look at what the stock has done over the past 10 to 12 years and then extrapolate roughly the same kind of performance into the future.
2. Based on alternative investment opportunities, arrive at the *benchmark rate of return* you'd like to earn on this stock.
3. Estimate the kind of yield you could earn on this stock from dividends alone. This means you're not anticipating any appreciation in the price of the stock; all you're assuming is that you'll be able to sell the stock for what you paid for it. To get an idea of a stock's *expected dividend yield,* simply divide the average annual dividends you expect to receive by the current market price of the stock. (While this may sound a lot like dividend yield, it's actually a variation of the fully compounded approximate yield formula, with capital gains assumed to be zero.)
4. Compare the expected dividend yield to your desired benchmark return. If the expected dividend yield is fairly close to your benchmark, the stock doesn't have to go up much in price in order to meet your desired rate of return; on the other hand, if the expected dividend yield is not even close to your benchmark return, you'll need a lot of capital gains to come up with the return you'd like. As a rule, the more income-oriented the stock, the less you'll need from capital gains.
5. Based on the results of your comparison, adjust the stock price change in the approximate yield formula until you come up with an approximate yield that equals, or is reasonably close to, your desired benchmark return.
6. Finally, evaluate the likelihood of the stock going up in price by the amount necessary to give you the return you need. The

logic here is that it's easier to assess the likelihood of reaching a *target price* than trying to come up with an uncertain future price from scratch. Obviously, if all the stock has to do over your anticipated holding period is go up $4 or $5, you'll be facing a lot less risk than if the price has to, say, double or triple over the same time span. Again, look at what it's done over the past 10 to 12 years; that'll help you put the needed future price performance into perspective.

To see how this whole yield process works, return to the Texas Utilities example and assume it's early 1988. What you want to know is: if you buy the stock today and hold it for, say, 10 years, what kind of return can you expect? In trying to get a handle on what the future holds, you have to recognize that market forces have a lot to do with a stock's performance, and certainly, the future market environment will play an important role in defining the future behavior of Texas Utilities. But that doesn't mean you should ignore the past altogether, for it does provide an indication of how well management is doing and how the company is able to perform. As such, the past can become a starting point in looking at the future. This is especially true with high-quality stocks, which tend to be somewhat predictable in behavior.

Consider dividends, for example. Coming up with an estimate of what future dividends are likely to be is the first step in our yield estimation process. As reported by Value Line, Texas Utilities' dividends have been growing at an average annual rate of about 7% over the past 5 to 10 years. For safety's sake, let's be a bit conservative here, and assume that *future dividends* are going to grow by only 5%. We can now find future dividends by simply multiplying each successive annual dividend by 1.05, where .05 represents the assumed 5% rate of growth. Starting with 1987 dividends of $2.77 per share, we have $2.77 × 1.05 = $2.91 × 1.05 = $3.05, and so forth for the rest of the 10-year period of investment. The bottom line is that dividends should gradually increase to about $4.51 a share over the next 10 years.

We can now find average annual dividends by adding the beginning and ending dividends and dividing this sum by 2: ($2.77 + $4.51)/2 = $3.64.

The general level of dividends is usually pretty easy to forecast with blue chips and quality income stocks, because such issues tend to follow a fairly stable pattern of dividends. You may not be right on the button every year, but you probably won't be far off either. Knowing this makes your job a lot easier, since dividend income is often an important source of return for these stocks.

The second step is to come up with a desired rate of return. Earlier we said you should consider investing in high-quality stocks only so long as you feel reasonably sure that you can earn 2 to 3 percentage points more than what you can get from high-grade corporate bonds—after all, more risk deserves more return. Let's say in early 1988, high-grade corporates were yielding around 10%. With a 3% risk premium tacked onto this base rate, you should expect a yield of around 13% from Texas Utilities. Given this desired benchmark rate of return, the third step is to see what kind of return we can expect from dividends alone. Dividing the expected average annual dividend of $3.64 a share by the current price of the stock ($27 in early 1988), we get an expected dividend yield of around 13.5% ($3.70/$27.00). Given this expected dividend yield, the fourth step is to compare it to your desired rate of return. In this case, all you have to do is get back what you paid for the stock and you'll earn your desired rate of return (13%). Should you sell your stock for more than what you paid for it, any capital gains would be pure gravy!

But what if you had a desired return of, say, 15%? Now the dividend yield falls short of your benchmark, so you'll need some capital gains to make up the difference. Fortunately, the shortfall is not that great (15% − 13.5% = 1½ percentage points), so you won't need much price appreciation. Moving to the fifth step in the yield calculation process, use a small stock price change in the full approximate yield formula to see what kind of return you end up with. Our objective here is to find out how much the price of the stock has to go up in order to give us a yield of 15%. For example, if you assume the price of the stock goes up by just $5.00 (that's certainly not a lot over a 10-year period of time), you'll earn a yield of 14.1%. Since that's still short of the mark, try a $10 increase; doing that boosts the yield to 14.5%. That's reasonably close to your benchmark return of 15%, so you now know the stock has to go up by around $10 to $15 over the next 10 years in order to give you a fully compounded rate of return of approximately 15%. In short, if you receive average annual dividends of $3.64 *and* the price of the stock goes up by $10 to $15, you stand to make roughly 15% on your money over this 10-year holding period.

The sixth and final step in this process is to assess the likelihood of realizing a $10 to $15 capital gain on the stock. That kind of appreciation amounts to about a 40% increase in price, which is about what the stock did over the last 10 years. Now, if you feel the odds are pretty good for a repeat performance, then perhaps you ought to view the stock as a viable investment candidate. Don't forget, however, that in our actual example, no capital gains are necessary to reach the benchmark return. Without question, the more return you can derive from dividends, the less you need to rely on capital gains. This is why a nice, steady, growing stream of dividends is so highly valued by safety-conscious investors: *by reducing the need for future price appreciation, a generous stream of dividends greatly reduces your exposure to risk.*

The Hunt for Quality Stocks

Unlike bond selection, selecting stocks is a lot more open ended. After all, stocks don't carry call provisions, and they don't have sinking fund features, maturity dates, or annual coupons. As a result, you're not concerned with trying to lock in a yield, or to shorten maturities so as to reduce price volatility. Rather, selecting the stock that's right for you is more a matter of getting the kind of quality you want, and the kind of current income and price performance you'd like. You can deal with the quality issue by sticking to stocks that are highly rated by Value Line and/or Standard & Poor's. If you're really concerned about quality, then stay with blue chips; if you want a little more in dividends, then lean more toward quality income stock.

A LIST OF BLUE CHIPS Using some pretty basic selection criteria, we can come up with a list of blue chip stocks. To meet the needs of someone who's investing for safety's sake, the stock selection procedure should first screen on the basis of safety and then on performance. With that in mind, we set up six standards of performance that we looked for in a stock. As a safety-conscious investor, these are the kinds of screens that you might want to use when selecting blue chips. More specifically, in order to be included in our list, the stock or the issuing company had to meet *each one* of the following criteria:

- To meet our rigid standards of safety, the stocks had to carry a Standard & Poor's rating of A or better *and* a Value Line Safety rank of 1 with a financial strength rating of A+ or better and a stock price stability rating of 80 or better.
- To make sure our selections were confined to big, well-established companies, we chose only firms with annual sales of $1 billion or more in 1987 or, if a bank, total assets of $3 billion or more (this was done since banks don't generate revenues like other companies).
- To provide a measure of dependability, a company had to have an uninterrupted record of profits for the 15 years from 1973 to 1987; even a small loss in just one year would result in elimination from the list. The decade and a half from 1973 to 1987 covers a variety of different market and economic environments, and if a company can do well through all those ups and downs, that says a lot about the firm and its management.
- To meet our criterion for stability, profits and earnings per share (EPS) over the period from 1973 to 1987 had to be on a generally increasing path *and* for the 10 years from 1978 to 1987, EPS had to be relatively stable as well. Even if earnings were trending upward, the stock was eliminated if there was substantial up-and-down volatility in EPS.

- To screen for reasonably priced securities, we looked for stocks that carried P/E multiples of no more than 15 to 18 times earnings. (We used the latest 1987 earnings to calculate P/E ratios.)
- To pass a fairly strenuous dividend pay-out test, the company had to have an uninterrupted record of generally increasing dividends for the 15-year period 1973 to 1987. Just one small cut was all it took to drop a stock from the list. Note that with this list of blue chip stocks, dividend yield wasn't as important as the ability of the company to pay a consistently increasing level of dividends.

Applying these selection criteria to over 1,500 of the biggest and best-known companies in the country resulted in a list of some 41 blue chip stocks. This list is indicative of the kinds of stocks you can come up with by applying the six selection screens we set up above. It's not meant to be an exhaustive tabulation of every blue chip in the market (indeed, a lot of household names are missing because they failed to meet one or more of our selection criteria). Nor should it be viewed as a finite set of recommendations, for as always, the decision to buy, sell, or hold a stock (or any security, for that matter) rests solely with the individual investor.

One message that should come through from even a casual perusal of this list is that putting some of your money into high quality stocks may make sense—so long as you have the risk tolerance to ride out the occasional ups and downs in the market, and you're willing to invest for the long haul. For even though stock performance was *not* one of the selection criteria, long-term (fully compounded) returns from this sampling of stocks turned out to be fairly attractive in most cases, and in a number of instances, downright substantial. Now, of course, this is all in the past, and there's no assurance that history will repeat itself. But no matter how you look at it, the numbers clearly are indicative of the type of performance that is possible with blue chip common stock.

Most of the companies listed here are well known to much

A Representative List of Blue Chip Stocks

| Stock | Latest (1987) Performance | | | |
	Dividends per Share	Year-End Share Price	Dividend Yield	Beta
Abbott Labs.	$ .96	$ 48	2.0%	1.15
American Brands	2.16	44	4.9	1.05
Am. Home Products	3.34	73	4.6	.95
Borden	1.24	50	2.5	1.00
Bristol-Myers	1.40	42	3.3	1.05
Campbell Soup	.72	28	2.6	.85
Centel	1.68	35	4.8	.85
Coca-Cola	1.12	38	2.9	.95
Consol. Nat. Gas	1.50	36	4.2	.80
Donnelley (R.R.)	.70	33	2.1	1.15
Dun & Bradstreet	1.45	55	2.6	1.15
Emerson Electric	.98	35	2.8	1.05
Fifth Third Bancorp	.99	35	2.8	.70
First Wachovia	1.20	34	3.5	.85
Gannett	.92	39	2.4	1.15
Gen. Electric	1.29	44	2.9	1.10
Genuine Parts	.90	35	2.6	1.00
Grainger (W.W.)	.78	59	1.3	1.05
Heinz (H.J.)	1.12	40	2.8	.95
IBM	4.40	115	3.8	1.00
Johnson & Johnson	1.61	75	2.2	1.00
Kimberly-Clark	1.39	50	2.8	.95
Eli Lilly	2.00	78	2.6	1.05
McDonalds	.48	44	1.0	1.00
Merck	2.45	158	1.6	.90
Minnesota Mining	1.86	64	2.9	1.05
Natl. Serv. Ind.	.64	21	3.0	.85
Norstar Bancorp	1.40	27	5.2	.70
No. States Power	2.02	30	6.7	.70
Pfizer	1.80	47	3.8	1.05
Philip Morris	3.00	85	3.5	1.00
PNC Financial	1.60	38	4.2	.85
Procter & Gamble	2.70	85	3.2	.90
Quaker Oats	.85	42	2.0	.95
Raytheon	1.80	67	2.6	.95
RJR Nabisco	1.76	45	3.9	1.05
SmithKline Beckman	1.62	48	3.4	.90
Washington Post	1.28	187	0.6	.90
Weis Markets	.41	36	1.2	.80
Wisconsin Energy	1.41	23	6.1	.65
Wisc. Pwr. & Lgt.	3.08	44	7.0	.60
Averages	$1.56	$ 54	3.2%	.94

All but three of these stocks are listed on the NYSE. The three stocks traded elsewhere are Fifth Third Bancorp (OTC), PNC Financial (OTC), and The Washington Post (AMEX). Also, all but four of the firms have dividend reinvestment plans—the four that don't are Dun & Bradstreet, Procter & Gamble, RJR Nabisco, and the Washington Post.

10-Year (1978–87) Performance			
Change in EPS	Change in Div/Share	Change in Share Price	Average Annual Rate of Return
343%	380%	586%	17.0%
122	137	300	17.6
156	151	161	13.5
147	121	400	16.3
225	367	425	17.0
103	85	250	14.2
60	46	119	13.0
143	93	217	13.8
56	111	260	16.1
200	218	450	16.2
313	326	686	18.4
104	145	192	12.7
314	230	600	18.2
186	275	325	16.0
190	207	388	15.8
133	105	267	14.9
123	173	250	13.9
115	117	269	13.0
256	261	700	18.8
64	53	64	8.8
190	182	212	12.5
133	114	400	16.7
130	141	310	15.1
260	700	340	13.6
226	188	485	15.9
63	86	190	13.1
161	191	425	17.0
113	103	238	15.7
82	89	114	14.3
186	206	262	15.3
364	488	431	17.1
145	202	322	16.9
48	100	123	10.9
181	227	740	18.1
152	177	319	15.2
164	144	275	15.9
231	315	300	15.4
253	327	938	17.2
211	241	620	16.4
118	90	130	14.4
98	79	110	14.5
167%	195%	346%	15.3%

Sources: Basic performance data were obtained from *Value Line, S&P Stock Guide,* and *The Wall Street Journal;* beta values were obtained from *Value Line.*

of the general public, as well as to most of the investing public—
though there probably are a few surprises. While they're generally
not perceived as hot growth stocks, the 10-year earnings per share
(EPS) performance of a good number of these stocks has been
considerable. And even though most of these are not income-
oriented securities, note that the amount of dividends paid grew
in nearly every case at a fairly hefty clip. As a result of this kind
of dividend growth—and a strong market in the latter half of the
period—stock prices behaved in a fairly predictable fashion: they
went way up! And keep in mind that the listed 10-year share price
appreciation takes into consideration the market crash of October
19th, 1987, as well as a few other rather "soft" years in the early
part of the period (1978 to 1981). Look at the last column. There
you can see how the growth in dividends per share and share price
appreciation have combined to generate some highly attractive
rates of return. And keep in mind that due to the widespread
availability of dividend reinvestment plans, these fully compounded rates of return were well within the grasp of any individual investor.

A LIST OF QUALITY INCOME STOCKS There are three good reasons
why a safety-conscious investor would be attracted to quality
income stocks:

1. For someone who's looking for current income, these stocks
   can offer not only highly attractive and highly competitive
   dividend yields, but also a level of current income that moves
   up over time.
2. Quality income shares tend to have low price volatility, so they
   offer a considerable measure of safety as far as market risk is
   concerned.
3. Even if you don't need the income for current consump-
   tion purposes, income stocks still hold a lot of appeal because
   with so much coming from dividends, you don't need a lot
   of highly uncertain capital gains to obtain a suitable rate of
   return.

The chart on the next page compares the coupon income from a hypothetical 10-year bond to the dividend income stream from a typical quality income stock—in this case, a public utility stock: Central and South West Corp. The chart covers the 10-year period from 1978 through 1987, and it's assumed that a $1,000 investment is made in each security. The bond is assumed to offer a very generous yield of 9½%, while the stock starts with a dividend yield of 8.38% on a dividend of $1.34 a share (the actual dividends paid on Central and South West stock).

Note that while the bond paid a fixed amount of $95 a year, annual stock dividends got progressively bigger. Indeed, even though the stocks started on the low side, they quickly passed the bonds and ended the 10-year period paying a lot more in current income—all of which means more return and higher yields for the stockholder. Such behavior also favorably affects stock prices since an increasing level of dividends puts upward pressure on stock prices. For like bonds, high-grade income stocks are priced on the basis of their dividend returns.

As you might expect, public utilities account for the biggest number of quality income stocks; in a distant second place are bank stocks. If you look at our list of blue chip stocks, you'll find that some of them also have relatively high dividend yields. A number of these blue chips, in fact, have traditionally been viewed by the market as income shares, including the following:

- American Brands
- American Home Products
- Centel Corporation
- Consolidated Natural Gas
- Norstar Bancorp
- Northern States Power
- PNC Financial
- Wisconsin Energy
- Wisconsin Power & Light

These stocks offer not only the ultimate in quality, but historically high dividend yields as well.

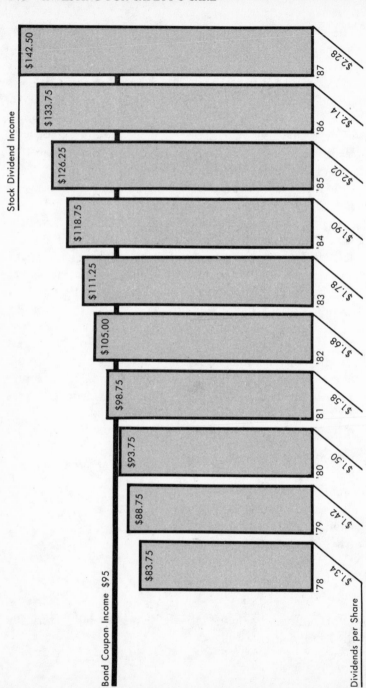

Stock Dividend Income

Bond Coupon Income $95

$142.50	'87 $2.28
$133.75	'86 $2.14
$126.25	'85 $2.02
$118.75	'84 $1.90
$111.25	'83 $1.78
$105.00	'82 $1.68
$98.75	'81 $1.58
$93.75	'80 $1.50
$88.75	'79 $1.42
$83.75	'78 $1.34

Dividends per Share

Much as we did with blue chips, we also came up with a list of quality income stocks. For obvious reasons, we confine our selection to public utility and bank stocks—after all, if that's where the vast majority of the action is, then that's where we ought to do our looking. In our search for quality income stocks, we again used a system of screens similar to those used with blue chips. Indeed, we used basically the same profits, EPS, and P/E screens. In addition, the stocks or their issuing companies had to meet the following quality and dividend performance criteria:

- As far as quality was concerned, the stocks had to carry one of the A ratings by S&P, *and* a Value Line Safety Rank of 1 or 2, with a financial strength rating of A or better and a stock price stability rating of 85 or better. We felt a slightly lower quality rating was justified so long as we stuck to the generally less risky utility and bank stocks; also, the move seemed justified in view of the more stable stock prices that normally accompany income shares. As we'll see, stock betas are significantly lower for income shares than they are for blue chip stocks.

- As far as dividends were concerned, we looked for stocks that were able to maintain dividend yields that were consistently well above the market average; of course, we also expected to see dividends growing at a sustained healthy rate. Here, the dividend payout test was much like the one used with blue chips (no missed dividends and the dollar amount of dividends paid had to be getting progressively larger over time), but we also required a hefty dividend *yield* as well. Accordingly, given that the average yield on non-utility stocks in early 1988 was about 3% to 3½%, to be included as a quality income stock, it had to yield about twice that amount, or roughly 6%.

- Finally, we redefined our size screen as follows: if it was a public utility, it had to have annual sales or total capital of $1 billion or more; the bank screen remained at total assets of $3 billion or more.

Applying these standards resulted in a list of 22 quality income stocks, as shown in the table. Throughout the screening, the standard of quality was never sacrificed for yield, stock performance, or any other measure of return. Yet, the performance figures in the table provide further evidence that attractive returns are possible by investing over the long haul in high-quality, low-risk common stocks. At the same time, if you're looking for a source of regular income, it's clear you can get that, too—in growing amounts—from income stocks.

Not surprisingly, the performance figures show consistently attractive dividend yields, along with a nice rate of growth in

A Representative List of Quality Income Stocks

| | Latest (1987) Performance | | | |
Stock	Dividends per Share	Year-End Share Price	Dividend Yield	Beta
Allegheny Pwr.	$2.94	$37	8.0%	.65
Atlantic Energy	2.65	31	8.6	.60
Baltimore G&E	1.85	30	6.2	.70
Bank of N.Y.	1.71	26	6.6	.95
Boatmen's Bancsh.	1.84	31	5.9	.80
Brooklyn Union Gas	1.66	22	7.5	.55
Central & So. West	2.28	30	7.6	.75
Delmarva Pwr.	1.41	18	7.8	.70
Duke Pwr.	2.74	43	6.4	.65
FPL Group	2.10	29	7.2	.70
IPALCO Ent.	1.80	21	8.6	.70
Kansas Pwr. & Lgt.	1.64	23	7.1	.65
Minnesota Pwr.	1.66	21	7.9	.70
Oklahoma G&E	2.18	29	7.5	.65
PacifiCorp.	2.49	32	7.8	.70
Potomac El. Pwr.	1.30	22	5.9	.60
Pub Serv. Ent. Grp.	2.00	24	8.3	.75
San Diego G&E	2.47	30	8.2	.80
SCANA Corp.	2.30	28	8.2	.70
So. Cal. Ed.	2.33	31	7.5	.85
S.W. Pub. Serv.	2.12	24	8.8	.70
Texas Utilities	2.77	27	10.3	.70
Averages	$2.10	$28	7.6%	.71

All of these stocks are listed on the NYSE except one: Boatmen's Bancshares is traded in the OTC. Every one of these companies offers a dividend reinvestment plan.

dividends. In contrast, the stocks tend to have relatively low P/E multiples, and their price appreciation is generally much less than that of the blue chip group. The reason for this, of course, is the very low betas that are so common with utilities and income stock. Low betas mean low price volatility, but stocks with low betas have one major drawback: they generally produce less price appreciation. Fortunately, with income stocks, low price appreciation is offset by much higher dividend yields. The net result, as you can see in the last column of the table, is a highly attractive fully

10-Year (1978–87) Performance			
Change in EPS	Change in Div/Share	Change in Share Price	Average Annual Rate of Return
113%	71%	85%	14.1%
79	59	41	11.6
101	64	114	14.0
62	111	160	15.9
86	130	182	15.8
61	77	120	15.6
76	70	88	14.0
38	62	100	15.1
70	58	96	13.3
41	110	107	14.2
109	80	75	13.9
79	76	109	14.6
50	80	110	15.4
32	42	61	12.6
47	32	52	12.4
153	94	175	15.9
38	44	50	12.5
63	76	100	15.3
44	42	48	12.2
88	103	138	16.1
33	77	50	12.3
81	82	35	12.1
70%	75%	95%	14.0%

Source: Basic performance data were obtained from *Value Line, S&P Stock Guide,* and *The Wall Street Journal;* beta values were obtained from *Value Line.*

compounded rate of return. Income stocks don't require a lot of capital gains to produce nice rates of return because they have such high-dividend yields to start with—that, of course, translates into less risk and is one very important reason why these securities are so appealing to safety-conscious investors.

So we don't get accused of looking at things through rose-colored glasses, a word of caution is in order at this point: don't be lulled into thinking that things can go only one way with these securities. For no matter how blue their blood, they're still common stocks and they're still subject to sustained soft markets. Just because there's not a lot of price volatility with these securities doesn't mean their prices can't fall. Consider what would happen if our economy goes through another period of rising/high interest rates—make no mistake about it, with income stocks, that would have a devastating effect on stock prices. That's one of the reasons why it's so important when you get into stocks—quality income stocks included—to get in for the long haul. That way you can ride out the market's ups and downs.

You may find that some well-known income stocks are not on our list; perhaps one of your favorites is missing, or your local utility was left off. The reason: they probably failed to meet one or more of the quality/performance screens. If you've found an income stock that's not on the list, run it through the tests—if it meets all the criteria, fine; if it doesn't, then you'll have to decide if it's appropriate to relax the standards.

WHAT ABOUT PREFERRED STOCK? Before we leave the area of income stocks, we should say a few words about preferred stocks. These securities are popular with some income-oriented investors; indeed, they derive their value and are priced in the market on the basis of their annual dividends. A lot of investors mistake a preferred's prior claim on income with a bond's legal obligation to pay principal and interest payments in a prompt and timely fashion. It's true, preferred dividends have to be paid before dividends can be paid to common stockholders, *but the company is under no legal obligation to pay preferred dividends.* If the company doesn't have the earnings, it just doesn't have to pay preferred dividends. If the preferreds are cumulative (and most are), the only requirement is that all missed preferred dividends have to be paid before the company can start paying dividends to common stockholders. That, in fact, is about the only protection preferred stockholders have.

Now, even though there's more risk with a preferred stock than with a bond, preferred stocks consistently yield *less* than comparably rated corporate bonds! Indeed, you can normally expect preferreds to yield only about 90% of what you can get from bonds. The reason for this unusual behavior is that corporations (but not individuals) enjoy a special tax break when they receive preferred dividend income; under current tax law, 80% of it is tax-free. Thus, you're left with more risk, but less return. So, should you invest in preferred stocks? Probably not. For the individual investor they're just not a very good deal. Here's why:

You don't get the protection of a bond.

Yet, yields are less than what you could earn from comparable debt securities.

And because dividends are fixed, there's no possibility of increase as with income stocks.

The Good Points:

- *Attractive current income and capital gains opportunities* from high-quality common stocks.
- *Low risk* with carefully selected blue chip and quality income stocks.
- *Active secondary market* for major common stocks, so the securities are *highly liquid.*
- *Steadily increasing level of dividends* is common with blue chip and quality income stocks.
- *Tendency for stock prices to go up over the long haul,* though you certainly have no guarantee that they will.
- *Reasonably priced,* so it doesn't take a lot of capital to get into stocks. Most of them sell for less than $50 a share and you can buy any number you want.

And the Bad:

- *More risk* than with either bonds or short-term investment vehicles, because common stock is a residual type of security. No matter how good they are, any common stock can fail to live up to your expectations, thereby exposing you to reduced return or even outright loss; the company itself, the economy, and/or the market can all do less than you hope or expect.
- *Subject to broad swings in market prices.* Even with blue chips and quality income stocks, prices can head down and stay down for extended periods of time, since there's no par or principal value to buoy them up.
- *Requires a long-term perspective.* Even though you can get in and out on short notice, to reduce your exposure to risk when investing in stocks, you generally have to commit your capital for the long run. If prices move against you, it may take a while to come out ahead.

Taxes:

There are no special tax provisions for common stocks. Both dividend income and capital gains are subject to normal income tax. The dividends are subject to taxes when earned, and the capital gains are taxable when realized. If you belong to a dividend reinvestment plan, you still have to pay taxes on the dividends as if they were received in cash rather than in the form of additional shares of stock.

7

Invest in Mutual Funds and Put the Big Guys to Work for You

Some people buy them because they're such an easy and convenient way to invest; others like the sense of security they provide, or the services they offer. We're talking about *mutual funds,* and for whatever reason, they have become one of the hottest forms of investing. Indeed, among individual investors, their popularity today easily rivals, and often surpasses, that of stocks and bonds. Mutual funds are quite unlike most other investment products. The reason: you're not investing directly in a security, as you are when you buy stocks, bonds, or CDs. Rather, when you buy shares in a mutual fund, you're buying part of a professionally managed *portfolio of securities.*

Basically, a mutual fund combines the investment capital of people with similar investment goals and then invests the money, for the mutual benefit of the shareholders, in a wide variety of securities. The individual investor receives shares of stock in the mutual fund and is thus able to enjoy much greater investment diversification than could otherwise be achieved. As the securities held by the fund move up and down in price, the market value of the mutual fund shares moves accordingly. When dividend and interest payments are received by the fund, they are distributed to shareholders on the basis of prorated ownership. When a security held by the fund is sold for a profit, that too is passed on to fund shareholders. The whole mutual fund idea, in fact, rests on the concept of pooled diversification and works in much the same way as insurance: individuals pool their resources for the collective benefit of all contributors.

The kind of return you can expect from a fund depends in large part on whether you invest in a bond fund or an equity (stock) fund. Generally, bond funds are less risky and therefore provide less return than stock funds. So, much like you decide what kind of risk exposure you want when you buy a bond rather than a stock, you make the same kind of decision with mutual funds by selecting a bond fund over an equity fund. The same principles and philosophies that were discussed in the preceding chapters on stocks, bonds, and short-term securities apply here, since you're still investing in many of the same types of securities; you're just doing it through a different medium.

The Ever-Expanding World of Mutual Funds

The first mutual fund was started in Boston in 1924; by 1940, there were 68 funds with $448 million in assets and nearly 300,000 shareholder accounts. That was only the beginning, however, as the growth in funds really took off in the late 1970s. Indeed, by 1988, assets under management had grown to nearly three-quarters of a *trillion* dollars, as 45 *million* investors held shares in over 2,000 publicly traded mutual funds. The fact is, we've reached the point where there are more mutual funds today than there are stocks on the NYSE! Mutual fund investors come from all walks of life and all income levels. And they all share one common view: they've all decided, for one reason or another, to turn over all or a part of their investment management activities to professionals.

What Funds Have to Offer

Considering the growth in mutual funds over the decade of the 1980s, you might say they must be doing something right. Well, yes and no. To begin with, the mutual fund industry just happened to be in the right place at the right time, for there's no doubt that it benefited enormously from two events that occurred in the 1980s. First, there was the introduction/liberalization of self-directed individual retirement accounts (IRAs), which in itself created a huge demand for mutual fund products. And second, both stocks and bonds took off on record-breaking bull markets and attracted investors in unprecedented numbers to Wall Street.

But mutual funds themselves also had a good deal to do with their growth. Clearly, they put together a product that the investing public found appealing. Much of that appeal is due, of course, to the things that mutual funds offer their investors, things like:

• **Diversification** This has long been a major attribute of mutual funds. Rather than buying just one or two stocks or bonds, with a mutual fund you're buying into a portfolio that might carry hundreds of different stocks and/or bonds. Such diversification is beneficial since it reduces risk; the more securities you hold, or have an interest in, the less chance that you'll be hard hit if some of them move against you.

• **Full-Time Professional Management** Few individual investors can compete with the talent and experience of mutual fund money managers. Not only do these experts take day-to-day investment decisions off your shoulders, they also handle the arduous record-keeping chores.

• **Convenience** Mutual funds are relatively easy to acquire; they handle all the paperwork, and their prices are widely quoted.

• **Modest Capital Requirements** In most cases, you can open a mutual fund account with relatively little money; sometimes there is no minimum investment requirement at all. And once you're a fund investor, you can usually purchase additional shares in small amounts, even fractional shares. Mutual funds, in fact, are ideal for people who don't have a lot of money to invest; they're an excellent way to get started in the market.

• **Investor Services** As you will see later in this chapter, such mutual fund services as automatic reinvestment of dividends, withdrawal plans, and exchange privileges are strong draws to many investors who want to invest with the same ease as they bank. In many ways, today's mutual funds are truly a one-stop investment service.

Some Drawbacks

While mutual funds do have a lot to offer, they are by no means perfect. On the contrary, like other investment products, they have their share of drawbacks, too. It seems a bit ironic, but in the opinion of many market experts, the number-one drawback of mutual funds is their *performance*. Supposedly, people buy funds because of their highly touted abilities to produce attractive investment returns. And yet, despite the expertise of professional money managers, average fund performance over the long haul is, at best, just about equal to what you would expect from the market as a whole. There are some notable exceptions, of course, but most funds do little more than just keep up with the market. Look at the accompanying chart. It shows the investment performance of 15 different types of equity funds over the 5½-year period from June 1982 through January 1988 (which, not by coincidence, covers all of the 1982–87 bull market). These are fully compounded returns, and assume that all dividends and capital gains distributions are reinvested into additional shares of stock.

Note that when compared to the S&P 500, only two types of funds outperformed the market, and many others fell far short of the mark. The lesson is clear: consistently beating the market is no easy task—not even for professional money managers. Even though a handful of funds have given investors above-average, and even spectacular, rates of return, most mutual funds do not meet this level of performance. This is not to say that the long-term returns from mutual funds are substandard, or that they fail to equal what you could achieve by putting your money into a risk-free savings account. Quite the contrary: the long-term returns from mutual funds have been substantial. In fact, if you were to compare the performance of these same 15 groups of funds over a 10-year—rather than a 5-year—period, you'd find

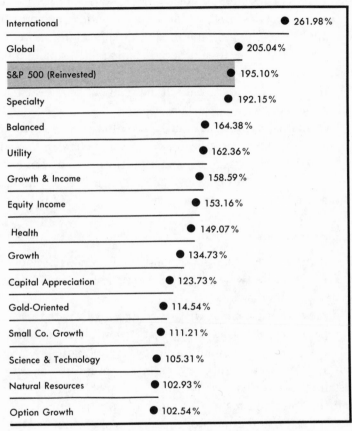

Fund Performance

(From June 30, 1982, to Jan. 31, 1988)

International	● 261.98%
Global	● 205.04%
S&P 500 (Reinvested)	● 195.10%
Specialty	● 192.15%
Balanced	● 164.38%
Utility	● 162.36%
Growth & Income	● 158.59%
Equity Income	● 153.16%
Health	● 149.07%
Growth	● 134.73%
Capital Appreciation	● 123.73%
Gold-Oriented	● 114.54%
Small Co. Growth	● 111.21%
Science & Technology	● 105.31%
Natural Resources	● 102.93%
Option Growth	● 102.54%

Source: Lipper Analytical Services Inc.; *Barron's,* February 15, 1988, p. 64.

that the vast majority were able to meet or exceed the S&P 500. Thus, in contrast to their short-term behavior, the performance of mutual funds over the long haul is a lot better.

Another serious drawback is lack of *liquidity.* Although funds are easy to buy, they are not as easy to sell. More often than not, you'll have to sell your shares back to the fund on your own. At best, your broker will be, shall we say, unenthusiastic about helping, since there usually are no commissions on mutual fund sales. This, of course, assumes that either the fund doesn't offer a *phone switching* service, or you're not taking advantage of it. If a fund offers such a service, that will lick your liquidity problems. For with phone switching, you can quickly and easily move your money from one fund to another, including one or more money funds. There's just one big hitch, however: you have to stay within a given family of funds (we'll talk more about phone switching later in the chapter).

Substantial up-front *costs* may also discourage you from investing. Many funds carry sizable commission charges (known as *load charges*) as well as annual management fees. You can expect the fund to collect this management fee regardless of whether it has made or lost money for you.

And Then There Are the Risks . . .

Mutual funds have their good points and their bad. They also have their risks. Let's take a look at how the four major types of risk apply to mutual funds.

• **Business and Financial Risk** Essentially, this is the risk that a company will falter financially; that it won't be able to live up to its obligations, or maintain a steady level of earnings. Buying a mutual fund won't eliminate these risks, but it can reduce them substantially—and with some funds, it can be reduced to the point that such risk really isn't much of an issue. Funds do this in two ways: First, they employ the services of professional money managers who are trained to select securities and know how to spot quality (or the lack of it) in a security. And, second, mutual fund portfolios are so well diversified that all but a tiny bit of this risk is literally diversified away. But just because funds have the ability to protect you from business and financial risks doesn't mean they all want to eliminate this kind of risk from their portfolios. Indeed, many funds seek out such risks as a way to improve their return! For a mutual fund is merely *a reflection of* *the securities it holds.* So the extent to which you're exposed to business and financial risk in a mutual fund will depend, in large part, on the investment philosophies and objectives of the fund itself. When it comes to mutual funds, the best way to control your exposure to business and financial risk is to pay attention to the stated investment objective of the fund and the kinds of securities it's investing in.

• **Market Risk** While funds have been able to do a reasonably good job of dealing with business and financial risk, the same cannot be said of market risk. For in spite of all the professional money management and extensive diversification, most funds are still exposed to a fair amount of price volatility. Indeed, it's because mutual fund portfolios are so well diversified that they tend to reflect the behavior of the marketplace itself—or certain segments of the market. Thus, if the stock market is drifting downward, most funds that invest heavily in stocks will also drift down in price. You just can't diversify away market risk, so you can't eliminate price volatility by simply investing in a mutual fund.

Stock funds and bond funds go up and down in price as the stocks and bonds they hold in their portfolios go up and down in price. If you're not comfortable with the kind of price volatility that's common in the stock market, don't buy stock funds; similarly, if you don't like the volatility of long-term bonds, stick with short- or intermediate-term bond funds. Again, pay attention to the stated investment objectives of the fund; as a safety-conscious investor, look for funds that stress *preservation of capital* along with a satisfactory rate of return. Professional money managers know how to spot securities that typically are subject to low price volatility (like income or low-beta stocks), and they know how to combine different kinds of securities to keep portfolio price variability down. It's not that they have great market timing abilities, it's just that they know which segments of the stock and/or bond markets have the least volatile securities.

• **Purchasing Power Risk** There's little you can do about purchasing power (inflation) risk except try to outperform it. And that's exactly what the mutual fund's managers are trying to do: generate a long-term rate of return that exceeds the rate of inflation, and preferably by a wide margin. How much protection you obtain will depend on whether you buy a stock or bond fund, and whether we're hit with high or low rates of inflation.

• **Liquidity Risk** As a rule, you're likely to find that buying and selling mutual funds is not only a bit more time-consuming than dealing with stocks and bonds, it also involves a little more work on your part. The reason for this is that in most cases you're dealing directly with the fund distributor. It's not like placing an order with your broker. Instead, you have to open an account at the fund, send in a completed form, mail in your checks with your buy orders, and possibly even submit certification of your signature with sell orders. All this, of course, has to do with mutual fund accounts and the mechanics of mutual fund orders, and really has very little to do with the underlying liquidity of the mutual funds themselves. That's the key issue here. And in that respect, we can conclude that mutual funds are a highly liquid form of investing. For once an account is open, you can buy or sell a fund on any trading day of the week and know your transactions will be executed at prevailing market prices—prices that are fairly set on the basis of the fund's net asset value. Thus, mutual fund shares are bought and sold on a continuous, orderly basis, and the share prices are fairly set in the market.

Getting to Know Your Fund

Questions of which stock or bond to select, when to buy, and when to sell have plagued investors for about as long as there have been organized securities markets. Such concerns lie at the very heart of the mutual fund concept and, in large part, are behind the growth in funds. Face it, a lot of people lack the time, the know-how, or the commitment to manage their own securities. As a result, they turn to others. And more often than not, that means mutual funds. But as many investors quickly learn, not all mutual funds are alike. Not only are there different types of funds offering different types of services, there are also differences in organizations, and differences in the costs and fees charged to investors.

OPEN-END FUNDS—THE BIGGEST OF THE LOT When the term *mutual fund* is used, it usually refers to an open-ended investment company. Open-end mutual funds are the dominant type of investment company, and account for more than 90% of the assets under management. In this type of operation, investors actually buy their shares from, and sell them back to, the mutual fund itself. When you buy shares in an open-end fund, the fund issues new shares of stock and fills the order with these new shares. The fund is considered open-ended because there is *no limit on the number of shares the fund can issue.* All open-end mutual funds stand behind their shares and buy them back when investors decide to sell; there is never any trading between individuals.

As a safety-conscious investor, you have no reason to invest in any other type of investment company. Or put more bluntly, if you're investing for safety's sake, *stick with open-end mutual funds!* There are a couple of thousand open-end funds in existence, so you'll have no trouble finding the kind of investment you're looking for. In addition to return, open-end funds provide all the services you could possibly want, and their prices aren't subject to exogenous supply and demand forces, or market whims.

THERE ARE ALSO CLOSED-END INVESTMENT COMPANIES While the term *mutual fund* is supposed to refer only to open-end funds, as a practical matter it's used to refer to closed-end investment companies as well. Closed-end investment companies operate with a fixed number of shares of stock outstanding and do not regularly issue new shares. In effect, they have a capital structure like that of any other corporation, except that the corporation's business happens to be investing in marketable securities. Closed-end company shares are actively traded on the secondary market, just like any other common stock. Most are traded on the NYSE, but they're also found on the AMEX, and in the OTC market.

The share prices of closed-end companies are determined not only by their net asset value (NAV), but also by general supply and demand conditions in the market. As a result, the shares generally trade at a discount or premium to net asset value. For example, if a fund has an NAV of $10 per share and is trading at $9, it is selling at a discount of $1; it would be selling at a premium of $1 if it were quoted at a price of $11. *Share price discounts and premiums can at times become quite large.* For example, it's not unusual for such spreads to amount to as much as 25% to 30% of NAV. Even worse, perhaps, these share price premiums and discounts are constantly changing and thus are continuously affecting investor return. Such variability from the true underlying value of the fund is why you should *avoid closed-end funds.* These funds really operate no differently than open-end funds, so all you get from a closed-end company is another element of price volatility and therefore more risk. Chances are you'll find it very difficult to come up with more long-run return by going with a closed-end fund, so why take on the added risk? Obviously that's something a safety-conscious investor can do without!

AND THEN THERE ARE UNIT TRUSTS A unit trust represents little more than an interest in an unmanaged pool of investments—a portfolio of securities held in safekeeping for investors under conditions set down in a trust agreement. The portfolios usually consist of corporate, government, or municipal bonds, with tax-free municipal bonds and mortgage-backed securities being the most popular investment vehicles. There is no trading in these portfolios; as a result, the returns, or yields, are fixed and usually predictable. Whereas the managers of conventional mutual funds actively trade the funds' securities, the manager of a unit trust merely puts together a portfolio of securities, and that's it. After the securities are deposited with a trustee, no new securities are added and, with rare exceptions, none are sold or removed from the portfolio unless they mature or are called by the issuer. Unlike normal bond funds, these trusts have finite maturity dates and will expire when the securities in the portfolio mature.

Various sponsoring brokerage houses put these pools of

securities together and then sell units in them to investors. Each *unit* is like a share in a mutual fund. The sponsoring organization does little more than routine record-keeping, servicing the investments by clipping coupons, and distributing the income (often on a monthly basis) to the holders of the trust units. If you decide to sell your units before they expire, the sponsor will usually buy them back at a price equal (or close) to their prevailing net asset value, less a commission, of course.

Unit trusts hold the most appeal for individuals who want to live off the income—particularly those who want to receive a regular stream of monthly income from their fixed income investments. Indeed, in our opinion, that's the only legitimate reason for owning an investment trust, but even then, it's not a very good one. The reason: you'll probably be much better off with a standard (open-ended) mutual fund. Don't confuse these trusts with normal mutual funds. For one thing, you can get far more in the way of services from a regular mutual fund. In addition, you have to use a good deal of care when buying these trusts, because the trust sponsors will often load them up with low-quality issues to drive up yields. That, of course, will make the advertised return look better, but it also means more risk. Perhaps just as important, these trusts have absolutely nothing to offer that you can't get from a regular open-ended mutual fund. If you want a regular stream of monthly income, you can get that from a mutual fund, plus a whole lot more. About the only possible advantage these have over regular bond funds is that their portfolios are fixed and, therefore, they have finite maturity dates. Thus, *so long as you can hold on until maturity,* you know you'll get your money back and swings in market prices really won't affect you. But a fixed portfolio with its fixed return can work against you, too, because if rates do rise, you'll miss out completely.

GETTING THE LOWDOWN ON LOADS AND OTHER CHARGES One thing you quickly learn with mutual funds is that the fund sponsors and distributors certainly don't seem to have much trouble in coming up with a full menu of fees and charges. But not all funds levy all the different types of fees and charges, nor do they all levy them at the same rate. Some funds have very low expense rates; others have very high rates. Worst of all, the expense rates have absolutely nothing to do with fund performance—very poorly performing funds can still have very high expense rates! To help you sort out the costs of buying, selling, and owning a fund, here's a rundown of the types of fees you could encounter when investing in open-end mutual funds:

• **Load Charge** This is just another way of describing the commission you have to pay when buying a fund. Funds that charge commissions up front are known as *load funds;* about half of the funds have front-end loads. Those that do not charge such commissions are known as *no-load funds;* less than a third of all mutual funds are pure no-loads, charging nothing to buy—or sell—their funds. Load charges can be fairly substantial and often amount to as much as 8½% of the purchase price of the shares. Invest $1,000 in an 8½% load fund and all you'll get is $915 in stock—the other $85 goes to pay commissions.

Rather than charge the maximum allowable 8½% load, a lot of funds charge much lower commissions. These are the so-called *low-load funds;* their load charges amount to only 2% or 3%. While load charges usually only apply to initial purchases, some funds also hit you with a load charge when you reinvest dividends and capital gains. This is nothing more than a rip-off, since there probably are no sales commissions to pay anyway. When looking at funds, keep in mind that there's absolutely no evidence that shows that load funds provide better returns than no-loads. In other words, fund performance has absolutely nothing to do with the amount of load charge you'll pay.

• **Redemption Fees** Although most funds that charge commissions do so only when you purchase the shares, some funds charge you a commission when you cash in (sell) your shares. This is known as a *back-end load* and it can amount to as much as 5% or 6% of the investment. While they're usually used by funds that don't charge front-end loads as a way to hide their commissions, they can also be employed by load or low-load funds.

• **Contingent Deferred Sales Charge** This charge is about as ominous as it looks. What it boils down to is this: should you, for any reason, decide to sell your fund within a certain period of time (generally within 3 to 5 years from the date of purchase), you will be hit with a sales charge—of as much as 6% of the amount sold. The bite usually goes down a percentage point or so a year until it eventually disappears. A contingent deferred sales charge is, in effect, a type of redemption fee with a twist. You only pay it if you cash in your shares too quickly. It's allegedly designed to discourage frequent switching of investments between funds, but it actually discourages all types of sales, whether you're switching or not.

• **12(b)-1 Fees** This is a devious little fee that can really add up over time. Also known as a *hidden load,* this fee has been allowed by the SEC since 1980, and was originally designed to help no-load funds cover their distribution and marketing expenses. Not surprisingly, the popularity of these fees (among fund distributors) spread rapidly, so that they are now used by about 40% of the funds. The fees are assessed annually and can amount to as much as 1¼% of assets under management. In good markets or bad, they're paid, right off the top, in addition to annual management fees. And that can take its toll. Consider, for example, $10,000 in a fund that charges a 1¼% 12(b)-1 fee. That translates into an annual charge of $125; certainly no small amount, since that means there's $125 a year less for you.

• **Management Fees** These fees are also assessed annually and usually run from ½% to 2% of assets under management. This is the cost you incur to hire the professional money managers. All funds have these fees, and like 12(b)-1 fees, they bear watching, since high expenses will take their toll on performance. As a rule, the size of the management fee is totally unrelated to the performance of the fund—you'll pay the same amount whether it's been a winning year or a real loser.

It should go without saying that whenever you're thinking about buying a fund, you should get all the facts about the fund's fee structure. Critics of the mutual fund industry have come down hard on the proliferation of fund fees and charges. Indeed, some would argue, as we do, that all the different kinds of charges and fees are really meant to do one thing: confuse the investor. Until the SEC stepped in, a lot of funds were going to great lengths to make themselves look like something they weren't— lower a cost here, tack on a fee there, hide a charge somewhere else. The funds were all following the letter of the law and, indeed, they were fully disclosing all their expenses and fees. Trouble was, the funds were able to neatly hide all but the most conspicuous of their charges in a bunch of legalese. No one's arguing that the fund distributors and money managers don't deserve to be fully compensated for their efforts. In fact, if they want to charge a big fat fee (or structure of fees), that's up to them. All the critics were asking was that the funds be up front with the charges and let the investing public decide whether or not they wanted to pay the fare.

Fortunately, some steps were finally taken to correct this problem. The federal government (in the form of the SEC) intervened and forced the funds to fully disclose all their expenses in a standardized, easy-to-understand format. Now, every fund prospectus must contain, right up front, a fairly detailed *fee table*. The table has three parts. The first section specifies all *shareholder transaction expenses*. In effect, this tells you what it's going to cost to buy and sell shares in the mutual fund. Included here are load charges on fund purchases, the loads if any on reinvested dividends, redemption or exchange fees, and any contingent deferred sales charges. The next section lists all the *annual operating expenses* of the fund. Showing these expenses as a percentage of average net assets, the fund must break out management fees, those elusive 12(b)-1 fees, and any other expenses. The third section provides a complete rundown of the *total cost over time* of buying, selling, and owning the fund. This part of the table contains both transaction and operating expenses and shows what the total costs would be over hypothetical 1-, 3-, 5-, and 10-year holding periods. To assure consistency and comparability, the funds have to follow a rigid set of guidelines when constructing the illustrative costs.

As a safety-conscious investor, you should pay close attention to the fee table whenever you're considering an investment in a mutual fund. Other things being equal, look for low initial charges as well as low expense ratios over time. As a rule, the longer you intend to hold a fund, the more willing you should be to trade a higher load charge for lower annual management and 12(b)-1 fees. That'll help you keep your total holding period costs down. In the final analysis, keep in mind that costs are only one element in the decision. Another very important variable is performance. There may be times when higher costs are justified; there may be other times when they're not. When it comes to costs, you might want to follow these guidelines:

- Consider a *more expensive* fund if it has a better performance record (and offers more return potential) than a less expensive fund—it's all a matter of whether you'd rather own a costly performer or a low-cost dog!
- If there's little or no difference in performance records or return potential, go with the *less expensive* fund. In this case, lower expenses will make a difference in comparative returns.

There's a Wide Range of Funds to Choose From

When it comes to your pocketbook, if there's ever a perceived demand, you can bet Wall Street will come up with a financial product to fill the need. That's precisely what's happened in the case of mutual funds. Over the past decade or so, the mutual fund industry has made enormous sums of money by developing mutual funds for just about every investment purpose imaginable. Today, you can find mutual funds that specialize in stocks, bonds, convertibles, options, and foreign securities; funds that are aggressive, others that are conservative; some that seek capital gains, others that go after high income and preservation of capital. You name it, and chances are there's a fund out there to fill the bill.

Each type of fund has a particular investment objective, including what the fund is established to achieve and, generally, how it intends to attain those stated goals. Fund objectives are supposed to be clearly stated in the fund prospectus, which you should obtain—and read—before investing any money. However, a note of caution is in order; for as far as fund objectives are concerned, the prospectuses provided by many mutual funds today are not as detailed as they once were. In fact, since many are little more than warmed-over sales pitches, you have to read between the lines to be sure you're getting exactly what you expect. If you want more detailed or factual information about fund objectives and investment strategies, you'll have to look to an awkwardly named document known as a *Statement of Additional Information.* But funds do *not* have to send them out, so you'll probably have to ask for one.

If you're investing for safety's sake, then there are a lot of funds you should stay away from. These are mutual funds that put too much emphasis on capital gains and not enough on preservation of capital, that go after high income by investing in high-risk securities, and that experience a lot of price volatility. In general, they involve a good deal more risk than you'd like to incur. Here's a rundown of the kinds of funds a safety-conscious investor should *avoid:*

Aggressive growth, or performance, funds
Growth, or capital appreciation, funds
Small company growth funds
International, or global, funds
Options funds
Commodities funds
Convertible funds
Most types of specialty funds
Gold funds
Sector funds
High-yield bond funds
Yield-enhanced bond funds
International bond funds

It's pretty easy to see why most of these should be avoided by conservative investors. With others, the reasons are not so obvious. For example, international funds: while many of these invest in nothing but high-quality firms, the problem is that, in addition to everything else, you have to deal with international economics and foreign exchange rates, all of which adds another layer of risk. Or sector funds: the problem here is not necessarily the quality of the securities, but the lack of diversification; so much concentration goes against the whole spirit of the mutual fund concept and often adds to fund volatility and risk exposure.

Even after you eliminate all these, you'll still be left with plenty of funds to choose from! As a safety-conscious investor, you should be looking for mutual funds that offer such things as:

- Preservation of capital
- Reasonably low price volatility
- A policy of investing in a highly diversified portfolio of high-quality/low-risk securities
- A generous amount of current income from dividends and/or interest
- A level of return that's reasonably attractive and fully compensates you for any risks incurred

In addition to money funds, which we discussed in chapter 4, there are several different kinds of stock funds you could invest in, and several different kinds of bond funds. If you're a conservative investor who wants to invest in a low-risk stock fund, you might want to consider:

- Equity-income funds
- Balanced funds
- Growth and income funds

These are all reasonably safe investment outlets, and you should have no trouble finding a fund with the kinds of investment attributes you're looking for. In contrast, if you want to stick with a safe bond fund, you ought to consider:

- U.S. government bond funds
- High-grade corporate bond funds
- High-grade municipal bond funds

EQUITY-INCOME FUNDS These funds emphasize current income and they do so by investing primarily in high-yielding common stocks. Capital preservation is also important, and so are some capital gains, although capital appreciation is not a primary objective of equity-income funds. These funds invest heavily in high-grade common stocks, some convertible securities and preferred stocks, and occasionally even some investment-quality bonds. As far as their stock holdings are concerned, these funds lean heavily toward blue chips, public utility shares, and financial stocks. They like securities that generate hefty dividend yields, but also consider potential price appreciation over the longer haul. In general, because of their emphasis on dividends and current income, these funds tend to hold higher-quality securities that are subject to considerably less price volatility than the market as a whole. They're generally viewed as a fairly low-risk way of investing in stocks.

BALANCED FUNDS These funds are so named because they tend to hold a balanced portfolio of both stocks and bonds, and they do so for the purpose of generating a well-balanced return of both current income and long-term capital gains. In many respects, they're a lot like equity-income funds, except that balanced funds usually put much more into fixed income securities; generally they keep at least 25% to 50% of their portfolios in bonds, and sometimes more. The bonds are used principally to provide current income, and stocks are selected mainly for their long-term growth potential. The funds can, of course, shift the emphasis in their security holdings one way or the other. Clearly, the more the fund leans toward fixed income securities, the more income-oriented it will be. In fact, funds that place major emphasis on current income are known in the market as *income funds*. Call them what you like, they're basically a type of balanced fund that invests heavily in fixed income securities and high-yielding common stocks. For the most part, balanced funds tend to confine their investing to high-grade securities. They use mostly growth-oriented blue chip stocks, high-quality income shares, and high-yielding investment-grade bonds. As such, they're usually considered to be a relatively safe form of investing, one where you can get a nice level of return without having to endure a whole lot of price volatility.

GROWTH AND INCOME FUNDS This particular type of fund also seeks a balanced return made up of both current income and long-term capital gains, but it places a greater emphasis on growth of capital. Moreover, unlike balanced funds, growth and income funds put most of their money into equities—indeed, it's not unusual for these funds to have 80% to 90% of their capital in common stocks. Many of them put little or nothing into bonds, and when they do, it's mostly for defensive purposes, like riding out a soft market. In essence, these funds seek both long-term growth and current income from common stocks. However, they do tend to confine most of their investing to quality issues, so you can expect to find a lot of growth-oriented blue chip stocks in their portfolios, along with a fair amount of high-quality income stocks. One of the big appeals these funds hold for safety-conscious investors is the fairly substantial returns many of them have been able to generate over the long haul. But then, higher return is something you should expect from investments that involve more risk. And make no mistake about it, while growth and income funds are considered to be a relatively low-risk form of investing, they involve more risk and more price volatility than either equity-income or balanced funds—if for no other reason than their greater emphasis on stocks and capital gains. As such, growth and income funds are probably most suitable for those conservative investors who are seeking a "measurable" exposure to equities, and who can tolerate a bit more risk and price volatility.

U.S. GOVERNMENT BOND FUNDS If you're looking for more security and stability than you can get from even low-risk stock funds, you might want to consider a bond fund. As the name implies, U.S. government bond funds invest exclusively in securities issued by the U.S. Treasury or agencies of the U.S. government. These funds generally seek a combination of high current income, liquidity, and security (preservation) of principal. Capital gains, if they exist at all, are little more than a pleasant by-product. While these funds offer a good deal of price stability, they are not without their ups and downs. For as noted earlier in this chapter, if the bond market's drifting down in price, then it's very likely that bond funds will move down as well—even one made up of U.S. government securities. If you want to reduce your exposure to price volatility, *stick with funds that invest mostly in short- to intermediate-term bonds.*

Basically, there are three types of government bond funds, those that invest in:

1. Both U.S. Treasury and agency issues
2. U.S. Treasury issues only
3. Mortgage-backed securities of the U.S. government

Regardless of the type, they're all low-risk investments that will appeal to those who like their returns chiefly in the form of current income. Obviously, if you're looking for absolute security, stick with bond funds that invest only in U.S. Treasuries. Also, if you like mortgage-backed securities, but don't like the way the principal is repaid in small amounts over time, you should consider mutual funds that invest in these securities—they'll automatically reinvest the principal for you, so all you'll ever see is the interest income (unless you want that reinvested, too).

HIGH-GRADE CORPORATE BOND FUNDS These funds invest chiefly in corporate bonds rated triple-B or better. They may also invest in U.S. government securities and sometimes put a little (seldom more than 10%) into lower-rated corporates. Most of these funds seek a high level of current income along with preservation of capital. Here again, if you want to reduce price volatility, look for funds that invest mostly in short- to intermediate-term bonds. In other words, look for funds that have "average maturities" of 3 to 5 years, and certainly no more than 10 years. This is especially important when you're investing in funds, because unlike the outright purchase of bonds themselves, bond funds do *not* have maturity dates. Therefore, there's nothing forcing the price of the fund toward a par value. Instead, because the funds are constantly buying and selling securities, their maturities don't change much over time, and as a result, there's no way of telling what the fund will be trading at 5 or 10 years down the road—you're strictly at the mercy of market interest rates. If market rates are way up, the price on long-term bond funds will be way down!

Also, be careful when selecting a corporate bond fund not to confuse *high-grade* funds with *high-yield* funds. They definitely are not the same thing. High-yield funds are risky investment vehicles that buy low-quality (junk) bonds as a way to drive up yields.

HIGH-GRADE MUNICIPAL BOND FUNDS If you feel you're being eaten alive by taxes, then municipal bond funds may be right for you. They're most suitable for high-income investors who are looking for shelter from income taxes. That means people who are in either the 28% or 33% federal tax brackets. If you're not in one of these tax brackets, stay away from municipal bonds in any form, including muni bond funds. High-grade municipal bond funds are just like the corporate version of this product except that they invest in high-grade, investment-quality municipal obligations. The municipal funds might even be a little more quality-conscious, as many of them only invest in bonds rated A or better, and a lot of them only buy bonds that are guaranteed against default by third-party municipal bond insurers. As you might expect, some muni funds emphasize long-term issues, while others emphasize short- to intermediate-term maturities.

Like their corporate counterparts, municipal bond funds seek both preservation of capital and a high level of current income, which in this case is exempt from federal and possibly state income tax. An added feature of these funds, and one that's often overlooked by investors, is their liquidity. For in sharp contrast to municipal bonds themselves (which are terribly illiquid), municipal bond *funds* are highly liquid, and can be bought and sold just as easily as any other security. Because of this feature, individual investors can get their tax-free income and still have plenty of liquidity to boot. And keep in mind, this same liquidity feature applies to any type of bond fund—not just municipals.

Fund Services—What You Need Is What You Get

Ask most people why they buy a particular mutual fund and they'll probably go on about how the fund provides the kind of income and return they're looking for. Now, no one would question the importance of return in the investment decision, but there are some other reasons for investing in mutual funds, not the least of which are the services they provide. Mutual funds have done a terrific job of meeting the needs of investors, and today you'll find that most funds provide a full array of attractive investor services. Indeed, many investors find these services so valuable that they often buy the funds as much for their services as for their returns. Some of the most sought-after fund services include savings and reinvestment plans, regular income programs, conversion and phone switching privileges, and retirement programs.

SAVINGS PLANS In a savings plan, you agree, either formally or informally, to add a certain amount of money to your account on a regular basis. For example, you might agree to add $250 every quarter. The money is then used to buy additional shares in the fund. Because the funds deal in fractional shares, every penny of your money is put to work immediately. While some of these plans may be more formal than others, none of them are contractually binding, since they can't force you to buy their funds. Actually, once a mutual fund account is open, you can add any amount to it at any time. But the nice thing about a savings plan is that it encourages savings and is an excellent way to build up investment capital.

Many funds offer *voluntary savings plans*, which are a great way of regularly adding to your investment program. In contrast, *contractual savings plans* that involve substantial front-end loads should be avoided! If you get hooked into one of these plans, you may find yourself paying for the plan's commissions long before you ever start getting full credit for your investments.

AUTOMATIC REINVESTMENT PLANS We've stressed throughout this book the importance of earning fully compounded rates of return, and that's exactly what you get with an automatic reinvestment plan. This is one of the real draws of mutual funds, and it's a service offered by virtually every open-ended mutual fund. A lot like the dividend reinvestment plans we looked at with stocks, the automatic reinvestment plans of mutual funds enable you to keep all your capital fully employed. Through this service, dividend and/or capital gains income is used to buy additional shares in the fund. Keep in mind, however, that even though you reinvest your dividends and capital gains, the IRS treats them as cash receipts and taxes them in the year in which they are paid. The funds deal in fractional shares, and these purchases are often commission-free. The important point is that by plowing back your earnings, you can generate substantially more earnings than would be possible without this reinvestment option. There's no question, *automatic reinvestment plans are a service that every safety-conscious investor should seriously consider signing up for.*

REGULAR INCOME PROGRAMS While automatic reinvestment plans are great for the long-term investor, how about the investor who's looking for a steady stream of income? Once again, mutual funds have a service to meet this kind of need. It's called a *systematic withdrawal plan,* and it's offered by most open-ended funds. Once enrolled in one of these plans, you'll automatically receive a predetermined amount of money every month or quarter. In most cases, you have to keep a minimum balance of $5,000 or more in order to participate in the plan. The size of the minimum payment is normally $50 or more per period, but there is no limit on the maximum amount you can withdraw. These monthly or quarterly withdrawals usually come from dividends or capital gains, although they can also be taken from principal if there aren't enough earnings in your account to cover them.

CONVERSION PRIVILEGES AND PHONE SWITCHING For one reason or another, you may at times find it necessary or desirable to switch out of one fund and into another. It may be because you feel you've held the fund long enough, or maybe your investment goals are changing. For whatever reason, conversion privileges were devised to make this type of exchange possible. A word of caution is in order here: even though conversion privileges make switching funds easy and convenient, *don't try to use them for market timing purposes.* In the vast majority of cases, market timing just doesn't work, and it's certainly not something a safety-conscious investor ought to get involved in. However, as a serious long-term investor, conversion privileges are something you might want to use sparingly as your investment program or goals gradually change over time.

Investment companies that offer a number of different mutual funds usually provide conversion privileges that enable you to simply pick up the phone to move money from one fund to another. This is known as phone switching. Most companies charge little or nothing for these shifts, although funds that offer free exchange privileges often place a limit on the number of times you can switch each year. Of course, you must confine your switches to the same family of funds. For example, you can switch from a Dreyfus balanced fund to a Dreyfus money or income fund, or to any other fund managed by Dreyfus. Despite the advantages in switching, there is one major drawback that may discourage you from changing the status quo. For tax purposes, the exchange of shares from one fund to another is regarded as a sale transaction, followed by a subsequent purchase of a new security. As a result, if any capital gains existed at the time of the exchange, you are liable for the taxes on that profit even though the holdings were not truly liquidated.

RETIREMENT PROGRAMS As a result of government legislation, self-employed individuals are permitted to divert a portion of their pretax income into self-directed retirement plans. Moreover, wage earners can put up to $2,000 a year into individual retirement accounts (IRAs). Even after the Tax Reform Act of 1986, every employed person can still invest in an IRA, although only certain individuals can deduct the capital contributions from their income tax. All earnings from IRA investments are still tax-deferred, however. Today, nearly all mutual funds provide a special service that enables individuals to quickly and easily set up a tax-deferred retirement program—as either an IRA or Keogh account. The funds set up the plans and handle all the administrative details in such a way that the shareholder can take full advantage of available tax savings. There is usually a small fee for this service (of perhaps $25 to $50 a year).

Getting a Handle on Mutual Fund Performance

If you were to believe all the sales literature, you'd think there was no way you could go wrong by investing in mutual funds. Just put your money into one of these funds and let the good times roll! Oh, if it were only that easy, we'd all be rich. Unfortunately, the hard facts of life are that when it comes to investing, it's performance that matters. And that applies just as much to mutual funds as it does to any other form of investing. Perhaps even more so, because with mutual funds, the single variable that drives a fund's market price and return behavior is the performance of the fund's portfolio of securities.

Sources of Return

Open-end mutual funds have three potential sources of return: (1) dividend income, (2) capital gains distributions, and (3) change in the price (or net asset value) of the fund. Depending on the type of fund, one source may be more important than another; for example, you would normally expect income funds to produce much more in dividend income than in capital gains distributions.

Mutual funds publish periodic reports summarizing their investment performance. One such report is the *summary of income and capital changes,* an example of which is shown here. This statement, usually found in the fund's prospectus or annual report, gives a brief overview of the fund's investment activities, including income and expense ratios and portfolio turnover rates. The top part of the report is especially interesting, since it reveals the amount of dividend income and capital gains distributed to shareholders, along with the change in the fund's net asset value. Using this summary report, we can take a closer look at the three principal sources of mutual fund return.

• **Dividend Income** This source of income, shown as item 4, is derived from the dividend and interest income earned on the security holdings of the mutual fund. When the fund receives dividend or interest payments, it first deducts operating expenses and then passes on all or most of what's left to shareholders in the form of dividend payments. The fund accumulates its current income and then pays it out on a prorated basis—usually this is done quarterly, though a number of funds pay dividends only once a year. Really, it makes no difference whether dividends are paid quarterly or annually, since the amount of accumulated dividends will be reflected in the NAV of the fund.

• **Capital Gains Distributions** This source of return, item 6 on the summary report, works on the same principle as fund dividends, except these payments are derived from the capital gains earned by the fund. Note that this distribution applies to *realized* capital gains only—that is, the capital gains actually earned when security holdings are sold.

• **Change in Share Price** Unrealized capital gains (or paper profits) are what make up the third and final element of return, shown as item 7. When the fund's holdings go up or down in price, the net asset value of the fund moves accordingly. Suppose an investor buys into a fund at $10 per share, and some time later it is quoted at $12.50. Assuming there are no accumulated dividends, the difference of $2.50 per share is the unrealized capital gains contained in the fund's security holdings. It represents the profit shareholders would receive (and are entitled to) if the fund were to sell its holdings.

Summary of Income and Capital Changes
(Per share data, for a share outstanding throughout the year)

		1988	1987	1986
INCOME AND EXPENSES				
	1. Investment income	$ .76	$ .88	$ .67
	2. Less expenses	.16	.22	.17
	3. Net investment income	.60	.66	.50
Dividend income →	4. Dividends from net investment income	(.55)	(.64)	(.50)
CAPITAL CHANGES				
	5. Net realized and unrealized gains (or losses) on security transactions	6.37	(1.74)	3.79
Capital gains distributions →	6. Distributions from realized gains	(1.75)	(.84)	(1.02)
Change in share price →	7. Net increase (decrease) in NAV*	4.67	(2.56)	2.77
Beginning share price →	8. NAV at beginning of year	24.47	27.03	24.26
Ending share price →	9. NAV at end of year	$29.14	$24.47	$27.03
Expense ratio →	10. Ratio of operating expenses to average net assets	1.04%	.85%	.99%
	11. Ratio of net investment income to average net assets	1.47%	2.56%	2.39%
	12. Portfolio turnover rate**	85%	144%	74%
	13. Shares outstanding at end of year (000s omitted)	10.568	6.268	4.029

*Net increase (decrease) in NAV, line 7 = line 3 − line 4 + line 5 − line 6.

** Portfolio turnover rate relates the number of shares bought and sold by the fund to the total number of shares held in the fund's portfolio; a high turnover rate (for example, in excess of 100%) would mean the fund had been doing a lot of trading.

Measuring Return

A simple yet effective way to measure mutual fund performance is to describe the fund's return in terms of the three major sources noted above: dividends earned, capital gains distributions received, and change in price. These payoffs can be converted to a convenient yield figure by using a holding period return formula like the one we introduced in chapter 2. The computations necessary are illustrated below using the 1988 figures from the summary report. According to the report, this hypothetical no-load fund paid 55 cents per share in dividends, another $1.75 per share in capital gains distributions, and had a price at the beginning of the year of $24.47, which rose to $29.14 by the end of the year. Summarizing this investment performance, we have:

Price (NAV) at the *beginning* of the year	$24.47
Price (NAV) at the *end* of the year	29.14
Net increase	$ 4.67
Return for the year:	
Dividends received	$ .55
Capital gains distributions	1.75
Net increase in price (NAV)	4.67
Total return	$ 6.97
Holding period return (total return/beginning price)	28.5%

Based on a total dollar return of $6.97 and a beginning investment of $27.47, we were able to realize an annual rate of return of 28½%.

GETTING A FIX ON FUTURE FUND PERFORMANCE There's no question that the HPR figure is a handy measure of return. Unfortunately, looking at past performance is one thing, but how about the future? Ideally, you want to evaluate the same elements of return as we looked at above. The trouble is, when it comes to the future performance of a mutual fund, it's extremely difficult—if not impossible—to get a handle on what the future holds as far as dividends, capital gains, and NAV are concerned. The reason: a mutual fund's future investment performance is directly linked to the future makeup of its securities portfolio, which is something that is next to impossible to get a clear reading on. It's not like evaluating the expected performance of a share of stock, where you're keying in on one company. With mutual funds, investment performance depends on the behavior of many different stocks and bonds.

So, where do you look for some insight on the future? Most market observers suggest you look at two things. First, give careful consideration to the future direction of the market as a whole. This is important because the behavior of a well-diversified mutual fund tends to reflect the general tone of the market. Thus, if the feeling is that the market is going to generally be drifting up, that should bode well for the investment performance of mutual funds.

Second, take a good hard look at the past performance of the mutual fund itself. The reason: it's a good way to get an indication of how successful the fund's investment managers have been. In essence, the success of a mutual fund rests in large part *on the investment skills of the fund managers.* So, when investing in a mutual fund, look for consistently good performance, in up as well as down markets, over extended periods of time (5–7 years or more). Although past success is certainly no guarantee of future performance, a strong team of money managers can have a significant bearing on the level of fund returns. Put another way, when you buy a mutual fund, you're buying a formula (investment policy + money management team) that has worked in the past, in the expectation that it will work again in the future.

WHERE TO FIND THE INFORMATION Given the importance of a fund's past performance, where can you find the kind of information you're looking for? Believe it or not, a good place to start is with the mutual fund itself. Not too long ago, you would have been putting your financial health in considerable jeopardy if you'd followed such a course of action. But with some recent changes instituted by the SEC, that's no longer so. For along with their load charges and management fees, mutual funds must now report historical return behavior in a standardized format. Understand, the funds are *not* required to report such information, but if they do cite performance in their promotional material, they must follow a standardized, full-disclosure manner of presentation. In particular, the funds must disclose the average annual, fully compounded, total return for the preceding 1-, 3-, 5-, and 10-year periods. The returns must include not only dividends and capital gains distributions, but also any increases or decreases in the fund's NAV. This is precisely the kind of return we've been advocating in this book.

You can also find a lot of valuable information about comparative mutual fund performance in publications like *Barron's, Financial World, Forbes,* and *Donoghue's Mutual Funds Almanac.* These sources provide a wealth of operating and performance information in a convenient and easy-to-read format. What's more, publications like *Sylvia Porter's Personal Finance, Money,* and *Changing Times* regularly list the top-performing funds. And, of course, there are services available that provide background information and assessments for a wide variety of funds. Some of the best in this category include Morningstar's *Mutual Fund Values* and Wiesenberger's *Investment Companies.* From these sources, you can obtain information on such things as investment policy summaries, portfolio analyses, services offered, historical statistics, and reviews of past performance.

Investing in Mutual Funds

Are mutual funds right for me? A lot of people have asked themselves that question, and apparently many have concluded that funds are, indeed, right for them. The investing public likes mutual funds because, among other things, they can be used to meet a variety of investment objectives. For example, in addition to earning a nice rate of return on your money, they can be used as a storehouse of value, to accumulate wealth over the long run, or as a source of regular income.

Mutual funds are especially attractive to individuals who don't have a lot of money to invest—less than $10,000 to $20,000 in capital. Most investment advisers strongly recommend that beginning investors, or those with limited capital, stick to mutual funds. And that's very good advice. If you want to leave the safety of CDs and Treasury securities to venture into the world of stocks, corporate bonds, agency securities, and municipals, you ought to travel with mutual funds at least until you pick up some knowledge and experience in the market.

Now, just because funds are so well suited to small investors does not mean you shouldn't invest in them if you happen to be well-heeled. Nothing could be further from the truth! Mutual funds can meet the needs of just about any type of investor, and particularly those who lack the time and/or market expertise to do it themselves. But regardless of how much you have to invest, before you put any money into a fund, *ask yourself whether you want to invest in stocks or bonds to begin with.* If you don't have the risk tolerance it takes to invest in these securities, you're likely to find that buying them through mutual funds won't help much. Once you get over that hurdle, you can start thinking about mutual funds.

What to Look for in a Fund

Suppose you're confronted with the following situation: you have money to invest and are trying to find just the right place to put it. Being a safety-conscious investor, you obviously want to pick a security with acceptable risk; but you also want one that will generate an attractive rate of return. The problem is, you have to make the selection from a list of over 2,000 securities. Sound like a mission impossible? Well, this is exactly what you're up against in trying to select a mutual fund. With a full range of choices, the task ahead of you can be demanding. But if you approach the selection process in a systematic way, you're likely to find that the chore is not as formidable as it first appears.

In many respects, selecting a mutual fund is no different from selecting any other kind of investment vehicle. You begin by clarifying your own investment objectives and work from there. Here's a quick rundown of what to do when making a mutual fund investment:

• **Match Your Objectives with the Fund's** You have your own tolerance for risk and your own set of investment objectives. Let these investment constraints and goals serve as a target—then, once you have a target to shoot for, you can find a vehicle to get you there. That's where the fund's investment objectives come into play: look for funds with investment objectives that are compatible with yours. If you want to go with equities, then confine your selections to the three types of low-risk stock funds: equity-income, balanced, and growth and income. Going a step farther, if you view yourself as more conservative than aggressive, then stick with equity-income or balanced income funds. In a similar fashion, if you want to go with fixed income securities, decide whether you want governments, corporates, or the tax-free income of municipal bond funds. Then go with one of the three types of low-risk bond funds: U.S. governments, high-grade corporates, or high-grade municipals.

• **Search for Funds with Proven Track Records** Now that you've got the list whittled down to certain types of funds that meet your risk and investment objectives, the next step is to deal with the matter of return. In this regard, look for funds that not only provide generous rates of return, but equally important, look for consistency! The best funds aren't necessarily the ones that hit an occasional home run: they're the ones that are consistently good hitters in both good markets and bad. They may not appear in the top 10 year after year, but they're close enough to the top year in and year out to be solid long-term performers. As a rule, don't buy a fund unless it's been around for at least 5 years, and preferably 10, and look for funds that have been able to build up good solid performance records over those 5- or 10-year periods.

• **Check Out the Charges and Fees** The idea here is to know what you're getting into. There's nothing wrong with paying load charges—so long as they're backed up by performance. But watch out for funds with abnormally high management fees. These can really hurt your returns, because they're taken out year after year, regardless of how well (or poorly) the fund does. To give you an idea of what's high and what's not, the table below lists median (midpoint) operating expenses for stock and bond funds. Ideally, you'd like to find a no-load fund that's one of the top performers and charges annual management fees of something less than the figures below.

Type of Fund	Median Annual Expenses Stated As a Percent of Assets under Management	
	$100 million to $250 million	$500 million and up
Stock funds	1.04%	0.68%
Taxable bond funds	0.99	0.76

Source: Money, May 1988, p. 39.

• **What Kinds of Services Are You Looking For?** One of the big attractions of mutual funds is the wide array of services they offer. If these are important to you, then check to make sure the funds you're looking at offer the services you want. For example, if you need something to supplement your current level of income, then make sure the fund has a distribution program that fits your needs. In contrast, if it's total long-term return you're after, then make sure the fund has a dividend reinvestment program. Such services add to the value of a fund, so you might as well make the most of them.

A List of Quality Stock Funds

Okay, so you know what you want out of a fund and what type of fund you want to invest in. All that behind you, there's still one big hurdle left, and that is: which particular mutual fund are you going to invest in? As a quality-conscious investor looking for a good stock fund, you ought to confine your selections to equity-income funds, balanced funds, or growth and income funds. Unfortunately, there are literally hundreds of these funds available. What we have to do is whittle down the alternatives to come up with a much shorter and more manageable list.

Just as we did with common stocks, we employed some fairly basic selection criteria to come up with a list of quality stock funds. We used the same tests you should use when picking a fund—like consistency of performance, a proven track record, adequacy of current income, and exposure to a tolerable level of risk. Indeed, because of our penchant for safety, the screening process started with the matter of risk, and then moved to performance and other characteristics. Roughly 200 major, actively traded equity-income, balanced, and growth-and-income funds were evaluated. To make it on our list, a fund had to meet all four of the following tests:

- In order to meet our standard of safety, the fund had to carry a low or below-average risk rating in Morningstar's *Mutual Fund Values;* in addition, we looked for funds with low price volatility indexes in Wiesenberger's *Investment Companies.* We wanted funds that followed low-risk investment policies, and whose fund shares had reasonably low price volatility.
- Because money management talents play such an important role in determining investment success, we looked for funds that had been around for a period of at least 5 years, and preferably 10 or more. We ignored all newcomers, no matter how good their short-term performance.
- To avoid the really small funds, we confined our selections to those nationally traded funds that had at least $10 million in assets under management at the end of 1987.
- When it came to performance, we selected only those funds that had been able to provide consistently strong levels of performance over sustained periods of time. We looked for

funds that were near the top (for their respective risk categories) when it came to long-term (5- to 10-year) investment performance. Consistency was also important and in that regard, we considered the ability of the fund to generate profits in good years as well as bad—thus, funds that had more than 1 out of 5 (or 2 out of 10) losing years (defined as a negative total return) were dropped from the list.

The table provides information on the 28 funds that qualified for our list. A lot of funds didn't make the cut because they were too risky and/or not profitable enough. Some didn't make it because they were too small or too young (they lacked a track record). Others—like Windsor Fund—were not included because they're closed to new investors. What we're left with is a list of high-quality stock funds, all of which are suitable for safety-conscious investors. These are the funds that have shown that they can consistently provide attractive rates of return without taking on unnecessary risks. Not surprisingly, many of these regularly show up on someone's "honor roll" or list of "all-weather" funds. As a group, they probably derive a greater portion of their return from dividends than any other type of stock fund, so they tend to be more price-stable. This is especially true with equity-income and balanced funds, which clearly are more income-oriented.

In addition to price (NAV) and dividend/income distribution information, the table also lists 10-year returns. These are fully compounded rates of return, and show the kinds of long-term performance results that are possible with high-quality stock funds. No matter how you look at it, these are pretty impressive performance numbers, especially for low-risk funds. Although not reported in the table, another impressive statistic is that 18 of the 28 funds had positive returns in every one of the years covered by the period of analysis—that means they never had a losing year over the time span covered! Because mutual funds are so susceptible to market forces, you can't expect their returns to constantly grow, or even remain steady, over time. But you can expect a fund

A Representative List of Quality Stock Funds

Fund	1987				10-Year (1978–87) Average Annual Total Return	Latest Load Charge	Latest Expense Ratio	Minimum Initial Investment
	Year-End NAV	Dividends per Share	Dividend Yield	Capital Gains Dist'n/Share				
EQUITY-INCOME FUNDS								
Decatur Fund I	$14.73	$0.93	6.3%	$1.75	16.32%	8.5%	0.69%	$ 25
Fidelity Equity-Income	21.85	1.51	6.9	3.92	19.24	2.0	0.63	1,000
Financial Industrial Income	7.24	0.36	5.0	0.89	15.44	0	0.74	250
Founders Equity Income	6.55	0.41	6.3	0.87	13.14	0	1.84	1,000
Lindner Dividend	19.87	1.87	9.4	1.16	19.68	0	1.00	2,000
Oppenheimer Equity Income	7.85	0.60	7.6	0.88	17.52	8.5	0.91	1,000
SAFECO Income	12.64	0.99	7.8	0.84	15.09	0	0.94	1,000
Stratton Monthly Dividend	23.44	2.44	10.4	0.65	13.62*	0	1.24	1,000
United Income	15.08	0.66	4.4	2.60	15.63	8.5	0.63	500
Averages	$14.36	$1.08	7.1%	$1.51	16.18%		0.96%	
BALANCED FUNDS								
Alliance Balanced	$11.42	$0.59	5.2%	$2.75	13.33%	5.5%	1.17%	$ 250
Fidelity Puritan	11.53	0.94	8.2	0.77	15.89	2.0	0.70	1,000
Franklin Income	2.11	0.22	10.4	0.02	15.81	4.0	0.64	100
Mass. Fin. Total Return	9.63	0.57	5.9	0.45	13.84	7.25	0.66	250
IDS Mutual	11.22	0.78	7.0	1.33	13.82	5.0	0.63	2,000
Income Fund of America	10.72	1.08	10.1	0.38	14.10	8.5	0.54	1,000

Seligman Income	11.80	1.01	8.6	0.13	12.20	4.75	0.79	None
Wellesley Income	14.57	1.04	7.1	0.38	12.93	0	0.48	1,500
Wellington Fund	15.15	0.98	6.5	0.14	14.87	0	0.43	1,500
Averages	$10.90	$0.80	7.7%	$0.70	14.09%		0.67%	
GROWTH AND INCOME FUNDS								
Affiliated Fund	$ 8.93	$0.58	6.5%	$1.34	16.02%	7.25%	0.32%	$ 250
American Leaders	12.20	0.43	3.5	0.47	15.29	4.5	1.09	500
American Mutual	17.05	1.06	6.2	0.71	17.69	8.5	0.45	250
Evergreen Total Return	15.66	1.33	8.5	0.88	16.06*	0	1.02	2,000
Investment Co. of America	12.61	0.52	4.1	0.75	17.19	8.5	0.41	250
Merrill Lynch Capital	19.79	0.61	3.1	5.37	17.71	6.5	0.62	250
Mutual Qualified	19.34	0.88	4.6	1.44	19.41*	0	0.68	1,000
Smith Barney Income & Growth	10.05	0.50	5.0	0.63	16.30	5.75	0.46	2,500
Strong Total Return	18.37	1.66	9.0	3.17	20.02*	1.0	1.10	250
Wash. Mutual Investors	11.45	0.52	4.5	0.59	17.41	8.5	0.54	250
Averages	$14.54	$0.81	5.5%	$1.54	17.31%		0.67%	
Dow Jones Industrial Average			3.7%		13.93%			

Sources: Basic issue and performance data were obtained from Morningstar's *Mutual Fund Values, Barron's,* and *The Wall Street Journal;* 10-year return figures are fully compounded rates of return given full reinvestment of dividends and other income. All data are as of, or for the period ending, December 31, 1987.

* 10-year returns are not available; figures shown are for 5 years of performance (from 1983 to 1987).

to keep losing years to an absolute minimum, and to maintain some consistency in generating attractive rates of return; that's just a sign of good money management. Each of the listed funds has been able to do that, and they've been able to hold their own against the Dow Jones industrial average, too.

A List of Quality Bond Funds

We used a similar set of standards to find bond funds that would make good, safe investment vehicles. Here we looked at U.S. government funds, high-grade corporates, and high-grade municipals. We used basically the same four screens for the U.S. government and high-grade corporate bonds as noted above with the equity funds (that is, risk ratings, 5- to 10-year track records, size, and consistency of performance). In addition, we also considered the makeup of the portfolio and the average maturity of the bonds held. To maintain our standards of quality, at least 90% of the bonds had to be investment-grade or better; and to keep price volatility down, preference was given to funds with average maturities of less than 10 years. We had to do things a little differently with municipal bond funds, however. Because *Mutual Fund Values* doesn't track municipals, we needed to look elsewhere—chiefly *Financial World, Donoghue's Mutual Funds Almanac,* and *Forbes*—for risk and performance characteristics. Using these sources, it quickly became clear that due to the devastating effects that the market had on muni bond fund performance from 1978 through 1981, only one or two funds met the requirement of having no more that two losing years out of ten. The fact is all but a couple of the major funds lost money *every year* from 1978 through 1981. To compensate for this, we made a slight revision in one of the selection screens: to qualify for our list, the fund had to generate a profit in *each one* of the 6 years from 1982 through 1987 (even one small loss disqualified a fund); all the other selection criteria remained basically the same.

Applying these tests, we came up with the 28 bond funds listed in the table. This table contains the same information as the table of stock funds. And like their equity counterparts, these are not only low-risk funds, but they are consistently strong performers as well. Taking a closer look at the figures, a couple of things stand out. To begin with, the dividend yields on bond funds (that is, the dividends paid from the funds' interest earnings) are generally a lot higher than on stock funds; this isn't totally unexpected, however, as these funds are more income-oriented than most stock funds. Note also that while the 1987 dividend yields for the municipal bond funds may appear a bit low (the average yield was only 7.1%), those are *tax-free returns*. As such, they translate into an average yield of nearly 11% for someone in the maximum (33%) tax bracket!

On the other hand, the 10-year returns on bonds are considerably less than the returns earned on stock funds. The reason is obvious: less risk means less return. Even so, the fully compounded returns were quite respectable, and the 10-year results clearly indicate that attractive long-term returns can be obtained from high-quality bond funds. While 10% or 11% may pale next to the 14% or 15% earned on many stock funds, keep in mind that a fully compounded return of 10% to 11% means your money will *triple* in about 11 years!

Note that the short- to intermediate-term funds have been identified with an I to the left of the fund's name—these are funds with average maturities of less than 10 years. You can see that while these funds may occasionally involve a slight give-up in current yield, they usually have no trouble holding their own when it comes to total return over the long haul. As an investor, you'll have to decide whether the yield give-up is worth the added peace of mind that accompanies the reduced price volatillity of these funds. Certainly, if current income is of little interest to you, then the intermediate funds will probably hold more attraction, since you'll be able to get competitive long-term returns with less risk. In contrast, if you need the current income, then increased exposure to price volatility may be the price you'll have to pay to get it.

A Representative List of Quality Bond Funds

Fund	1987				10-Year (1978–87) Average Annual Total Return	Latest Load Charge	Latest Expense Ratio	Minimum Initial Investment
	Year-End NAV	Dividends per Share	Dividend Yield	Capital Gains Dist'n/Share				
U.S. GOVERNMENT BOND FUNDS								
Composite U.S. Gov. Secs. (M)	$ 0.99	$0.09	9.1%	$0	10.54%*	4.0%	0.88%	$1,000
Fund for U.S. Gov. Secs. (M)	8.29	0.77	9.3	0	9.18	4.5	0.95	500
(I) Hancock U.S. Gov. Secs.	8.83	0.83	9.4	0	10.02	8.5	0.97	500
(I) Kemper U.S. Gov. Secs.	9.14	1.01	11.0	0	12.47*	4.5	0.48	1,000
(I) Midwest Inc.—Inter.-Term Govs.	10.22	0.77	7.5	0	9.11*	2.0	1.03	1,000
Mutual of Omaha America Fund	9.85	0.83	8.4	0.03	9.15	0	0.98	250
Prudential-Bache GNMA Fund (M)	14.76	1.14	7.7	0.25	10.42*	0	1.60	1,000
(I) Twentieth Century U.S. Govs.	95.34	8.00	8.4	1.22	9.33*	0	1.00	None
Vanguard Fxd. Inc. Secs.—GNMAs (M)	9.35	0.89	9.5	0.01	11.74*	0	0.38	3,000
Averages	$18.53	$1.59	8.9%		10.22%		0.92%	
HIGH-GRADE CORPORATE BOND FUNDS								
Babson Bond Trust	$ 1.56	$0.20	12.8%	$0	10.33%	0	0.97%	$ 500
Dreyfus A Bonds Plus	13.36	1.35	10.1	0.22	10.79	0	0.84	2,500
(I) Fidelity Intermediate Bonds	10.05	1.61	16.0	0.10	11.82	0	0.75	2,500
(I) IAI Bond Fund	9.51	0.98	10.3	0.10	10.46	0	0.70	1,000
(I) Kemper Income & Capt. Preserv.	8.42	0.93	11.0	0	10.23	5.5%	0.69	1,000
(I) Merrill Lynch Corp. Bonds—I/T	10.99	0.94	8.6	0	11.58*	2.0	0.61	1,000

	NAV	Exp.	Yield		10-Yr.	Load	Risk	Min.
(I) Pioneer Bond Fund	9.05	0.79	8.7	0	10.92*	4.5	0.90	1,000
(I) T. Rowe Price New Income	8.55	0.75	8.8	0	10.39	0	0.65	1,000
(I) Vanguard Fixed Inc. Secs.—S/T	10.33	0.76	7.4	0.18	10.66*	0	0.38	3,000
Averages	$ 9.09	$0.92	10.4%		10.80%		0.72%	

HIGH-GRADE MUNICIPAL BOND FUNDS

	NAV	Exp.	Yield		10-Yr.	Load	Risk	Min.
Eaton Vance Muni. Bonds	$ 8.59	$0.66	7.7%	$0	11.31%*	4.75%	0.81%	$1,000
(I) Fidelity Ltd. Term Munis.	9.10	0.58	6.4	0	6.16	0	0.68	2,500
Kemper Municipal Bonds	9.37	0.72	7.7	0	7.36	4.5	0.54	1,000
M.F.S. Managed Muni. Bonds	10.09	0.72	7.1	0	9.44	4.75	0.60	250
Nuveen Muni Bonds	8.38	0.60	7.2	0.15	6.66	4.0	0.67	1,000
Oppenheimer Tax-free Bonds	9.12	0.68	7.4	0	6.63	4.75	0.78	1,000
SAFECO Muni Bonds	12.60	0.97	7.7	0.40	12.16*	0	0.59	1,000
Shearson Managed Munis	14.51	1.11	7.6	0.01	12.30*	5.0	0.55	500
SteinRoe Managed Municipals	8.50	0.61	7.2	0.14	8.21	0	0.65	1,000
(I) Vanguard Muni. Bonds—Intermed.	11.56	0.82	7.1	0.09	5.23	0	0.33	3,000
Averages	$10.18	$0.75	7.3%		8.55%		0.62%	
S&P High-Grade Corp. Bonds			10.3%		8.45%			

A minor variation was allowed for the quality screen with the U.S. government bond funds—in particular, a couple of funds with average risk ratings were allowed to appear on the list, since such a rating with a U.S. government bond fund still amounts to a very low level of risk.

(M) indicates the fund invests primarily, or exclusively, in mortgage-backed pass-through securities.

(I) indicates the fund invests primarily, or exclusively, in short- to intermediate-term bonds (i.e., funds have average maturities of less than 10 years).

Sources: Basic issue and performance data were obtained from Morningstar's *Mutual Fund Values, Barron's, The Wall Street Journal, Donoghue's Mutual Funds Almanac, Forbes,* and *Financial World;* 10-year return figures are fully compounded rates of return given full reinvestment of interest and other income. All data are as of, or for the period ending, December 31, 1987, unless indicated with an asterisk (*), in which case the return figures cover the 5-year period from 1983 to 1987.

The Good Points:

- A cost-effective way of obtaining the services of *professional money managers.*
- Provide a degree of *investment diversification* that most investors would find impossible to obtain on their own. This reduces your risk by spreading out your holdings.
- *Inexpensive to open a mutual fund account* so they're well within the financial reach of most individual investors.
- *Deal in fractional shares,* so every penny you put in is invested for you. This applies to your initial investment as well as any additions you make to your account.
- *Full menu of services,* including automatic reinvestment plans, systematic distribution programs, exchange privileges, and phone switching.
- *No commissions* if you confine your investing to true no-load funds.
- *Convenient.* They're easy to acquire, and they handle all the paperwork and record-keeping.
- *Fully compounded rates of return* available through automatic reinvestment plans.

And the Bad:

- *High transaction costs* if you deal in load funds. Be careful in this regard, because these expenses can take many forms: front-end loads, redemption fees, and deferred sales charges.
- *Annual fees* charged regardless of how well—or poorly—the fund performs. These fees can add up over time and be a real drag on your investment returns.
- *Returns are often average, at best.* Most funds have a tough time outperforming the market.
- *Price volatility of bond funds.* They tend to be more price volatile than the direct investment in bonds, because (except for target funds) they don't have maturity dates so there's nothing driving the price of the fund back to par.
- *Share prices subject to market swings,* because fund perform-

ance is so closely linked to the market. There's no way to hide from it: as the stock (or bond) market goes, so goes the share prices of most stock (or bond) funds.

Taxes:

Interest and dividend income, as well as capital gains distributions, are fully taxable at the federal level, *except* for the interest earned from municipal bond funds. Similar provisions generally apply to state and local taxes; with the following qualifications: the interest earned from U.S. government bond funds is exempt from these taxes; with municipal bond funds, that portion of the interest earned on in-state bonds is exempt from state and local taxes (the fund will provide you with a year-end statement indicating how much of the interest income qualifies as tax-exempt).

Capital gains earned through price appreciation of your mutual fund shares are fully taxable when realized (when the shares are actually sold).

Any dividends and/or capital gains distributions that are reinvested in the fund are fully taxable in the year they're credited to your account.

8

How to Build a Better Portfolio

The trouble with investing is that you really don't know what the future holds. What's going to happen to inflation? How are stocks going to perform? Which way are interest rates headed? As an investor, you have to deal with these and many other uncertainties, since these are the variables that can affect interest earnings, price stability, rate of return, and the like. If things go one way, you're in good shape; but if they move against you, that's another story.

There's a certain four-letter word that describes the kind of thing we're talking about here. That word is *risk*. This whole book has dealt with steps you can take to avoid risk when investing in various types of short- and long-term securities. But there's still one more thing you can do to control your exposure to risk even more—that is, make it a habit to develop and hold a well-diversified portfolio of securities. The key word here is *diversify;* don't put all your eggs in one basket.

You Can Have Your Cake and Eat It, Too

A well-diversified portfolio is one that provides:

- The highest return for a given level of risk *or*
- The lowest risk for a given level of return.

Any way you look at it, the net result should be a highly favorable risk-return trade-off, one in which the investor is fully compensated for any risk incurred. And the nice thing about reducing your risk through portfolio diversification is that it has absolutely no effect on your return.

Putting your money into several different investment vehicles allows the risk from individual securities to be dispersed in such a way that risk exposure declines. This assumes that the securities you're buying are sufficiently different in return characteristics. If that's the case, then a security's risk will always be less when held in a portfolio than in isolation. Put another way, while the contribution of a given security to the risk of a portfolio depends on its return behavior traits, it can never be greater than its risk when held in isolation. Thus, from a risk perspective, you can't go wrong by diversifying your holdings, for it can never increase your exposure to risk. On the other hand, while risk is reduced through portfolio diversification, return is unaffected by this process. For the return you earn on a given security is the same whether it's held in isolation or in a portfolio.

It Pays to Diversify!

To provide a simple illustration of how portfolio diversification works, consider two investment opportunities. One involves putting everything you have into one investment—let's call it security A. The other calls for putting an equal amount into two investments—half into security A and half into security B. If both security A and security B have expected returns of, say, 10%, then it really doesn't make any difference which portfolio you choose— you'll get the same 10% return from the one-asset portfolio as from the two-asset portfolio. So, as far as expected return is concerned, here's proof that this aspect of performance is unaffected by the diversification process.

But if you're going to make the same expected return with either investment, why waste your time buying two securities rather than one? The answer, of course, is that it reduces your exposure to risk. If you hold the two-asset portfolio and something goes wrong with one of the securities, it'll only hurt part of your portfolio. Indeed, up to a point, the more securities you hold, the more you can disperse (or dissipate) the impact of one or two bad apples. If the market turns against security A, the investor who holds it in a one-asset portfolio will see the whole portfolio experience a drop in return—perhaps a big one. Start increasing the number of securities in your portfolio and you reduce the chance of that happening; which, by itself, translates into less risk for the portfolio.

But it goes beyond that, because a well-diversified portfolio also increases your chances of earning a rate of return equal or close to your expected return. For example, assume your two-asset portfolio is made up of a long-term Treasury and a short-term brokered CD. Now, if interest rates move up, the price of the bond will fall, dragging down returns on that segment of the portfolio, whereas the yields on short-term securities will rise, causing the returns on that segment of the portfolio to move up. In essence, what you lose in one area you can at least partially make up for in the other. So even if things don't quite work out the way you expected, a well-diversified portfolio is far more likely than an undiversified one to provide a return in line with your expectations.

Building Your Own Portfolio

You need a portfolio in order to diversify. A portfolio breathes life into your investment program; it is the vehicle through which you should manage your investment holdings. A portfolio is not a physical thing—you can't hold it, you can't sit on it, there's nothing to kick around when things don't go right. Rather, a portfolio is represented by a collection of investment vehicles that are being held for a common goal. But a portfolio is far more than a collection of investments; it's an investment philosophy that provides guidelines for carrying out your investment program. A portfolio combines your personal and financial traits with your investment objectives to give some structure to your investments.

Throughout *Investing for Safety's Sake* we've stressed the need to follow certain investment principles: Invest for the long haul, keep it simple, don't try to time the market, add capital regularly to your investment program, and be sure to keep your capital fully employed. Above all, play it safe, stick with high-quality securities, and don't take on any more risk than you can tolerate. These are all sound investment principles and in no way should they be jeopardized for the sake of portfolio diversification. Indeed, they are just as relevant to portfolios of securities as they are to individual securities.

WHERE TO START To build a portfolio, start with your own personal and financial characteristics:

- Your age and experience as an investor
- The size of your family and ages of your children
- The level and stability of your income
- Your net worth
- Your need for income
- Your tolerance for risk

These are the variables that set the tone for your investments. They determine the kinds of investments you should consider and how long you can tie up your money. In order for your portfolio to work, it must be tailored to meet your personal financial needs. Therefore, start the portfolio process by taking a thorough inventory of these needs, and repeat this type of inventory every 3 to 5 years to make sure your portfolio is staying on the right course. Once you have a clear picture of your financial needs, you're in a position to set some investment objectives.

There are three factors that stand out here and have a pronounced impact on the tone of your portfolio:

• **Tolerance for Risk** The overriding theme of this book, this factor influences the amount of price volatility you're willing to tolerate, the quality of the securities you hold, and even the general areas you invest in (stocks versus bonds versus mutual funds).

• **Income and Return Requirements** This factor plays an important part in determining the kind of dividend and interest yield you look for, how important long-term capital growth is to you, and your need for reinvestment programs.

• **Investment Horizon** The longer you're able to stay invested, the more investment alternatives you have. Clearly, if you have important short-term needs, you shouldn't jeopardize them by mismatching maturities. *Liquidity* is also an issue here, as the more liquidity you need, the shorter your investments should be.

You Need an Asset Allocation Scheme

Once you've done a thorough inventory of your financial needs and have set your sights on one or more investment goals, your portfolio can start taking shape. But before you buy any stocks or CDs, take the time to develop an *asset allocation scheme* that's right for you. In asset allocation, emphasis is placed on *preservation of capital.* For the idea is to position your assets in such a way that you can protect your portfolio from potential negative developments in the market, while still taking advantage of potential positive developments. This is one of the most overlooked yet most important aspects of investing. Indeed, there's overwhelming evidence that, over the long run, the total return on a portfolio is influenced more by its asset allocation plan than by specific security selections.

Well, if it's so important, it must be difficult, right? Wrong! All asset allocations involves is a decision on your part about how to divide your portfolio among different types of securities: for example, what portion of your portfolio is going to be devoted to short-term securities, longer bonds, and/or bond funds and what if anything is going to stock and/or equity funds. Asset allocation deals with devising an asset mix by broad categories and does not tell you which individual securities to buy or sell.

An asset allocation scheme might look something like this:

Type of Investment	Asset Mix
Short-term securities	35%
Longer bonds (7- to 10-year maturities)	40
Equity funds	25
Total portfolio	100%

As you can see, all you're really doing here is deciding how to cut up the pie. You don't need to get any more specific than this. To be effective, however, you should design your asset allocation scheme for the long haul. Come up with an asset mix that you can live with for at least 7 to 10 years, perhaps even longer. Once you have it set, then stick with it. The key to success here is to force yourself to be faithful to your asset allocation scheme. By all means, fight the temptation to wander off course.

Don't Put All Your Eggs in One Basket

While a practical asset allocation scheme is a vital element in the diversification process, it deals in very general terms. You still have to decide which particular securities you should invest in. Okay, so you want to put, say, 35% of your money into short-term securities—just precisely which short-term securities do you have in mind? Enter the final step of the diversification process: *security selection.* This is where your asset allocation scheme is put into action and your portfolio becomes a reality. While devising a workable asset allocation scheme is, by nature, an episodic exercise, security selection and portfolio management are recurring activities that become an almost routine part of your investment program. You receive an interest or dividend check and you have to find a place to put it; you add new capital to your investment program, or one of the Treasury notes you're holding matures, and you have to decide what to do with the money. These events occur with considerable regularity, so you're likely to be faced with a series of little (and sometimes not so little) investment decisions over time.

Portfolio Management in Action

Portfolio management is a term used to describe the ongoing administration of a group or collection of securities and investments. It involves the buying, selling, and holding of various securities for the purpose of meeting a set of predetermined investment needs and objectives. Portfolio management is based on the concept of diversification and is an extension of your asset allocation scheme.

To see how portfolio management actually works, let's take a look at several different portfolios. While each one is structured to accomplish a slightly different investment objective, they all have one common objective: to maintain the highest standards of *safety.* Safe, low-risk investing has been the theme throughout this book and it continues to be so here. In chapters 4 through 7, we discussed the things you could do to minimize your exposure to risk—like laddering your CD investments, sticking with intermediate-term bonds and low-beta stocks, and buying only certain types of mutual funds. Each of those investment strategies can be put into practice within the context of a portfolio.

Besides safety, we also considered the matter of yield. Just because we don't like a lot of risk doesn't mean we should forget about return. So obtaining a satisfactory rate of return from our investments was also a major objective in our portfolios. Generally, we sought to do this by going after higher-yielding securities whenever they were compatible with the risk constraints we had established. In addition to risk and return, we also took into account such things as liquidity requirements, the need for current income, age of the investor, and the amount of capital the investor has to work with. In particular, we developed several different portfolios to show how the asset allocation schemes and security holdings might change with these conditions.

The portfolios demonstrated here can serve as benchmarks

to show what can be done under different sets of investment circumstances. Now, of course, specific needs and requirements will vary with individual investors, so you have to adjust your portfolio accordingly. For example, if you like the general thrust of one of the portfolios, but want a bit more debt or equity, then by all means alter the asset mix to meet your needs. Generally speaking, the portfolios are fairly generic in terms of what actually goes into them. We identify several different kinds of securities to hold for each segment of the portfolio, but we don't get down to specific names. Here's what you can expect: put X amount of money into a 7- to 10-year Treasury note or a high-quality income stock. We did this because, while it provides quite a bit of direction, it still gives you enough room to fill in the kind of details you'd like in a specific security.

This is also where the investment strategies that we discussed in chapters 4 through 7 come into play. You want to minimize your risk or maximize your return, then use the trading techniques we talked about. For example, it's assumed that every portfolio will be made up exclusively of high-grade investment-quality securities. A good place to start the hunt for such investments is the lists of high-quality securities we've provided in some of the previous chapters. Moreover, when making a security selection, bring in the issue characteristics you'd like: things like call and sinking fund protection, agency ratings, level of coupon and dividend income, stock betas, dividend reinvestment plans, and mutual fund services.

MODERATELY CONSERVATIVE PORTFOLIO We begin by building a middle-of-the-road portfolio for investors who are *moderately conservative* and who are looking for long-term growth in capital. These investors have little or no need for current income but want to earn a fully compounded rate of return on their money. For purposes of discussion, we'll be working with $50,000 in investment capital. This is neither a really big portfolio nor a small one, but it does allow us to go beyond the basics and get into some serious portfolio management. Later we'll look at how the investment decisions change when you're dealing with larger or smaller portfolios.

Moderately conservative investors want a high degree of safety, but not to the point where everything else is excluded. In this way, they're probably typical of most safety-conscious investors: they put a good deal of their money into various types of short-term securities, like CDs and money funds, while recognizing that there are also attractive return opportunities in certain types of investment-grade bonds and high-quality income-oriented equities. A respectable total return over the long haul is a principal objective of these investors. The accompanying table shows what the portfolio of a typical moderately conservative investor might look like.

This portfolio provides a nice balance of investment holdings, yet it doesn't involve a lot of different securities. That's one

Moderately Conservative Portfolio

Asset Allocation Scheme	Type of Investment	Amount Invested	Indicated Yield*
45%	SHORT-TERM SECURITIES		
	Money fund	$ 7,500	6.7%
	Laddered 2½-year CDs	15,000	7.6
		$22,500	
30%	BONDS		
	7- to 10-year Treasury note	$ 5,000	9.0
	7- to 10-year agency note	10,000	9.2
		$15,000	
25%	EQUITIES		
	High-quality income stock	$ 5,000	13.0
	1 or 2 high-quality equity-income mutual funds	7,500	15.0
		$12,500	
100%	Total portfolio	$50,000	
	Average portfolio yield		9.6%

* *Indicated yield* is as of mid-1988; yields are for current (interest and/or dividend) income only, except in the case of equity securities, where return also includes historical capital appreciation experience.

of the hallmarks of *investing for safety's sake:* to keep it simple. And that's just what we've done here (and will continue to do with the other portfolios we develop). In this case, depending on how many different maturities you have in your ladder of CDs (probably there are at least three), this whole portfolio is put together with only eight or nine different investments. The net result is a portfolio of low-risk securities, where there's plenty of liquidity (provided by the short-term securities), and price volatility is kept reasonably low through the use of intermediate-term bonds and low-beta income stocks. Indeed, about the only segment that's subject to much risk (and even then it's not a whole lot) is the equity-income mutual fund.

While this portfolio derives a good deal of its total return from current income, there's still room for some capital growth (stemming from the equity holdings). Look, only 25% of this portfolio is devoted to equities, yet it has an average indicated yield of around 9.6%. That's not bad for an investment program that's dedicated to safety. If it can be maintained, in 10 years this $50,000 portfolio will increase in value to something around $125,000! All of which provides support to the argument that respectable returns are, indeed, available from low-risk investment programs.

As indicated, about 25% of this portfolio consists of equity securities. Now, there are a lot of safety-conscious investors who, for one reason for another, just will not put their money into common stocks, or any other form of equity. They still consider themselves to be moderately conservative investors and they're still willing to take some risks—so long as it doesn't involve investing in common. No problem, it's relatively easy to modify our moderately conservative portfolio to *exclude equities,* as in the next table.

In this case, there's a little less devoted to the short end and much more put into longer-term notes and bonds. Also note that even though there's less in short-term securities, the liquidity of the portfolio has actually increased, as there's more held in money funds. With improved liquidity, more could be devoted to the

Moderately Conservative Portfolio—No Equities

Asset Allocation Scheme	Type of Investment	Amount Invested	Indicated Yield*
40%	SHORT-TERM SECURITIES		
	Money fund	$ 8,000	6.7%
	Laddered 2½-year CDs	12,000	7.6
		$20,000	
60%	BONDS		
	2 or 3 government or high-grade corporate bond funds	$20,000	9.2
	7- to 10-year double- or triple-A-rated corporate notes	10,000	9.5
		$30,000	
100%	Total portfolio	$50,000	
	Average portfolio yield		8.5%

* *Indicated yield* is as of mid-1988; the yields are for current (interest) income only.

longer end in an attempt to pick up yields. This portfolio consists of two or three bond funds, which provide not only return, but also a vehicle for conveniently reinvesting coupon income. Just because we're ignoring equities doesn't mean we're not interested in reinvesting our investment income. A fully compounded rate of return is still important, and that's something that's made all the easier with bond funds that offer automatic reinvestment plans.

Along this line, you might even want to consider high-grade *zero-coupon bonds* in place of, say, the corporate notes. They would be a nice complement to the bond funds, and they're a great way of earning a fully compounded return on your money. Overall, the level of risk in this portfolio has dropped with the removal of the equity securities, but so has portfolio return. However, note that return doesn't fall as much as might be expected—we're still able to earn about 8½% from our money.

ULTRACONSERVATIVE PORTFOLIO Some investors are able to tolerate risk much better than others. As a group, safety-conscious investors generally don't care much for risk and try to avoid it. But there are many investors who just can't tolerate it in any manner, shape, or form. Indeed, the number of such investors is probably greater than most people realize. Unfortunately, a lot of these investors—they often view themselves more as savers than investors—do little more than put their money into passbook savings accounts and 6-month CDs. This really is a shame, since there are a number of other equally safe investments that can produce big increases in return. The table shows an example of such a portfolio.

This portfolio has several notable attributes. For one thing, the securities are all of the highest quality—indeed, 60% of the portfolio is in Treasury obligations. Note, too, that if you invest in a money market deposit account rather than a money fund, this whole portfolio can be put together at your local bank. That's important to a lot of people, since they don't want to deal with brokers. Also, except for the Series EE bonds, the portfolio is kept fairly short. As such, there's plenty of liquidity and really no price volatility to speak of (rates have to move quite a bit in order for a 2- or 3-year Treasury note to undergo much price change).

Ultraconservative Portfolio

Asset Allocation Scheme	Type of Investment	Amount Invested	Indicated Yield*
70%	**SHORT-TERM SECURITIES**		
	Money fund (or money market deposit account)	$ 8,000	6.7%
	Laddered 2½-year CDs	12,000	7.6
	Series EE bonds	15,000	6.9
		$35,000	
30%	**BONDS**		
	2-year Treasury notes	$ 10,000	8.2
	3-year Treasury notes	5,000	8.4
		$15,000	
100%	Total portfolio	$50,000	
	Average portfolio yield		7.5%

* *Indicated yield* is as of mid-1988; the yields are for current (interest) income only.

The 2- and 3-year Treasury notes were included in the portfolio as a way to go after a bit more yield. If the longer maturities are a cause for concern (and they really should not be), then stick with short-term investment vehicles. You can do this, for example, by adding $10,000 to your ladder of CDs and $5,000 to the Series EE bonds. Added return is also the reason we put Series EE bonds into this portfolio—they not only provide absolute protection against capital loss, but also have floating rates so their yields go up and down with the market. Granted, they lack liquidity, because you have to hold them for a minimum of 5 years to earn the going yield; but even so, they can be sold any time after 6 months and they'll at least pay something in return. Overall, the yield on this portfolio amounts to a highly respectable 7½%, which really isn't bad given the amount of risk involved. It's especially nice when you consider that the same amount of money placed in a portfolio made up of a savings account and a 6-month CD would have yielded less than 6%.

AGGRESSIVELY CONSERVATIVE PORTFOLIO Whereas ultraconservative investors are on one end of the safety continuum, aggressively conservative investors are on the other. These latter investors are willing to take on more risk so long as they're fairly compensated in the form of added return. But only up to a point, for safety is still a paramount concern, and in no way are these investors interested in doing any speculating! Capital growth is normally a major consideration, so there's generally a good deal of emphasis on equities. The table shows an example of a portfolio that's structured so it can more aggressively go after return while still maintaining high standards of quality and safety.

Half of this six- to eight-security portfolio is devoted to equities. *That's about the most that should ever be committed to equities in any safe, quality-conscious portfolio.* Indeed, if you find that's too much, then cut the equity position back to, say, 40%. Regardless of what you decide on, however, it's likely that equities will play an important role in your portfolio, as they're usually the preferred way to picking up both added returns and increased

Aggressively Conservative Portfolio

Asset Allocation Scheme	Type of Investment	Amount Invested	Indicated Yield*
30%	**SHORT-TERM SECURITIES**		
	Money fund	$ 5,000	6.7%
	12- to 18-month brokered CD	10,000	7.5
		$15,000	
20%	**BONDS**		
	7- to 10-year investment-grade corporate note (or zero-coupon bond)	$10,000	9.5
50%	**EQUITIES**		
	1 or 2 blue chip, growth-oriented stocks	$10,000	15.5
	2 or 3 high-quality growth and income funds	15,000	16.5
		$25,000	
100%	Total portfolio	$50,000	
	Average portfolio yield		12.1%

* *Indicated yield* is as of mid-1988; yields are for current (interest and/or dividend) income only, except in the case of equity securities, where return also includes historical capital appreciation experience.

capital growth. With such a heavy emphasis on equity securities, it's more essential than ever to stick with high-quality investment vehicles—that's the best way to keep your risk in check. Also, be sure to diversify by holding three to five different stocks or equity funds, at the minimum. Finally, to get the most from this segment of the portfolio, it's important that you fully participate in available dividend reinvestment plans.

Actually, this would also be a great place to use something like a zero-coupon bond. It's a good risk modifier to use against the more uncertain equities, and it can serve to underwrite your capital position in case things don't work out as expected with the stocks. Put $10,000 into a 9½% zero-coupon and in 10 years you'll be able to cash it in for $25,000. If nothing else, that's a nice position to be able to fall back on. Aggressive portfolios do have their risks, but as you can see in the figures above, they also have their rewards in the form of highly attractive potential returns.

INCOME-ORIENTED PORTFOLIO So far, we've been constructing portfolios with the idea that the investor is working for a fully compounded rate of return over the long haul. As a result, we've assumed that the income from interest and dividends is constantly being plowed back into the investment program. While that may be a valid assumption in many cases, it's inappropriate for the investor who's living off the income. Under such circumstances, the current stream of income is not an additional source of investment capital, but a vital supplement to other sources of income. These investors look for both preservation of capital and high levels of current income and, indeed, dividend reinvestment programs are of no interest to them. Not surprisingly, many of these investors are retired.

While this portfolio appears to hold a lot of securities, a closer look reveals that there are really only about seven or eight

Income-oriented Portfolio

Asset Allocation Scheme	Type of Investment	Amount Invested	Indicated Yield*
30%	**SHORT-TERM SECURITIES**		
	Money fund	$ 5,000	6.7%
	12- to 18-month brokered CD	10,000	7.5
		$15,000	
35%	**BONDS**		
	1 to 2 government or high-grade corporate bond funds	$12,500	9.2
	7- to 10-year investment-grade corporate note	5,000	9.5
		$17,500	
35%	**EQUITIES**		
	1 or 2 high-quality income stocks	$ 7,500	7.7**
	1 or 2 high-quality income funds	10,000	7.5**
		$17,500	
100%	Total portfolio	$50,000	
	Average portfolio yield		8.1%

* *Indicated yield* is as of mid-1988; the yields are for current (interest) income only.

** Indicated rate is for dividend yield only and *ignores* any capital gains.

different investments, which is about in line with the other portfolios we've developed. A big chunk of this portfolio—about 45%
of it ($12,500 + $10,000 = $22,500)—is devoted to stock and
bond mutual funds. This was done not only for the return, but
also for the withdrawal plans these funds make available. Since a
steady stream of income is a top priority here, you can arrange for
the funds to distribute a certain amount of income on a regular
(monthly or quarterly) basis. Note also that, with the possible
exception of the money fund, all the securities were selected for
safety as well as high current income. More return is why we
selected a brokered CD rather than a local one; likewise, the
income stocks were included for their high dividend yields, *plus*
the fact that their dividends tend to grow over time at a fairly
hefty clip.

Now, you might wonder why we even bothered to include
equities in this portfolio, since you can usually get higher current
income from bonds. We did it because you can't ignore capital
growth altogether. You may need this income for a long time, so
you better take some steps to build up the capital. If you don't,
then sooner or later your portfolio income will start falling farther
and farther behind inflation. As a unit, this portfolio has an
indicated current yield of 8.1%. This is based on the return from
dividends and interest only. It does not include any potential
capital gains from the equity portion of the portfolio. At an 8%
rate, you can expect this $50,000 portfolio to generate interest
and dividend income of about $4,000 per year—or about $335 a
month.

THE MORE YOU HAVE, THE MORE YOU CAN DO Up to this point, the
portfolios have been put together assuming the investor has
$50,000 in capital. If you're fortunate enough to have more than
that, you have some obvious modifications to make. Actually,
there's no real reason to alter the basic asset allocation schemes—
at least not by much. The biggest change comes in the area of
securities selection. For the more money you have to invest, the
greater are your investment alternatives. Not only can you put

more into each of your investments, you can also increase the number of different securities held in your portfolio. For example, rather than holding only two or three blue chip stocks or equity-income funds, hold five or six. But don't overdo it; there's no need to hold a lot of different securities to achieve a high degree of asset diversification. Keep in mind that you're already diversifying across different types of securities, so there's not a lot to be added by increasing the amount of diversification within each type of security holding.

STARTING OUT SMALL Unfortunately, the situation is quite different when the amount of investable capital moves in the other direction. For as it drops below $50,000, the amount of asset diversification begins to slide as well. So what's a person to do if he or she has only $5,000 or $10,000 to invest? Well, as you can see below, all is not lost: asset allocation and portfolio management still have very important roles to play in low-dollar investment programs. Indeed, they may be even more important here, since you have to get as much diversification as possible from a very limited amount of money.

An $8,000 Portfolio

Asset Allocation Scheme	Type of Investment	Amount Invested	Indicated Yield*
70%	SHORT-TERM SECURITIES		
	Money market deposit account	$2,600	6.3%
	Laddered 2½-year CDs	3,000	7.6
		$5,600	
30%	EQUITIES		
	High-quality equity-income fund	$2,400	15.0
100%	Total portfolio	$8,000	
	Average portfolio yield		9.4%

* *Indicated yield* is as of mid-1988; yields are for current (interest and/or dividend) income only, except in the case of equity securities, where return also includes historical capital appreciation experience.

Here we assume once again that the investor is moderately conservative. Looking at this portfolio, it's readily apparent that in spite of the limited amount of capital, a good deal of diversification is possible, along with a fairly attractive rate of return—9.4%. This portfolio is kept very simple by holding only three kinds of investments, and it would be ideal for someone just starting out. Note that most of it can be set up at your local bank, as in the case of the short-term securities. Actually, we're just a step or two away from a basic starter portfolio, as most people would probably start investing by putting money into MMDAs and CDs. After $3,000 to $5,000 is built up there, we can start thinking about other types of investment vehicles, like equity-income funds, for example.

Our $8,000 portfolio has plenty of liquidity, and risk is held in check by devoting approximately 70% of the portfolio to short-term securities. In addition, the equity-income fund provides a bigger bang for the buck and is used to boot up return. This segment of the portfolio provides for capital growth, which is an important ingredient for younger investors. At the same time, the amount committed to this higher-risk form of investing is kept within reasonable limits.

Now, over time, the size of this portfolio will grow, especially if you regularly add funds to your investment program. Couple a steady input of fresh capital with a favorable market environment, and the portfolio will quickly double and then triple in size. Indeed, before you know it, you'll be managing a $25,000 portfolio. At that point, your portfolio is likely to start changing its look, as it begins the transition from a small portfolio to one of our full-sized benchmark portfolios. In particular, our moderately conservative portfolio at $25,000 might look more like what's shown in the table on the next page.

By this time, the portfolio has filled out a little more. Notice that we've added some Treasury notes, along with another mutual fund—in this case, a growth and income fund as a way to enhance growth in capital. On a percentage basis, there's considerably less in the lower-yielding short-term securities and a lot more in

A $25,000 Transitional Portfolio

Asset Allocation Scheme	Type of Investment	Amount Invested	Indicated Yield*
50%	SHORT-TERM SECURITIES		
	Money market deposit account (or money fund)	$ 5,000	6.3%
	Laddered 2½-year CDs	7,500 $12,500	7.6
20%	BONDS		
	3-year Treasury note	$ 5,000	8.4
30%	EQUITIES		
	High-quality equity-income fund	$ 3,500	15.0
	High-quality growth and income fund	4,000 $ 7,500	16.5
100%	Total portfolio	$25,000	
	Average portfolio yield		9.9%

* *Indicated yield* is as of mid-1988; yields are for current (interest and/or dividend) income only, except in the case of equity securities, where return also includes historical capital appreciation experience.

higher-yielding bonds and equities. Not surprisingly, the net result is a boost in the portfolio's indicated yield, from 9.4% to 9.9%. That's significant, because at that rate of return, the portfolio has reached the point where it is growing by over $2,400 a year—just from the average annual profits being generated by current holdings. Clearly, the benefits of compounding are about to really start taking hold!

INVESTING OVER A LIFETIME Whether we're aware of it or not, our style of investing tends to change with age. And that's appropriate, since we should follow different investment philosophies as we move through different stages of our lives. As a rule, people tend to be more aggressive when they're young and more conservative as they get older. This applies to safety-conscious investors, too, as our needs and responsibilities evolve over time. As a result, our asset allocation schemes and the composition of our portfolios should also change.

Most young investors—those in their 20s and 30s—tend to prefer investments that stress capital growth as much or more than current income. Often these investors don't have a lot in the way of investable capital and so capital appreciation is generally viewed as essential to building up a sizable pool of capital. Young safety-conscious investors are inclined to favor growth-oriented blue chips, growth and income funds, A-rated corporate notes, and other securities that offer higher yields and/or more price appreciation. And while they generally start small, most young investors have a tendency to eventually follow something like the *aggressively conservative* approach to asset allocation and portfolio management.

As investors move into their mid-40s, their investment programs start to undergo noticeable change. Family responsibilities grow, and pending retirement takes on increased importance. At this age their investment programs become decidedly more conservative. Capital appreciation is still important, but so is capital preservation, and because it's less risky, current income has also become a more important source of return. High-grade bonds (like Treasuries and agencies) begin playing a critical role in their portfolios. At the same time, they tend to show a greater preference for blue chips and high-quality income stocks, equity-income and balanced funds, possibly even zero-coupon bonds. As for the asset mix, it's probably beginning to look more like one of the *moderately conservative* portfolios.

Finally, as investors move into their retirement years, current income and preservation of capital become the principal concerns. Earning a fully compounded rate of return no longer matters; instead, emphasis is placed on generating a safe, secure, steady stream of income from interest and dividends. The objective at this point is to live as comfortably as possible on the income from their investments. The time has come to reap the rewards of a lifetime of saving and investing. High-quality income stocks, various types of income funds, and high-yielding fixed income securities are very likely to play prominent roles in this portfolio, which by now probably looks very much like a typical *income-oriented* portfolio.

Maintaining Your Balance

The whole idea behind asset allocation and portfolio management is to position your assets so that you're able to maintain a high degree of safety in your portfolio. Don't put everything into one part of the market, and you won't be subject to heavy losses if something goes wrong there. In addition, asset allocation helps you deploy your assets so that you can take advantage of return opportunities when they occur. For example, if you have a chunk of your portfolio in short-term securities, and interest rates go up, you'll be in a position to take advantage of it. In short, the goal is to situate yourself so that you can participate on the up side, and enhance your protection on the down side. Good steady performance in your portfolio is what you're looking for.

The asset allocation schemes we developed in the various portfolios above are, of course, subject to change over time. Indeed, you might think of these portfolios as snapshots that we took at given points in time. As events occur over time, our asset allocation scheme starts to get out of balance. When that happens, we have to do some *portfolio rebalancing* to get our asset mix back in line.

Stick with Your Asset Mix

As we've said, one of the key principles in investing for safety's sake is to maintain a long-term perspective in your investment program. In terms of your asset allocation scheme, this means that when you've finally settled on an asset mix you're comfortable with, stick with it for the long haul—go in with the idea that you're going to stay with your chosen asset mix for at least 7 to 10 years, perhaps longer. Pick one of the portfolios developed in this chapter; or find the one that comes closest to your investment objectives and alter it to meet your needs. For example, if you're leaning toward the moderately conservative portfolio but would like to put a bit more of your money into equities, do so.

Okay, so one way or another, you decide on an asset allocation scheme you can live with. Unfortunately, it seems that no sooner do you get everything in place, but the market prices of your securities start changing, and in so doing, your asset mix gets out of whack! This is bound to happen if you hold a number of marketable securities in your portfolio—particularly common stocks and mutual funds. Now, even though you only invest in securities with low price volatility, you still have to put up with some price swings. For example, if the market values of your common stocks and/or equity funds shoot way up (as they would have during the bull market of 1982–87), the proportion of equities in your portfolio will probably increase as well. When that happens, your asset mix will be out of balance; you'll be holding too much in equities, and you'll have to take steps to rebalance things.

What this means is that periodically—as often as every 3 to 6 months—you should run an inventory of your portfolio to determine if it's staying in line with your target asset mix. If it is, fine. But if it starts getting way out of line, then some rebalancing will be necessary. You'll get statements every month or so from your banker, broker, and/or mutual fund. Use these statements, along with the latest stock, bond, and mutual fund quotes, to figure your latest asset mix position. So long as everything is within a few percentage points or so, follow the same investment scheme you've been using. And by the way, don't worry about daily or weekly movements—if you do, you'll end up spending all your time on a bunch of insignificant details. It's the major moves over time that are of interest to you here.

Take corrective action only if you're starting to drift way off target. More often than not, such action will involve little more than redirecting the placement of fresh investment capital to the underfunded segment(s) of the portfolio. Presumably, you're following a regular savings plan, and systematically adding capital to your investment program. Let's say, for example, you're adding $1,000 to your portfolio every 3 to 6 months. If the level of equities has built up, just keep putting all the new capital into short-term securities and/or bonds until the portfolio gets back into balance.

In the vast majority of cases, that's about all it'll take to keep a portfolio in balance, especially for safety-conscious investors who stick with securities that are fairly price-stable. Sometimes, however, things will get so much out of line that more dramatic steps will be necessary. As a rule, big moves in the equities portion of your portfolio will be the underlying cause for such actions. Therefore, the greater the portion of your asset mix that's devoted to equities, the greater the likelihood that this could happen to you. For example, if the stock market really kicks into high gear, as it did in 1986 and 1987, you may well find that the values of your stocks and/or equity funds have shot way up as well. In such cases, major steps may be necessary to bring your portfolio back into balance.

Generally, that means actually selling part of your equity holdings. In other words, *sell enough of one or two of your stocks or equity funds to bring your portfolio back into balance with your target asset mix.* The idea here is to sell some of these securities so you can take your profits out and put them somewhere else. If you don't, what you'll probably find is that more and more of your money is being held in stocks as the market rises, which in turn makes your position ever more dangerous: when the bear strikes, and it will, you'll just have more to lose! In a similar fashion, if the market drops way off, as it sometimes does, you may find it's necessary to liquidate some short-term securities and/or bonds and, using your target asset mix as a guide, redirect those funds toward the lower-priced stocks and equity funds in your portfolio. In that way, you'll be increasing your equity holdings when the market is off and stocks are cheap, so you will be well positioned to take advantage of the situation when the market rebounds—as it ultimately will. No matter how you do it, the idea is to stick with your asset mix over time and in so doing, to position your assets so that you can obtain protection on the down side and still participate in the profits on the up side.

Dealing with Your Portfolio in Transition

As time goes by, the size of your portfolio will undoubtedly grow as you systematically add capital to your investment program, and even more important, as your investment program itself pays returns—in the form of interest, dividends, and capital gains. Guided by your asset mix, your portfolio is kept on course primarily through the ongoing administration of these investment earnings and new capital. The number and composition of the securities held in your portfolio may change—if for no other reason than because the amount of money being invested is probably building up. But the target asset mix will remain set for an extended period of time. However, in time, it's very likely that even that will change. And when that occurs, you'll have to take some steps to deal with the transition of your portfolio.

Clearly, our investment goals and financial needs change. And not just in subtle ways. When that happens, the makeup of our portfolio and the asset allocation scheme we've been living with should change as well. The best example of this is the aging process. As we saw earlier, most people go through some type of investment life cycle. But the change can be triggered by any number of things—the life cycle is just one of them. It can just as easily be something like a divorce, early retirement, or a big change in your health or the health of someone near to you. As we go through changes like this, our portfolios and asset allocation schemes should be gradually altered to reflect these new family traits and financial pressures.

In the vast majority of cases, this alteration can be both planned and gradual. It doesn't have to happen overnight. Indeed, probably the worst thing you can do is to effect sudden major changes in your portfolio. Here's an example of a much better way to deal with change in your portfolio. We'll use life cycle changes for purposes of illustration. Let's assume you've been following a conservative yet moderately aggressive approach to investing; you're now in your late 40s, and for a variety of reasons, you want to tilt your asset mix away from equities and more toward fixed income securities. In other words, you feel it's time to be a bit more conservative as far as your portfolio is concerned. Here's what your present asset mix looks like, and right next to it is what you'd like to change to:

	Present Asset Mix	Proposed Asset Mix
Short-term securities	30%	30%
Bonds	30	45
Equities	40	25
	100%	100%

You know where you are now; you know where you want to be. Now it's simply a matter of gradually bringing the change about. This could be done over a 3-year period by reducing your equity position approximately 5% per year and correspondingly increasing your bond holdings by the same amount. To begin with, you should divert any new capital and all investment earnings away from equities and toward bonds. If even more modifications are necessary, then pick one or two stocks or equity funds, and start liquidating them so that your equity position is down to 35% at the end of the first year, 30% after the second, and 25% by the end of the 3-year transition period.

When searching for candidates to sell, look for stocks and equity funds that have either way outperformed or way underperformed your expectations. In the first case, it might be time to take some of your profit out and put it someplace else. In the case of the underachiever, it might be a situation where things just didn't work out as planned and so it's perhaps best to cut your losses while there's still time. In addition to these guidelines, you should carefully evaluate the composition of the equity segment of your portfolio. You may find, for example, that there's a bit too much emphasis on growth and not enough on current income. You can obviously use this period of transition to reduce the emphasis on growth—if you have to do some cutting (selling), the first securities to consider ought to be the growth-oriented stocks and/or equity funds.

In short, this is a time of transition not only for your asset mix but also for your security holdings. No matter what the reason for the shift in direction, by following a gradual, well-thought-out plan, you can systematically, and with surprisingly little effort, bring about change in your portfolio. Once the transition is completed, you'll have a new asset allocation scheme in place, and a target portfolio you can follow for the next 7 to 10 years, or maybe even longer.

Why Settle for Anything Less?

Investing for safety's sake is based on the idea that caution does have its rewards—that it is possible to earn a respectable rate of return by putting your money into good, sound investments. Let the other guy take all the risks; you want nothing to do with it. Rather, you're willing to give up *some* return potential in exchange for security and peace of mind. Why? Because you're one of those investors who finds return *of* capital to be just as important as return *on* capital. And there's certainly nothing wrong with that, for as we've seen repeatedly in this book, you can have *both* safety and return. Indeed, there's no reason to settle for anything less.

Just because you want less risk, however, doesn't mean you have to take a bath on return. Far from it! It's been our position that you don't have to follow a complicated, aggressive, high-risk trading strategy to make some serious money in the market. Indeed, our approach has been quite the opposite! It's based on the notion of sticking with sound, high-quality investment outlets for the long haul and then seeing to it that you keep your money fully employed. You provide a steady stream of capital to your investment program, and your investment program, in turn, should be able to provide you with a growing stream of earnings. The hallmark of a successful investment program is a constantly growing capital base; and that's our objective, too. It's just that we feel the best way to achieve such an end is through an investment approach that emphasizes two things: *safety and simplicity*.

Consider, for example, a portfolio that earns an average rate of return of around 9%. As we saw in the portfolios developed earlier in this chapter, a return of 8½% to 9½% is well within the reach of a moderately conservative investor. Let's assume our investor starts with $10,000 in capital and every year for the next 25 years adds $2,000 in fresh capital. After 25 years of 9% returns, this portfolio will be worth just over $250,000. That's not too bad when you stop to think that only $60,000 of that is the investor's own money. All the rest—nearly $200,000—comes from investment earnings and interest-on-interest. Now, it's true that you may not be able to get an average return of 9% over a period of 25 years. But even if it's only 7½% or 8%, you'll still end up with a tidy sum of money at the end of 25 years. All by following a simple, safe approach to investing.

We've looked at the things that are important to safety-conscious investors, including, for example, how to reduce business or market risk (try low-beta stocks or intermediate-term bonds), how to set up a ladder of CDs or bonds, how to identify high-quality income stocks and equity funds, and how to get a fully compounded rate of return on your money (try a dividend reinvestment plan). We've also examined the four principal types of investment vehicles used by safety-conscious investors: short-term securities, longer-term notes and bonds, high-quality common stocks, and various types of mutual funds. You should have a better feel now for the investment options open to you—things like brokered CDs, agency securities, zero-coupon bonds, insured municipal obligations, high-paying income stocks, and equity-income funds, to name just a few. We've also explained how an asset allocation scheme and a diversified portfolio of securities can further reduce your risk, without getting in the way of potential return.

The ball's now in your court. You have to decide what you're going to do to get the most from your money, given the level of risk you feel you can tolerate. All things considered, the best way to do that is to be safe, be comfortable, be consistent, and be patient. Don't try to time the market and don't put all your eggs in one basket. Instead, invest for the long haul and follow a well-diversified asset allocation scheme. For if you can discipline yourself to do these things, you, too, will quickly find that *better returns and safe investments do, indeed, go hand in hand!*

Appendix: Becoming an Informed Investor

Staying informed about specific investments and general market conditions is a very important element of investing. Yet it's surprising how many investors ignore this aspect because they're too busy, they don't understand financial statements, or they have the attitude "that's what I pay my broker for."

Staying informed about investments doesn't mean trading in and out on every rumor. The reason: by the time you hear about it, it's usually too late! For example, if you read about some development in the popular press, as in Dan Dorfman's column in *U.S.A. Today*, it's probably too late to do anything about it. This doesn't mean that the popular press is useless. On the contrary, many of the business publications offer individual investors a wealth of information that helps them make informed decisions. This is particularly true when you're buying for the long term. Just remember to ignore the rumors and focus, instead, on the underlying fundamentals.

So what's the best source of information? The answer is there's really no single *best* source of information. Rather, there are numerous good, informative sources, and the problem most people have is information overload. We suggest you try to read two or three investment magazines or newspapers on a regular basis, as a way to keep up-to-date on general market news, and then use other sources for more specific information. Along this line, probably the most useful, yet most *unused,* source of investment information is a company's annual report. It's amazing how many people never look at these things even though they contain an abundance of information about the company. Now obviously you shouldn't believe everything you read in the annual report; instead, try to focus on the company's past performance and its future prospects.

In addition to annual reports, there are other useful, reader-friendly sources of investment information. They address such issues as the current state of the market, recent developments in various types of investment vehicles and strategies, and current interest rates and price behavior. Most of these publications are aimed directly at the nonprofessional, individual investor. They assume only a very basic and fundamental knowledge of investments and so provide an easy and convenient way of staying abreast of the market. The following tables list some of these sources, with particular attention given to the four main types of investment vehicles discussed in this book: short-term securities, bonds, stocks, and mutual funds. The list certainly is not exhaustive, but instead contains some of the more popular, more reader-friendly financial publications. We also tried to include only the more reasonably priced publications, those that won't put too big of a dent in your budget. (For completeness, and because they're such great sources of information, we did include several fairly costly publications in our list; if the costs of these publications are more than you care to spend, you can usually find them at your local library or brokerage office.) In our opinion, each one of these publications is a very good source of investment information, and we feel that by carefully selecting a few of them, you should be able to stay adequately informed at a very reasonable cost. Furthermore, by being a regular reader of publications such as these, you'll find that your level of investment sophistication will build up, too.

Periodicals for Investors

Publication	Frequency of Publication	Yearly Subscription Price	Publisher	Information
GENERAL FINANCIAL PUBLICATIONS, JOURNALS, NEWSPAPERS				
The Wall Street Journal	Daily	$107.00	Dow Jones & Co., Inc. 22 Cortlandt Street New York, NY 10007 (212) 416-2000	General business, financial, and world news, with market quotations.
Investors Daily	Daily	$89.00	*Investors Daily* P.O. Box 25970 Los Angeles, CA 90025 (213) 207-1832	Comprehensive coverage of investment vehicles; emphasis on statistical and graphical analysis.
Barron's	Weekly	$63.00	Dow Jones & Co., Inc. 22 Cortlandt Street New York, NY 10007 (212) 416-2000	Financial and investment news; information on commodities, international trading; tables on NYSE transactions.
Forbes	Biweekly	$45.00	Forbes, Inc. 60 Fifth Avenue New York, NY 10011 (212) 620-2200	General economic and financial news; reports on various corporations, executives, stocks and industries. August issue: annual performance review of mutual funds.

Publication	Frequency of Publication	Yearly Subscription Price	Publisher	Information
Fortune	Biweekly	$44.50	Time, Inc. 541 N. Fairbanks Court Chicago, IL 60611 (800) 621-8200	Business and economic developments; evaluates specific industries and corporations; notes banking and energy news.
Changing Times	Monthly	$15.00	Kiplinger Washington Editors, Inc. 1729 H Street, NW Washington, DC 20006 (202) 887-6400	Articles of general consumer interest; tax and personal financial planning.
Money	Monthly	$31.95	*Money* Time, Inc. Box 2519 Boulder, CO 80322 (800) 621-8200	Reports on personal finance; stock market trends, estate planning, taxes, tax shelters, and consumer affairs.
Sylvia Porter's Personal Finance Magazine	10 times a year	$19.97	SPPFM, Co. 380 Lexington Avenue New York, NY 10017 (212) 490-8989	Every aspect of an individual's financial life. Article topics range from bargains in auto insurance to pension planning, from coop education to divorce settlements.

Personal Investor	Bimonthly	$11.97	Plaza Communications, Inc. 18188 Teller Avenue Suite 280 Irvine, CA 92715 (714) 851-2220	Practical information for investors on everything from mutual funds to how to invest in thoroughbreds. Organized by "Outlook" sections on interest rates, futures, collectibles, and personal finances.

INVESTMENT ADVISORIES AND NEWSLETTERS

SHORT-TERM SECURITIES

Bank Rate Monitor	Weekly	$395.00	Robert Heady Box 088888 N. Palm Beach, FL 33408	Concentrates on highest-yield CDs at major banks and thrifts.
Income & Safety	Monthly	$100.00	Income & Safety The Institute for Econometric Research 3471 N. Federal Highway Fort Lauderdale, FL 33306 (305) 563-9000	A guide to safe places to save and invest for income, concentrating on money market funds, bank accounts, and tax-free income funds.

BONDS

Moody's Bond Record	Monthly	$125.00	Moody's Investors Service 99 Church Street New York, NY 10007 (212) 553-0300	Provides a wide variety of information, including call prices and agency ratings, on thousands of corporate and municipal bonds.

Publication	Frequency of Publication	Yearly Subscription Price	Publisher	Information
S&P Bond Guide	Monthly	$145.00	Standard & Poor's 345 Hudson Street New York, NY 10014 (212) 208-8000	Descriptive and statistical data on 3,000 corporate bonds. Nearly 10,000 state, municipal general obligation, and revenue bonds, over 650 convertibles, and more than 200 foreign bonds.
S&P CreditWeek	Weekly	$1,238.00	Standard & Poor's 345 Hudson Street New York, NY 10014 (212) 208-8000	Comments on trends and outlook for fixed-income securities, including money market instruments and corporate and government bonds. Money market rates, bond yields, federal figures, new offerings, and credit analyses.

STOCKS

Standard & Poor's Stock Reports	Periodically revised	$820.00	Standard & Poor's 345 Hudson Street New York, NY 10014 (212) 208-8000	Data on numerous NYSE issues, including financial data and latest developments.

Title	Frequency	Price	Publisher	Description
Value Line Investment Survey	Weekly	$495.00	Value Line, Inc. 711 Third Avenue New York, NY 10017 (212) 687-3965	Weekly looseleaf booklet covering the business activities of corporations in a variety of industries. Charts and graphs cover a variety of fundamental and technical data.

MUTUAL FUNDS

Title	Frequency	Price	Publisher	Description
Donoghue's Moneyletter	Bimonthly	$87.00	Donoghue's Moneyletter Box 540 Holliston, MA 01746 (617) 429-5930	Reports exclusively on money market mutual fund performance, portfolio composition, management, and current yields.
Donoghue's Mutual Funds Almanac	Annually	$19.95	Donoghue's Mutual Funds Almanac Box 540 Holliston, MA 01746 (617) 429-5930	Extensive statistical review, including expense ratios, covering 10 years of performance for over 1,800 funds.
United Mutual Fund Selector	Semimonthly	$103.00	United Business Service Company 210 Newbury Street Boston, MA 02116 (617) 267-8855	Evaluates mutual funds, including bond and municipal bond funds, reports industry developments, and includes tables and charts.

Publication	Frequency of Publication	Yearly Subscription Price	Publisher	Information
Morningstar's Mutual Fund Values	Biweekly	$295.00	Morningstar, Inc. 53 W. Jackson Boulevard Chicago, IL 60604 (800) 876-5005	Provides a thorough, in-depth analysis of the investment behavior and market performance of some 800 mutual funds; looks at both risk and return characteristics.
No-Load Fund Investor	Monthly	$79.00	*No-Load Fund Investor* Box 283 Hastings-on-Hudson New York, NY 10706 (914) 478-2381	Complete performance statistics, news, views, recommendations, and forecasts for no-load mutual funds.
Wiesenberger's Current Performance	Monthly	$66.00	Warren, Gorham & Lamont 210 South Street Boston, MA 02111 (617) 423-2020	A supplement to *Wiesenberger Services, Inc., Investment Companies,* providing detailed monthly data on mutual fund performance.
Wiesenberger Services, Inc., Investment Companies	Annually, updated quarterly	$295.00	Warren, Gorham & Lamont 210 South Street Boston, MA 02111 (617) 423-2020	Gives background, management policy, and financial record for all leading U.S. and Canadian investment companies. Available for reference in most public and college libraries.

Books for Investors

Title and Author(s)	Price	Publisher	Information
Investment Fundamentals: A Guide to Becoming a Knowledgeable Investor, Lawrence J. Gitman and Michael D. Joehnk	$24.95	Harper & Row Publishers, Inc. 10 East 53rd Street New York, NY 10022 (212) 207-7225	A primer for all investors; this book includes a wide-ranging discussion of all types of investments and the investing marketplace.
Barron's Finance and Investment Handbook	$21.95	Barron's Educational Series, Inc. 113 Crossways Park Drive Woodbury, NY 11797 (516) 921-8750	Analysis of investment fundamentals and discussion of personal investment alternatives. Explains how to read annual reports and financial news and contains a dictionary of 2,500 key terms. Includes addresses of NYSE, AMEX, and NASDAQ (NMS) stocks and directories with current and historical data on mutual funds, investment newsletters, and financial institutions.
Random Walk Down Wall Street, Burton G. Malkiel	$9.95	W. W. Norton & Co., Inc. 500 Fifth Avenue New York, NY 10110 (212) 354-5500	Observations on mortgage securities, zero-coupon bonds, and other investment vehicles available in the contemporary markets. It also includes Malkiel's now-classic examination of why stock prices are unpredictable.
How to Buy Stocks, Brendan Boyd and Louis Engel	$15.95	Little, Brown Publishers 34 Beacon Street Boston, MA 02106 (617) 227-0730	The classic guide of how the market works and how to deal with brokers and securities firms.

Index

Agency bonds, 102–3. *See also*
  Government bonds
Age of investor, portfolio management
  and, 216–17
Alternative minimum tax (AMT), 119
Annual reports, 227–28
Annuities, 6
Annuity factors, savings plan and, 38–39
Approximate yield, 25–27
  of common stock, 137–41
Asset allocation scheme, 202–3, 218–
  20
Automatic reinvestment plans, 177

Balanced funds, 172–73
Bank Rate Monitor, 231
Barron's, 229
Beta, 15
  common stock, 123, 129–30
Black Monday (October 19, 1987), 12,
  120
Blue chip stocks, 124–25, 142–46
Bond funds, 171, 173–76, 192–95
Bonds, 82–119
  call features of, 88–90
    government bonds, 100
  corporate, 87–88, 113–18
    convertible, 114–16
    ratings, 113–14
    yields, 93
    zero-coupon, 116–18, 208, 211
  cost of buying and selling, 47–48
  coupons, 82
    yields and, 93
  current income and, 83–84
  good and bad points of, 118–19
  government, 99–106
    agency issues, 86–87, 102–3
    call features, 100
    laddered approach to investing in,
      100–101
    mortgage-backed, 104–6

Bonds *(cont.)*
  reinvesting income from, 101–2
    taxes and, 119
  inflation and, 85
  issuers of, 86–88
  market interest rates and, 92–93
  municipal, 87, 106–13
    guaranteed (insured), 109–12
    maturities of, 108–9
    state income taxes and, 106–7
    taxable, 112–13
    tax bracket of investor and,
      108
    taxes and, 119
    yields, 93
  par value of, 82–83
  prices of, 96–98
  quality of, 84
  ratings of, 90–92
  with refunding provisions, 89
  risks of, 84–86
  safety of, 84
  taxes and, 119
  yields, 92–96
    measures of, 94–96
    yield spreads, 93–94
  zero-coupon, 116–18, 208, 211
Books for investors, 235
Brokers, 41–48
  certificates of deposit (CDs) sold by,
    63
  commissions of, 44–48
  corporate bonds and, 114
  discount, 43–44
  selecting, 41–42
  services provided by, 42–43
Bump-up CDs, 63–64
Business and financial risk, 14
  of bonds, 84
  of common stock, 123
  of mutual funds, 160–61
  of short-term securities, 55

237

About the Author

Michael D. Joehnk, Ph.D., is professor of finance at Arizona State University. He is a Chartered Financial Analyst (CFA) and has been a student of the market for more than 20 years. His articles on investments and finance have appeared in numerous professional journals, including *Financial Management* and *Journal of Portfolio Management.* Dr. Joehnk's last book, *Investment Fundamentals,* was cowritten with Lawrence J. Gitman, as were two bestselling finance textbooks. Dr. Joehnk is a member of the editorial advisory board of and a contributor to the *Handbook of Fixed Income Securities.* He lives in Scottsdale, Arizona.